The MAILBOX® SUPERBOOK™

GRADE 1

Your complete resource for an entire year of first-grade success!

Editor:
Sharon Murphy

Contributing Editors:
Darcy Brown and Susan Hohbach Walker

Contributors:
Elizabeth Almy, Amy Barsanti, Sherri Beckwith, Catherine Broome, Lisa Buchholz,
Candi Deal, Linda Gordetsky, Darcy Gruber, Lisa Kelly, Pamela Kucks,
Susan Majors, Rita Petrocco, Kathryn Shanko, Virginia Zeletski

Art Coordinator:
Cathy Spangler Bruce

Artists:
Jennifer Tipton Bennett, Cathy Spangler Bruce, Clevell Harris,
Kimberly Richard, Rebecca Saunders, Barry Slate, Donna K. Teal

Cover Artist:
Jim Counts

www.themailbox.com

The Education Center, Inc.
Greensboro, North Carolina

ABOUT THIS BOOK

Look through the pages of *The Mailbox® GRADE 1 SUPERBOOK™*, and discover a wealth of ideas and activities specifically designed for the first-grade teacher. We've included tips for starting the year, managing your classroom, maintaining parent communication, and motivating your students. In addition, you'll find activities for reinforcing the basic skills in all areas of the first-grade curriculum. We've also provided reference materials for every subject, literature lists, arts-and-crafts ideas, holiday and seasonal reproducibles, and bulletin-board ideas and patterns. *The Mailbox® GRADE 1 SUPERBOOK™* is your complete resource for an entire year of first-grade success!

Library of Congress Cataloging-in-Publication Data

The mailbox superbook , grade 1 : your complete resource for an entire
   year of first-grade success! / editor, Sharon Murphy ; contributing
   editors, Darcy Brown, Susan Hohbach Walker ; contributors, Elizabeth
   Almy ... [et al.] ; art coordinator, Cathy Spangler Bruce ; artists,
   Jennifer Tipton Bennett ... [et al.].
       p.   cm.
   ISBN 1-56234-197-9
   1. First grade (Education)—Curricula.   2. Education, Elementary—
Activity programs.   3. Teaching—Aids and devices.   4. Elementary
school teaching.   I. Murphy, Sharon (Sharon V.)   II. Mailbox.
LB1571 1st.M35 1997
372.24'1—dc21   97-47383
                                                        CIP

Manufactured in the United States
10 9 8 7 6 5 4

TABLE OF CONTENTS

BACK TO SCHOOL

BACK TO SCHOOL

WELCOME-TO-SCHOOL LETTERS

This welcome-back idea is sure to help students anticipate the first day of school. A week before the big day, mail a copy of the letter on page 18—accompanied by a photocopied picture of yourself performing a favorite activity—to each student. This thoughtful invitation to begin a new school year, along with a photograph of yourself, will certainly put your youngsters at ease.

To increase their enthusiasm on the first day of school, encourage each student to bring in a photograph or hand-drawn picture of himself performing a favorite activity. Then begin the day by asking students to introduce themselves to you and their classmates by sharing their photographs or pictures. It won't take long for students to see how much they have in common with their new classmates!

JUST THE TICKET

Here's the ticket to get the school year started right. Just before school starts, mail a letter to each of your students. Include a summary of your summer vacation as well as a brief description of some of the special projects planned for the new year. Also attach a signed "free-gift coupon" (pattern page 19) to each letter. On the first day of school, each student exchanges her coupon for a colorful party bag filled with a new pencil, sugarless candy or gum, some stickers, and other coupons for 15 minutes of free time and an evening of no homework.

Good for one
FREE GIFT

Ms. Carson
signed

Redeem on the first day of school.

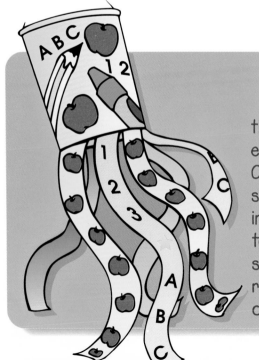

A GUIDING WINDSOCK

A colorful and decorative windsock displayed in the hallway outside your classroom door makes it easy for youngsters to identify their new room. Choose a windsock that ties in to your back-to-school theme. Then write each of your students an introductory letter before school begins telling them to look for that particular windsock. This easy-to-spot decoration also makes it easy for students to relocate their classroom when returning from recess or the restroom.

A NEW LOOK

Each school year brings new students and new experiences. So why not try a new look for your classroom? Peruse the list below and choose a theme. Then put your imagination in gear to design nametags, a helpers chart, a bulletin board, and a door decoration around this theme.

"Toad-ally" Cool In First Grade—Students will jump at the chance to be in a colorful classroom decorated with toad cutouts, lily pads, and other pond decorations.

A Royal Welcome——Roll out the red carpet for your students this year. Use king, queen, and castle cutouts to add that royal touch to your classroom.

Cruise Into A New Year—Welcome your youngsters all aboard the USS [your name]! Decorate your classroom with boats, life preservers, and cute ocean animals.

Tracking Down A Good Year—Get your supersleuths off to a great start in a classroom decorated with detectives and magnifying glasses.

It's Going To Be A Rootin'-Tootin' Year—Decorate your classroom with a cowboy motif, and your young buckaroos will be ready to hoot and holler with pride!

Making A Splash In First Grade—Students are sure to dive into learning when they enter a classroom decorated with fish, seashells, and other beach decorations. For even more fun, set up a small, plastic wading pool in the corner of the room to serve as a reading center.

Blast Off Into A New Year—Launch your students into a new year using a space theme. Decorate the classroom with rocket ships and stars for an out-of-this-world display.

The First-Grade Express—All aboard! Your youngsters will sure be all aboard when you choose a train theme for your classroom. Be sure to display a railroad track cut-out labeled with all the stops for learning they'll be making this year.

NIFTY NAMETAGS

These fashionable nametags are sure to win rave reviews from students. Purchase a large quantity of wooden beads (or cubes) at a craft store. For each child provide a length of durable string and enough beads for each letter in her name. Have each child string the beads and then tie the two string ends in a knot. Assist each child in using a black permanent marker to write each letter of her name on a different bead. (If students are using cubes, have them write the letter on each side of the cube.) Students will enjoy wearing these necklaces during the first few days of school and for substitutes. When they are not being worn, hang them on a coat hanger to avoid tangling. These handy nametags make great personalized gifts to take home at the end of the school year, too!

WELCOME BACK!

On the first day of school, ask your students what they hope to learn during the year. Tape-record their individual responses with each child identifying himself on the tape. Then store the tape recording in a secure spot. On the last day of school, replay the tape. Students will see just how much they've learned during the year!

Transportation Graph

Get your first day on the road by inviting youngsters to share how they plan to travel from school each afternoon. To prepare, duplicate the pattern from page 20 that best depicts each child's mode of transportation. Make extra patterns for those students who travel to school using several different means. Then program a sheet of chart paper labeled to correspond to each mode of transportation used.

Read aloud *This Is The Way We Go To School* by Edith Baer (Scholastic Inc., 1992). Encourage students to discuss the many different ways children around the world get to school. Then have each child tell how he plans to travel from school each afternoon. Ask him to select a pattern that corresponds with his mode of transportation. Have him color it, cut it out, and write his name on it. If the student rides a bus home, write the bus number beside his name. Then have him tape his pattern in the appropriate column on the graph. Discuss what the completed graph reveals.

At the end of the day, refer to the graph to group students based on their modes of transportation. Be sure to also group students in the bus group based on their bus numbers. When the dismissal bell rings, have students leave with the classmates in their group. What a great way to ease those first-day dismissal problems for youngsters with apprehensions!

Transportation Chart

FIRST-DAY FRIENDS

Try this welcome warm-up on the first day of school! Cut pictures from magazines, glue them onto construction paper, and then cut each picture into two irregular shapes. As you greet each child, ask him to choose a shape. After everyone has arrived, have each child find the person with the shape that completes his picture. Then let the new friends get acquainted for a few minutes. If desired, have each student exchange shapes with someone other than his partner and repeat the activity.

A CIRCLE OF NAMES

Sometimes it's difficult for students to learn the names of their new classmates, but this outside game—a variation of Duck Duck Goose—will make it easy and fun. Have students sit in a circle. Choose a student to be It. It walks around the outside of the circle and continuously says his own name. When he gets to a classmate he would like to have chase him, he taps that student on the shoulder. That student stands up and chases It. If It gets back to the chaser's place in the circle without being tagged, the chaser becomes It for the next round. If the chaser tags It, the chaser returns to his place and It must go another round.

A GINGERBREAD HUNT

Acquaint students with their new surroundings and help them get to know the support staff by taking them on a gingerbread hunt. To begin the activity, read aloud *The Gingerbread Man* and enlist your students' help in making gingerbread man cookies. Place the unbaked cookies on a baking sheet and invite your students to assist you in taking the cookies to the cafeteria to bake. Return with your students to the classroom. Make arrangements ahead of time with the cafeteria manager to have the cookies baked, secretly removed, and returned to the classroom when you go with students to get them.

After allowing time for the cookies to bake and be removed from the cafeteria, take your students to check on the cookies. When students discover the gingerbread men are missing, lead them on a hunt throughout the school for the runaway cookies. As you and your youngsters journey from room to room, introduce them to important people, such as the P.E. teacher, art teacher, librarian, and principal. When students arrive at the classroom, they'll be thrilled to discover the gingerbread men waiting to be eaten!

READING ALREADY

Oftentimes first graders come to school expecting to learn to read the very first day. Show these youngsters that they're already readers with this unique activity. In advance collect empty cereal boxes, soda cans, candy-bar wrappers, and magazine pictures of popular items. Then display the items, one at a time, for students to read. Won't they be surprised at all the words they already know!

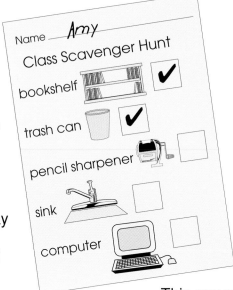

PICTORIAL SCAVENGER HUNT

Here's a first-day activity to put anxious students at ease right away. Make a look-and-find sheet that is made up of simple drawings of objects in different areas of your classroom. Duplicate a copy for each student. Have the child search to find each of the pictured items and to explore the area once she's found it. This scavenger hunt is a great way to familiarize youngsters with their new classroom.

Busy Bees

This beginning-of-the-year activity will have your students buzzing about their summer vacations. In advance cut a large beehive from yellow bulletin-board paper and duplicate a class supply of bees using the pattern on page 19. To begin, have each child color his bee cutout. Then ask him to name an activity he participated in during the summer. Write the activity and the child's name on his bee cutout; then mount the cutouts on the beehive. Display the hive on a classroom wall with the title " 'Bee-dazzling' Summer Vacations."

PERSONALITY BAGS

Getting to know each other is in the bag with this clever activity! Have each student bring a grocery bag containing five personal items. Each day choose a bag and unpack it in front of the class. Students try to guess the identity of the bag's owner. It's a fun way for students to share information about themselves with their classmates!

All About Dogs

1ST PLACE • A CLASS
Soccer Tournament

SPOTLIGHTING SPECIAL INTERESTS

At the beginning of the school year, ask each student to tell you a special interest. Then, during the school year, use each child's special interest at least once as a theme for bulletin boards, learning centers, or creative-writing projects. For example, you might choose to display a bulletin board about different kinds of dogs for all the dog lovers. Each child gets a chance to pursue his special interest at least once during the year.

MEMORY BOOK

Preserve special days as a treasured keepsake with a memory book. At the beginning of the school year, make a memory book for each student. To make a memory book, staple several pieces of blank paper between two construction-paper covers. Have each student personalize and add decorations to his front cover; then collect the books and store them until your class takes part in a special event, such as a field trip. At that time have each student write about his favorite part of the event; then have him illustrate the page accordingly. What a treasure each student will have at the end of the year!

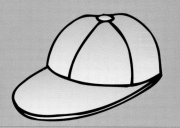

Today we went to the farm. We saw pigs, cows, and chickens.

August

June

Just A Growin'

During the school year, students will be growing and changing in more ways than one. At the beginning of the year, photograph each student. In addition, have each child draw and autograph a self-portrait. Save both the drawings and the photographs. In June repeat the activity. On pieces of brightly colored construction paper, attach beginning- and end-of-the-year portraits. Each child's parents will enjoy seeing how much their child has grown in first grade!

MORE THAN NAMES

Help students learn their classmates' names with this tasty game. Divide the class into small groups. Ask each child to think of a food that begins with the same letter as his name. Choose one group to begin. For example, Player 1 might say, "My name is Jonathan and I like jelly beans." Player 2 would then say, "Jonathan likes jelly beans. My name is Dee Dee and I like doughnuts." When one group is finished, start over with the next group. Repeat the activity throughout the year using larger groups and topics other than food, such as hobbies or toys.

COLOR COLLAGES

This unique beginning-of-the-year activity yields a practical, student-made display. Assign each child one of the eight colors found in a basic box of crayons. Have each child cut pictures from magazines of eight objects in her assigned color. Next group students by their assigned colors and provide each group with a piece of 12" x 18" construction paper in the corresponding color. Have the group members work together to glue their pictures onto the construction paper in a collage fashion. Label each collage with its assigned color; then mount the completed projects on a classroom wall titled "Colors In Our World."

red

Partner Portraits

This art project is great for becoming acquainted with new classmates or just fun to play on a rainy day. Pair students; then have each student—without looking—draw a picture of his partner and place it under his chair. Next have each student draw another picture of his partner while looking at him. When these illustrations are complete, have each student show both pictures to his partner. Challenge students to determine which picture their partners drew first.

FIRST GRADE OF LONG AGO

Show your youngsters that you were once a kid, too! Display photographs of yourself when you were in first grade. Then share some of your favorites from that time, such as your favorite game, TV show, and book. Students will be thrilled at the chance to get the inside scoop on their teacher!

KIDS SAY THE CUTEST THINGS!

The comments kids make can be both humorous and inspirational. Throughout the year record funny, insightful, or interesting comments made by your students. At the end of the year, bind all the comment pages into a class book to share with students and parents during your year-end activities. You're guaranteed to see lots of smiles!

CLASS DIRECTORY

Help students get to know their classmates with this informative idea. At the beginning of the school year, take a photo of each child. Next assist each child in completing a copy of the biography sheet on page 21. Glue each child's picture to his biography sheet and then laminate all the sheets. Finally, place the sheets in a three-ring binder. Have each child, in turn, take the finished directory home to share with his family. Parents will appreciate the chance to get to know their child's classmates, too!

See pages 88 and 89 for Open House ideas.

A CLASS COMPANION

Choose a colorful stuffed animal to be your class's very special friend, and the learning possibilities will go on and on!

Hi! I like my name, Puddles. We're going to have oodles of fun this year!

IT'S NICE TO MEET YOU

Students will be all smiles when they see you holding the class mascot. To create a sense of ownership, have your students cooperatively name the class mascot. Once a name has been chosen, have your new friend introduce himself to the class. The students will be thrilled to learn all his favorites!

THE LITERATURE LINK

Now that your mascot has made a successful debut, devote several sessions of storytime to reading stories that feature your mascot's animal type. Students' interest level is sure to soar when they are listening to a story about a personal friend of theirs!

A Visit To Puddles' World

We could visit Puddles at the pond. We would watch him swim around and we would feed him.

ACROSS THE CURRICULUM

Students will be ready to jump into science to learn what kind of habitat the real version of their animal mascot lives in. After sharing information about the real animal, have each child draw a picture of himself visiting the animal in its habitat. Compile the completed pictures into a class book titled "A Visit To [class mascot's name]'s World."

WEEKEND ADVENTURES

Help foster positive home-school relationships by giving each child the opportunity to take the mascot home for a weekend. In advance place a supply of story paper in a three-ring binder and label the cover "[Class mascot's name]'s Travel Log." Instruct the child to write and illustrate an entry in the travel log about an event that took place, with the mascot, during the weekend. On Monday morning, have the child share her entry about her weekend adventures with the mascot. At the end of the year, compile all the accounts into a book and send a copy home with each child.

Puddles'
Travel
Log

Puddles and I went on a picnic.

Molly

EXTRA ADVENTURES

Imagine the students' excitement when they hear that the class mascot will be going home with the principal! In advance ask your principal to participate in the activity. On the Friday of the event, have your principal visit the classroom to meet the mascot. Ask student volunteers to tell the principal what to do with the travel log. Then have students wave good-bye as your principal leaves with their special friend. Students will be more than eager on Monday to read the mascot's travel log! For added fun invite other school workers, such as your librarian or physical education teacher, to take the mascot home, too!

DAILY ACTIVITIES

Make routine activities more exciting by including the class mascot. Have the mascot help you with your morning greeting, attendance, or lunch count. Make construction-paper cutouts of the mascot to use as nametags, desktags, or center signs. Have the mascot host special class events, such as birthday parties or holiday celebrations. No matter where the mascot appears, he's sure to make the activity more enjoyable for your students!

Darren

Math

BRIGHT BOOKS

This collection of back-to-school books will start the school year off with glowing reviews.

THE DAY THE TEACHER WENT BANANAS

Written by James Howe
Published by
Dutton Children's Books, 1984

When the new teacher is sent to the zoo instead of the classroom, and someone who's supposed to go to the zoo ends up teaching the class, there's fun for all!

THE PRINCIPAL'S NEW CLOTHES

Written by Stephanie Calmenson
Published by Scholastic Inc., 1991

The famous Hans Christian Andersen tale about a vain emperor's invisible clothing gets an updated twist in this humorous tale. Youngsters will be delighted to see this principal parading in his underwear!

MISS NELSON IS MISSING!

Written by Harry Allard
Published by
Houghton Mifflin Company, 1985

When the students begin to take advantage of their dear Miss Nelson, a terrible thing happens. Miss Viola Swamp shows up to substitute in Room 207.

MY TEACHER SLEEPS IN SCHOOL

Written by Leatie Weiss
Published by Puffin Books, 1985

When a group of students begins pondering it, they're positive that their teacher sleeps at school. But the teacher soon clues them in.

"NEVER SPIT ON YOUR SHOES"
Written by Denys Cazet
Published by Orchard Books, 1993

Arnie tells his mother all about his exciting first day at school. From rule-setting to recess, Arnie describes the events of the day.

CHRYSANTHEMUM
Written by Kevin Henkes
Published by
William Morrow And Company, Inc.; 1996

Chrysanthemum thinks that her name is perfect—until her first day of school. Her classmates tease her about her unusual name. With the help of her teacher, Mrs. Delphinium Twinkle, Chrysanthemum realizes that her name really is perfect.

THE TEACHER FROM THE BLACK LAGOON
Written by Mike Thaler
Published by Scholastic Inc., 1989

You are sure to have some children who will relate to this story of a boy who imagines that his new teacher—Mrs. Green—will be rather beastly. Fortunately Mrs. Green turns out to be rather nice.

NOBODY'S MOTHER IS IN SECOND GRADE
Written by Robin Pulver
Published by
Dial Books For Young Readers, 1992

In this hilarious story, a mother visits her daughter's classroom disguised as a plant. To make this story more appealing to your class, substitute "first grade" any time the author refers to the story taking place in a second-grade classroom.

Dear _____,

    Welcome to the first grade! I am excited about having you in my class. I know that, together, we will have a great time this year.

    Our school day begins at _____. This year we will be
learning about _____
time
_____
_____
_____.

    Here are some things you might like to bring to school:
_____
_____
_____.

    I am eager to learn more about you and the things you enjoy. I look forward to seeing you on _____.
date

Your teacher,

_____

SCHOOL

Note To Teacher: Duplicate one copy of this page and program the necessary information. Then duplicate copies for your students.

Good for one FREE GIFT

_____
signed

Redeem on the first day of school.

©1998 The Education Center, Inc. • *The Mailbox® Superbook • Grade 1 • TEC450*

Use with "Busy Bees"
on page 10.

Patterns

Use with "Transportation Graph" on page 8.

Let Me Introduce Myself

Glue student's
picture here.

My name is _____.

I am _____ years old.

I have _____ brother(s) and _____ sister(s).

My favorite activity is

_____.

My favorite food is

_____.

My favorite book is

_____.

Here is my signature:

_____

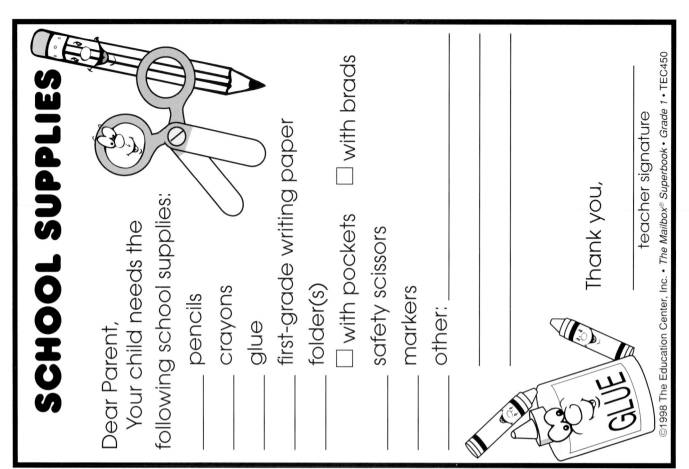

SCHOOL SUPPLIES

Dear Parent,
Your child needs the following school supplies:

- pencils
- crayons
- glue
- first-grade writing paper
- folder(s)
  - ☐ with pockets ☐ with brads
- safety scissors
- markers
- other:

Thank you,

_____
teacher signature

HOORAY!

_____

had a great first day in first grade.

_____
teacher signature

_____
date

Note To Teacher: Duplicate one copy of "School Supplies" and program it with needed supplies; then duplicate a class supply and send one home with each student. Duplicate a class supply of awards and send one home with each student on the first day of school.

BULLETIN BOARDS

To create this display, take a picture of each student. Mount each student's photo atop a playing card and have him personalize the card. Enlarge and color the character on page 38 and mount it to the board. Arrange the cards around the dealer and add the title as shown.

Spotlight your new student lineup with this eye-catching display. Have each student cut out, personalize, and decorate a construction-paper T-shirt (enlarge the pattern on page 39). Add the title and then display the T-shirts using clothespins and lengths of heavy string or plastic clothesline. Each day ask a few students to tell something special about themselves. Record each child's response on his T-shirt. What a fun way for students to get to know each other!

This back-to-school bulletin board is sure to put a polish on a great school year! Cut an apple shape from red, green, or yellow construction paper for each student. Instruct students to decorate their apple patterns to resemble themselves. (Provide construction paper of assorted colors, yarn, scissors, crayons, and glue for students to use.) Display the completed cutouts on a bulletin board covered with construction-paper branches.

This tail-waggin' job-assignment display will have your youngsters eager to perform classroom duties. Enlarge several copies of the doghouse pattern on page 40 and program each with a classroom job title. Color, cut out, and laminate each pattern. Cut a slit in each dog bowl; then mount the patterns on the board. Duplicate and cut out a class supply of bone patterns from page 40. Personalize one end of a bone for each child and then laminate. Assign a classroom duty by placing a bone cutout in each dog bowl, and you'll be ready for some hardworking hounds.

Student writing and fall colors add seasonal style to this fall bulletin-board idea! Mount the title and brown construction-paper tree branches. Duplicate a class supply of leaf-shaped writing paper on page 41. A student writes about the season and then draws a related picture in the blank space provided. Glue the writing paper atop a slightly larger leaf cut from fall-colored construction paper. To decorate, a child wraps one-inch fall-colored tissue-paper squares around the eraser end of a pencil, dips them in glue, and presses them onto the border of the leaf. When the glue has dried, mount the leaves on the branches.

Ask students to cut pumpkin shapes from orange bulletin-board paper. Then have students cut out, personalize, and attach green paper stems to the resulting cutouts. Display a pumpkin for students to observe; then have them brainstorm words that describe the pumpkin. Record students' responses on the chalkboard. Have each child write a different description of the pumpkin on his pumpkin cutout; then mount each pumpkin on the bulletin board. What a crop of descriptions!

Sail into learning about Columbus and his journey with this seaworthy display. Enlarge, color, and cut out the Columbus pattern on page 42; then mount it and the title on the bulletin board. Have students brainstorm objects that Columbus may have seen on his journey. Record students' responses; then have each child draw and cut out a different object. Mount each child's object and then add a label for each one to complete the display.

Create this interactive display to recognize National Children's Book Week (the third week in November) and to encourage reading success. Mount the title, road, trail markers, and starting and finishing lines. Have each student color, cut out, and personalize a runner (pattern on page 43). Laminate the runners; then use pushpins to post them at the starting line. As students accomplish their goals, they move their runners along the reading road. Reward each student when his runner reaches the finish line. Ready, set, read!

Students can show their thankful thoughts when they create this fine-feathered friend. Enlarge, color, and cut out the turkey on page 44. For turkey feathers, students trace and cut out their footprints from sheets of light-colored construction paper. Have each child write her thankful thought on the cutout. Mount the turkey, the feathers, and the title as shown. Gobble, gobble!

Hanukkah greetings abound from this festive display. Mount a large menorah cutout and the title. Have each child place a blue, five-inch construction-paper square in between two white, five-inch construction-paper squares. Have him fold the squares in half and place a star pattern (page 44) on the fold. He then traces the pattern, cuts it out, opens the fold, and staples on the crease. Separate the star layers and mount it on the board for a three-dimensional effect.

Filling Santa's sleigh with presents is a "ho-ho-ho" lot of fun! Mount a large sleigh cutout, the title, and one 9" x 12" sheet of wrapping paper per student. Have each student personalize a gift tag; then attach the tags and self-adhesive bows above the sheets of wrapping paper. Have each student select a sample of his best work. Attach the work samples to the presents as shown. Replace students' work samples weekly.

You'll receive a jolly response when you display these student-made projects. Enlarge, color, and cut out the Santa pattern on page 45. Have each student cut out snacks for Santa and his reindeer, and glue them onto a paper plate. Next have each child glue his plate onto a 9" x 12" sheet of colored construction paper. On his resulting placemat, have him write a short message to Santa. Mount the title, Santa cutout, and placemats on the board as shown. Ho! Ho! Ho!

Ring in the New Year with this festive, three-dimensional display. Using a variety of arts-and-crafts materials, have students decorate face-shaped cutouts to resemble themselves. Next have each child write a self-improvement goal on a light-colored triangle and glue it to the top of his face cutout. Assist each student in making a cut by the mouth and inserting a party blower through the hole. (Use tape as needed.) Mount the completed projects and title as shown.

Set the mood for wintertime writing with this motivational display. Mount a large igloo cutout and the title. Have each student write a story about winter on writing paper; then attach each story to a white circle cutout. Mount the resulting snowballs in a pile around the igloo. Scatter snowflake cutouts around the board to complete the frosty display.

Celebrate Dr. Martin Luther King, Jr.'s birthday in January with this inspiring bulletin board. With students, discuss Dr. King's life and his work for equality and peace. To follow up the discussion, have each child use a variety of art supplies to decorate the pattern on page 39 to resemble himself. Each child then writes his own dream on a cloud-shaped piece of white paper and glues cotton balls around its edges. Mount the student replicas with their cloud cutouts on the board for a dreamy display!

Spotlight the great musician, Louis Armstrong, during Afro-American History Month. Enlarge and cut out two copies of the musician pattern (page 46) on black construction paper. Mount the musician cutouts, the title, and a half-globe cutout as shown. Play a recording of Armstrong's song "What A Wonderful World" for your students. Write each line from the song on a different piece of white construction paper; then have students illustrate the lines. Mount the completed pages. Cut out music notes to complete the display.

Spread the message of friendship with this simple, yet heartwarming bulletin board. Mount the title and a large, red, construction-paper heart. Have each student draw a picture of herself being a good friend. Trim the drawings and glue them to the heart in a collage-fashion. Add a border of smaller hearts if desired.

Salute our country's possible future greats with this patriotic bulletin board! To begin, discuss the qualities of a good president. Then assist each student in creating a silhouette cutout of himself. Next, on a piece of writing paper, have each child write why he would make a good president. Mount students' writing assignments on pieces of construction paper and display them next to students' silhouettes.

Your lucky youngsters can share their creative talents on this shamrock-filled display. Duplicate a class supply of the shamrock pattern (page 47) onto green construction paper. After a brainstorming session of green items, have each student cut out his pattern and write a riddle about a green item. Then have each child trace and cut out a matching shamrock shape from lined paper and write the answer. Display completed shamrocks and answers (one atop the other) as shown. To complete the display, have students sponge-paint a shamrock border.

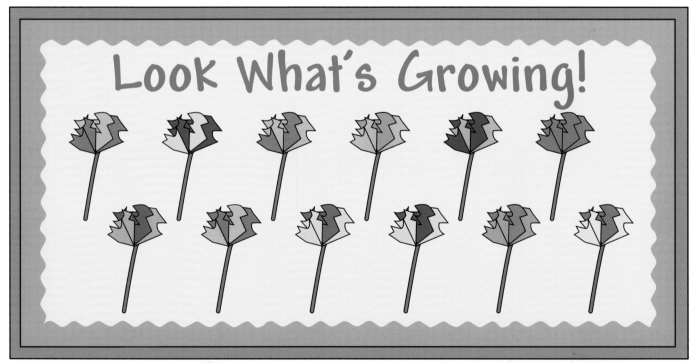

Welcome spring with this eye-catching display. Have each child place four tissue-paper squares atop each other and then fold them accordion-style. Next have the student pinch together the center of the folded tissue-paper squares and tightly bend a length of green pipe cleaner around the pinched area to secure the pipe cleaner in place. Carefully pull the tissue-paper squares apart to open the flower. Mount the flowers and the title on the display. Happy spring!

Guess who's hatching. Your students, that's who! Duplicate the egg pattern from page 48 onto pink, yellow, or light blue construction paper for each student. Have each student write a description of himself on the lines and then decorate the top of his egg. Then have each child cut his egg pattern on the bold line. Glue a photograph of each child to the top edge of the egg's bottom half; then use a brad to attach the two halves on the left edge. Mount the completed projects, the title, and some cellophane grass on the board for an "egg-citing" display.

This interactive display guarantees that the last week of school will be memorable. Mount bulletin-board paper to represent the water, the sky and the sand as shown. Ask students to brainstorm objects they would see at the beach; then have students use construction paper to make the objects. (You will need one object for each remaining day of school.) Number the front of each object and write an end-of-the-year surprise, such as lunch outdoors, on the back of each object. Mount the items on the board; then, on the remaining days of school, remove the daily item and enjoy the resulting surprise for the day.

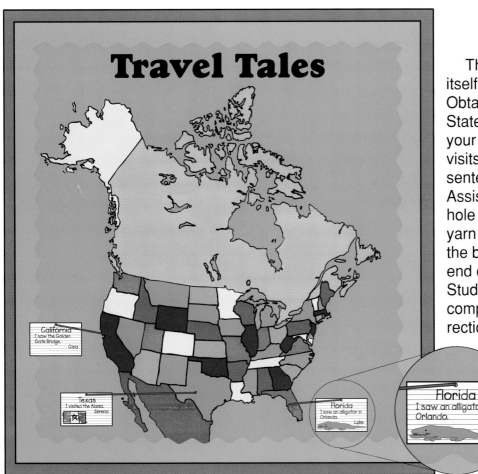

Travel Tales

California
I saw the Golden Gate Bridge.
Gina

Texas
I visited the Alamo.
Serena

Florida
I saw an alligator in Orlando.
Luke

Florida
I saw an alligator in Orlando.
Luke

This bulletin-board display lends itself to an instant geography lesson! Obtain a large map of the United States and Canada and mount it on your bulletin board. After a student visits another area, have him write a sentence about it on a large card. Assist the student in punching a hole in the card, tying a length of yarn through it, pinning the card to the board, and attaching the loose end of the yarn to the featured area. Students will have a visual aid to compare distances traveled and directions of their journeys.

We're Stuck On Doing Our Best Writing!

Pre-Write
Edit
Draft
Revise
Publish

The Writing Process

Students' enthusiasm for writing is sure to stick with this year-round display. Cut out a globe and base to resemble a gumball machine; then cut out five gumball shapes and label each with a different step in the writing process. Glue the gumballs to the gumball machine, laminate it, and mount it on the bulletin board. Invite youngsters to submit writing samples for the display. Mount students' edited writing atop a gumball cutout. Students will bubble with excitement when their work is displayed!

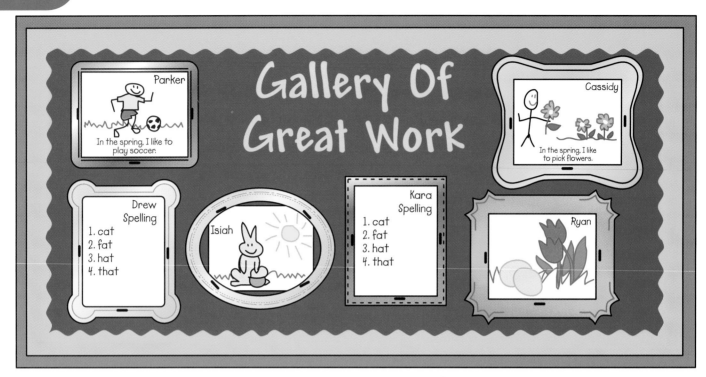

Showcase your students' greatest work in this class gallery. Cut gold or silver poster board into various-sized picture frames with standard 8 1/2" x 11" openings. Laminate each frame; then staple each frame to the board, leaving an opening at the top. When a student's work merits extra recognition, simply slip her paper into a mounted frame. Now, that's a stunning display of work!

Extra! Extra! Read all about this appealing idea to spotlight students' work. Mount 10 1/2" x 13" pieces of newspaper on the board. Mount the newspaper pieces, the title, and a newspaper border on the board as shown. Have each student attach his work atop a newspaper. Encourage students to keep their displays current.

Motivate students to cook up some good work with this eye-catching bulletin board! Suspend various kitchen accessories—such as an oven mitt, a spatula, and a spoon—from the board. Then mount students' best papers around the accessories. It won't be long before students are serving up gourmet work!

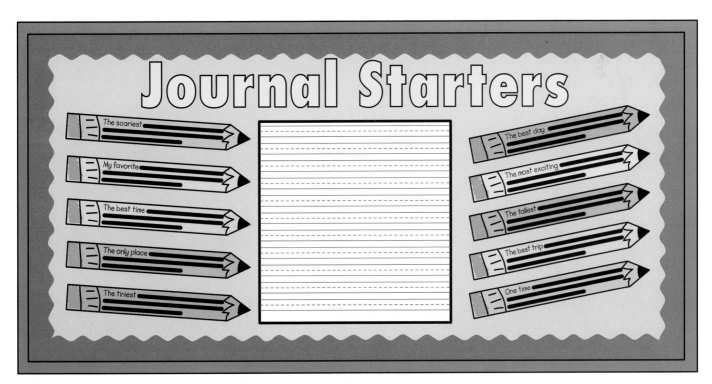

Students sometimes needs a jump start to come up with ideas for writing in their journals. Have each child write a journal starter on a piece of writing paper. After editing students' work, have each student decorate a 3" x 12" piece of light-colored construction paper so that it becomes a giant pencil; then instruct her to copy her edited journal starter on the pencil. Mount the pencils on the board. Now when a student is stumped for a writing topic, she can choose one from the board.

Patterns

Use with "This Year's Lineup" on page 24.

Use with "We All Have Dreams" on page 31.

Patterns

Use with "Helping Hounds" on page 25.

by _____

Pattern
Use with "Columbus Sights" on page 27.

Patterns

Use with "Thinking Thankful Thoughts" on page 28.

Use with "Happy Hanukkah!" on page 28.

Pattern

Use with "What A Wonderful World!" on page 31.

Pattern
Use with "Look Who's Hatching!" on page 34.

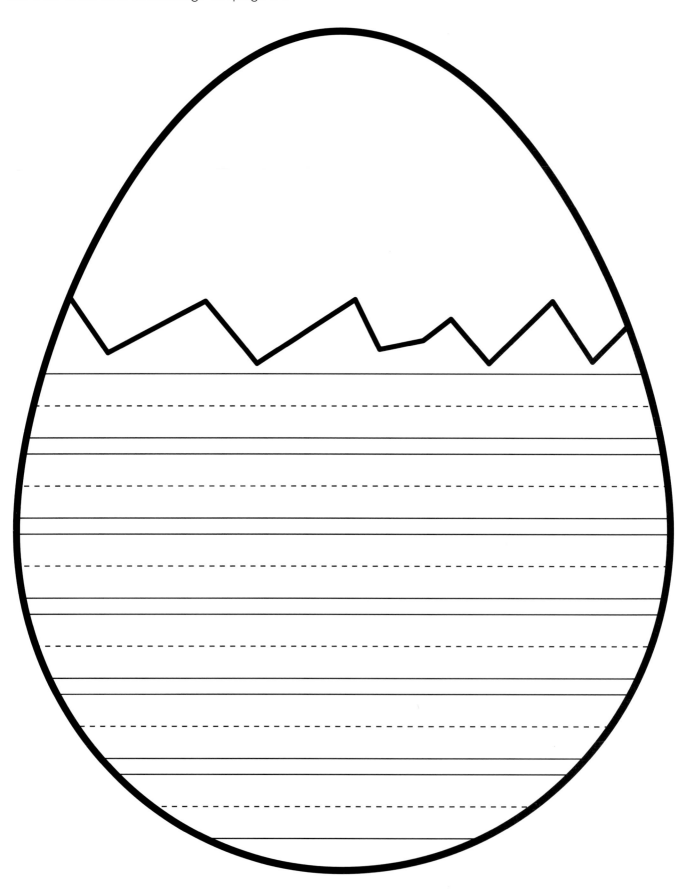

CLASSROOM MANAGEMENT

ROUTINES

Checking In

Here's an idea for combining daily attendance and lunch count. Duplicate a copy of the reproducible on page 60. White-out "Birthday," "Parent Name," "Home No.," and "Work No." and program as shown. Write each student's name on the list; then duplicate several copies and place one copy on a table near the door each morning. As students arrive, have them check the "I'm here" column and the appropriate lunch column. You'll know at a glance which students are at school and what their plans are for lunch.

Class Information

	Name	I'm here	Buying lunch	Buying milk only	Boxed lunch
1.	Beth	✓			✓
2.	Hannah	✓	✓		
3.	David	✓			
4.	Mike	✓		✓	
5.	Zach	✓	✓		
6.	Kim	✓	✓		
7.	Rob	✓			
8.	Mary				✓
9.	Pam				
10.	Shelia	✓			
11.	Becky	✓	✓	✓	
12.	Barry	✓	✓		
13.	Donna				
14.	Cathy	✓			
15.	Jennifer	✓		✓	
16.	Clevell	✓			✓
17.	Susan	✓	✓		
18.	Amanda	✓			✓
19.	Lisa				
20.	Karen	✓			✓
21.	Stephen	✓			✓
22.	Chris	✓	✓		
23.	Irv	✓			
24.					
25.					
26.					
27.					
28.					
29.					
30.					

©1997 The Education Center, Inc. • The Mailbox® Superbook • Grade 1 • TEC450

Take A Number

During times you're busy, use this orderly technique to handle students' requests for help. Number ten 4-inch construction-paper squares from one to ten. Laminate each card; then punch a hole at the top of each card. Suspend the cards in numerical order from a prominently located hook. When a student needs your help, he simply takes a card and waits for you to call his number when you are available.

Colorful Table Teams

Use color-coded student desks to help manage your classroom. Arrange your students' desks in groups of four; then attach a different color of construction-paper circle or self-adhesive dot to each desk in a group. Determine four jobs, such as paper collector, roll taker, table manager, and materials distributor. Then, during cooperative-learning activities, assign jobs by making a color choice. This teamwork will help keep the room more organized, and it will help students feel more responsible for their tasks.

HOMEWORK

OTHER IMPORTANT PAPERS

Fantastic Folders

Personalized homework folders help ensure that homework and other important papers reach home safely. Personalize a two-pocket folder for each student. Label one pocket "Homework" and one pocket "Other Important Papers." Near the end of each day, have students tuck their homework papers and any other important notes into the appropriate pockets of their homework folders. Request that parents check the contents of their children's folders each day and ensure that the homework assignments are returned in the folders the next day. These handy folders will become a regular part of your students' daily routines in no time at all!

Lights, Camera, Action!

Are you tired of repeating the classroom rules every few weeks? Here's the tip for you! After determining your classroom rules and discussing them as a class, have small groups of students role-play situations concerning each rule. Videotape the sessions; then watch them with students several times throughout the year to refresh those forgetful minds!

Discussion Corner

Help students take responsibility for their own behavior with a Discussion Corner. Arrange two small chairs in a quiet corner of the classroom. When two children have a minor argument, ask them to go to the Discussion Corner. Once they are sitting facing each other, each student should tell his side of the story without yelling or any interruptions. Each child must agree the argument is settled before they can leave the corner. At first you will need to direct the discussions, but as time goes by, students will learn to settle their problems on their own.

The Stop Card

Grab the attention of students who are misbehaving with a Stop Card. To make a Stop Card, draw a stop sign on a blank card and below it write "Please stop what you are doing"; then laminate the card. Keep the card handy, and when a student is disruptive, simply place the card on his desk. What a great way to discipline a student without interrupting your lesson or embarrassing him in front of his classmates.

Attention, Please

What do students do when they hear a rhythm of clap, snap, clap? Join in, of course! To help quiet students down between activities or to gain their attention, establish a simple pattern of claps, snaps, and/or slaps. Pause; then repeat the pattern again. Continue in this manner, challenging students to repeat the rhythmic pattern during each pause. It won't take long before you have their undivided attention, and that will be music to *your* ears!

STOP

Please stop what you are doing.

ORGANIZATION

EASY-TO-FIND REPRODUCIBLES

Try organizing your favorite reproducibles with this helpful tip. Label a divider page for each month of the school year or for each subject area. Hole-punch your favorite reproducibles and place them into the binder according to when they will be used or the subject area. Your reproducibles will be right at your fingertips when you need them.

Theme Storage

Organize theme-related books, art ideas, and center activities in theme storage boxes. Label a large, clear storage box (or plastic sweater container) for each theme used during the school year; then sort your teaching materials into the boxes. Store the stackable containers in a cabinet. This system makes retrieving your materials a snap!

File It!

Help students keep track of their ongoing work with this organizational tip. Using students' first names, label a tab on an accordion folder for each child. Have each student place any unfinished work in his file at the end of the day. Then, the following morning, have him retrieve his work to complete. Say good-bye to crumpled, incomplete papers in the back of your students' desks.

Whole-Language Organization

This organizational method is sure to be a hit if you use a literature-based approach. To organize your whole-language ideas, store a book in one side of a pocket folder and tuck ideas for related activities and sample art projects into the other pocket. Now when you go to look for teaching ideas related to a specific book, they'll be a cinch to find!

Storage Tips

If it seems like there are never enough cabinets or shelves for storing all your materials, then we have what you need! Peruse the storage ideas listed below—you're sure to find some nifty ways to organize clutter in your classroom.

- **Funnels**—Place a ball of yarn in each of several old funnels and pull the yarn end out of each spout.

- **Bandage Boxes**—These handy boxes can be used to store cards for different games. For easy identification, attach labels to the front of the boxes.

- **Videocassette Boxes**—Use these nifty containers to store small manipulatives.

- **Hardware Storage Boxes**—These boxes are great for organizing and holding stickers, as well as craft supplies such as sequins, beads, and buttons.

- **Hang-Up Shoe Bags**—Shoe bags with pockets work great for storing materials such as scissors, rulers, markers, and glue.

- **35mm Film Containers**—Students can use old film containers to store their lunch money or lost teeth.

- **Ice-Cube Trays**—These convenient trays work well for holding small amounts of colorful paints, as well as an assortment of mini supplies.

- **Peanut-Butter Jars**—Use these plastic containers to store game pieces and other small manipulatives.

- **Tennis-Ball Containers**—Students can use these containers instead of pencil boxes to store their pencils and crayons.

- **Margarine Tubs**—Another nifty container for storing small manipulatives.

- **Silverware Trays**—These trays work well for holding paintbrushes, rulers, markers, and colored pencils.

Tracking Progress

Record each student's progress in your classroom with this easy record-keeping system. Set up a notebook with a divider tab for each child. Place several sheets of notebook paper behind each tab. Each day circulate with a clipboard and sticky notes. Write your anecdotal notes and stick them to the clipboard. At the end of the day, simply transfer the notes for each child onto one of her pages in the notebook.

Portfolio Folders

Encourage your students to take an active role in maintaining their portfolios with these nifty tips. To begin, provide a variety of arts-and-crafts supplies, including glue, markers, crayons, cutouts for tracing, and scraps of construction paper. Have each student personalize the cover of her portfolio, then decorate it to reflect her likes and interests. Laminate the completed works of art for durability.

Once the folders have been decorated, give each student a sheet of smiley-face stickers. When a student wants a paper filed in her portfolio, she attaches a sticker to it; then she returns it to a designated basket. If desired, change the color of the stickers to reflect the start of a new grading period. Students will enjoy earmarking their papers. And later, during teacher-student portfolio reviews, it will be easy to tell which papers were student-selected.

Picture The Progress

Here's a simple idea to help keep track of your students' individual progress. Purchase a flip-top photo album like the one shown. Personalize a card for each student and insert each card into a different plastic sleeve. When you wish to make a note about or check on a student's progress, his card is readily available.

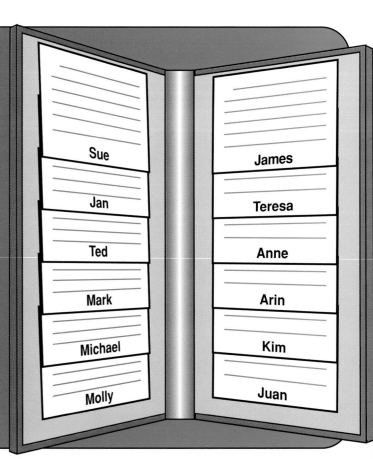

Sue

Jan

Ted

Mark

Michael

Molly

James

Teresa

Anne

Arin

Kim

Juan

The Birthday Visor

The birthday boy or girl will receive lots of special attention when he or she wears a special birthday visor. Create a birthday visor for each of your students to wear on his special day. Purchase a plastic visor from your local craft store. Use a paint pen or permanent marker to write "Happy Birthday" across the visor; then add birthday-themed stickers or imitation jewels. (Be sure to clean the visor thoroughly between each wearing.)

A Cake That Lasts And Lasts

A reusable cake helps you celebrate youngsters' birthdays all year long. Decorate a sturdy box with a lid to look like a birthday cake. Insert candleholders in the top of the lid. When it's time to celebrate a child's birthday, place the appropriate number of candles in the holders (not lit) and strike up a chorus of "Happy Birthday." If desired, place small items, such as pencils or stickers, inside the box cake, and invite the birthday child to reach in and choose one.

Summer Birthdays

Honor students who have summer birthdays with a day-long celebration at the end of the school year. Plan a day filled with birthday-related activities and treats. Be sure to include the usual birthday activities that are done throughout the year, too. Now each student with a summer birthday will be able to share his special occasion with his classmates!

Birthday Certificate

No matter how you choose to celebrate students' birthdays, be sure to present each child with a copy of the birthday certificate on page 61.

CLASSROOM HELPERS

Helper Chart—Of The Garden Variety

Assign classroom helpers with this attractive chart. Cut a picture from a seed catalog or seed packet for each classroom job; then add a classroom job—such as Snapdragon Snack Helper, Marigold Messenger, Dahlia Door Holder, or Tulip Trash Helper—to each. Next attach a craft stick to each picture, and mount the pictures, along with the title, on a piece of poster board as shown. Personalize a laminated, green leaf shape for each child, and store the shapes in a small container nearby. To assign jobs, simply use tape to attach a leaf cutout beside each picture.

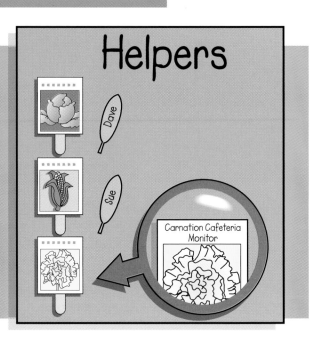

Help To The Rescue!

This easy-to-make chart will make assigning helpers a cinch! Duplicate the helper cards on page 62. Color the job cards as desired. Cut the cards out and glue each one to the front of a library card pocket. Display the pockets on a chart. Then label 3" x 5" index cards with the names of students who will be responsible for the jobs, and insert a card into each pocket.

Monitor Tags

Looking for a simple way to assign monitors? Then use this idea! Cut four 6-inch *M*s from cardboard or wood. Spray-paint each with a bright color and allow to dry. Each day—or week—choose four students to be the monitors and give an *M* to each child to place on his desk. Whenever you need assistance, simply announce, "Monitors needed."

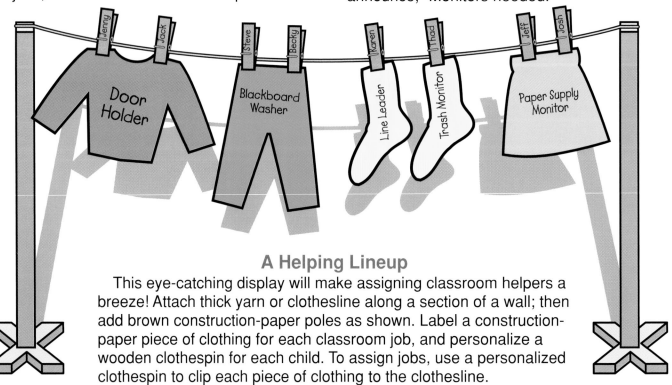

A Helping Lineup

This eye-catching display will make assigning classroom helpers a breeze! Attach thick yarn or clothesline along a section of a wall; then add brown construction-paper poles as shown. Label a construction-paper piece of clothing for each classroom job, and personalize a wooden clothespin for each child. To assign jobs, use a personalized clothespin to clip each piece of clothing to the clothesline.

EARLY FINISHERS?

What Next?

Looking for a way to eliminate the phrase "What do I do now?" from your students' vocabularies? Try this tip! At the beginning of the school year, have students brainstorm an "I'm All Finished" list. Tell students to imagine that everyone else in class is working quietly and they have finished early. What could they do without disturbing others? Record their responses, along with the suggestions below, on a piece of poster board, and display it in a prominent location.

Read a book.	Use flash cards.	Read a magazine.	Read a class-written story.	Write the numbers 0–100.
Write a story.	Count the months to their birthdays.	Design a school T-shirt.	Visit the school or classroom library.	Play a quiet game.
Make an art project.	Work on a puzzle.	Draw a map of the classroom.	Design a book cover for a favorite book.	Write a letter to the principal.
Clean and organize their desks.	Write in their journals.	Go to a center.	Write a poem.	Make a puppet.
Use a calculator to solve math problems.	Work on the computer.	Write a letter to a friend.	Make a card for parents or a friend.	Study spelling words with a friend.
Practice their handwriting.	Check the extra-work box .	Make a gameboard.	Write a recipe for a favorite food.	Write word problems for a friend to solve.
Draw a picture.	Clean an area of the classroom.	Work on a class newspaper.	Create an ad for a new kind of candy.	Draw a family portrait.

Field-Trip Treasure Hunt

Make any field trip a day to remember by making a treasure guide. In advance contact your tour guide to find out what points of interest will be discussed and toured. On a sheet of paper, draw some of the things that the youngsters are likely to see. Make a copy of this treasure guide for each child. Have each student carry his guide and a crayon with him on the trip. As your class encounters the different points of interest on the tour, have each child mark the picture on his treasure guide. When students take their guides home, they will easily remember the highlights of the trip and be eager to share them with their families.

Name Kim

barn ✔

cow

scarecrow ✔

pumpkin patch

Easy Identification

Make it easy for you and your chaperones to keep track of your class on field trips. The day before the field trip, send home a note with each child asking that he wear a specific color T-shirt. Now, that's an easy solution to an often-difficult problem.

Chaperone Nametags

Here's a handy idea that will help chaperones remember the students in their groups. Make a nametag similar to the one shown for each chaperone. Then write the names of the students in his group on the back of his nametag. If a student is missing, the chaperone simply checks the back of his nametag for a quick reference.

Field-Trip Video

Bring a video camera along on your next field trip. Ask a parent to take lots of footage of the trip. Then, on a rainy day, pop some popcorn and let your students watch themselves on television. Students are sure to enjoy the viewing—especially since they are the stars!

Mr. Noon

John   Brent
Carol   Sophia
Sam   Charida

FIELD-TRIP POSSIBILITIES

Try one of these exciting destinations the next time your class hits the road for a field trip.

COMMUNITY SERVICES

water department
police station
public library
fire station
bank
post office
hotel
factory
nursing home
newspaper press
TV station
radio station
recycling center
courthouse
hospital
bus depot
airport
train station

RETAIL STORES

bakery
computer store
restaurant
grocery store
florist

ANIMALS AND NATURE

animal shelter
aquarium
farm
orchard
park
pet shop
planetarium
science museum
veterinarian's office
zoo
horse ranch

EXHIBITS

planetarium
art museum
local historical site
children's museum

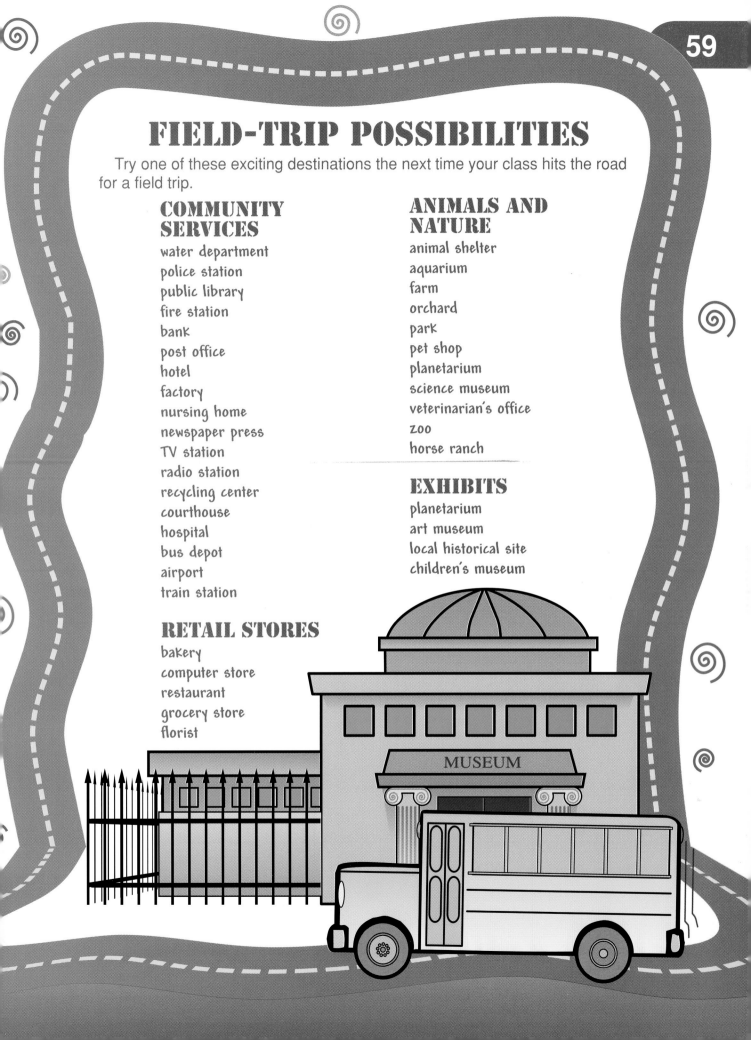

Class Information

	Name	Birth-day	Parent Name	Home No.	Work No.
1.					
2.					
3.					
4.					
5.					
6.					
7.					
8.					
9.					
10.					
11.					
12.					
13.					
14.					
15.					
16.					
17.					
18.					
19.					
20.					
21.					
22.					
23.					
24.					
25.					
26.					
27.					
28.					
29.					
30.					

Note To Teacher: Duplicate a copy; then program with the necessary information. Also use with "Checking In" on page 50.

Work Watchdog

How did you do on _____?
Color a face to answer each question.

1. Did I listen?

2. Did I work quietly?

3. Did I do my best?

4. Am I proud of my work?

5. Did I enjoy my work?

Happy Birthday,

_____!

From: _____

Date: _____

Note To Teacher: Duplicate several copies of the Student Evaluation Sheet. Have each student complete the sheet when evaluating his work. Use the certificate with "Birthday Certificate" on page 55.

Line Leader	Door Holder	Pencil Monitor
Paper/Supply Monitor	Board Washer	P.E. Equipment Monitor
Attendance Clerk	Light Monitor	Trash Monitor
Library Monitor	Rest Room Monitor	

Note To Teacher: Use with "Help To The Rescue!" on page 56.

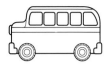 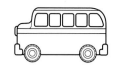

We're Going On A Field Trip!

Dear Parent,

We are planning a trip to

_____ on _____,

_____. Your child will need to bring:

- field-trip permission form (below)
- _____
- _____
- _____

Keep this note and post it at home as a reminder. Thank you.

_____
teacher's signature

Cut here and return the form below.

- -

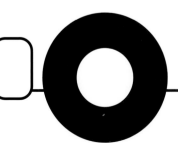

_____ has my permission to go on

the field trip planned for _____.
date

☐ I would like to be a chaperone.
☐ I'm not able to be a chaperone.

_____
parent's signature

_____
date

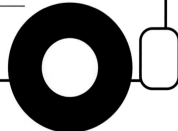

- -

Note To Teacher: Duplicate one copy of this page and program the necessary information. Then duplicate copies for your students' parents.

Student Information Card

First name _____   Last name _____

Address _____

City _____   State _____   Zip _____

Mother's name _____   Father's name _____   Home phone _____

Mother's work phone _____   Father's work phone _____   Student's birthdate _____

Comments:	In an emergency call:
Medical concerns:	

Hall Pass

teacher _____

Rest Room Pass

teacher _____

Note To Teacher: Duplicate a supply of the Student Information Cards and send one home with each student. Have parents complete the cards and return them to school. Duplicate the passes on the bottom half of this page. Color, cut, and then laminate the passes for durability. Using a hole puncher, punch a hole in the top of each pass. Tie a length of yarn through each hole.

Broken-Rule Notice

_____
date

Dear Parent,

Your child, _____, has broken a school rule by _____

_____

The following disciplinary action was taken at school: _____

_____

Your child's plan for improved behavior includes _____

_____

It is important to us that all our students have a positive and successful learning environment. Please support our efforts by visiting with your child to encourage appropriate behavior.

Please sign this notice and return it to school. If you have any questions concerning this notice, please contact me. Thank you.

Comments: _____   Sincerely,

_____   _____
                                                         teacher's signature

_____   _____
                                                         parent's signature

Mini Message

To:

From:

Note To Teacher: Duplicate a supply of the Broken-Rule Notice and send one home with students as needed. Duplicate a supply of the messages on the bottom half of this page to use as needed.

WEEKLY HOMEWORK ASSIGNMENT SHEET

Monday _____
date

Tuesday _____
date

Wednesday _____
date

Thursday _____
date

Friday _____
date

Note To Teacher: Duplicate one copy of this page and program the necessary information. Then duplicate copies for your students.

Transportation List

Teacher: _____

Room No.: _____

Grade: _____

BUS RIDERS   BUS

_____

_____

_____

_____

_____

_____

_____

_____

_____

_____

AFTER-SCHOOL-CARE STUDENTS

_____

_____

_____

_____

👟 WALKERS 👟

_____

_____

_____

_____

_____

_____

_____

_____

_____

_____

🚗 CAR RIDERS 🚗

_____

_____

_____

_____

_____

_____

_____

Note To Teacher: Duplicate one copy; then program with the needed information. Display the list in a prominent location.

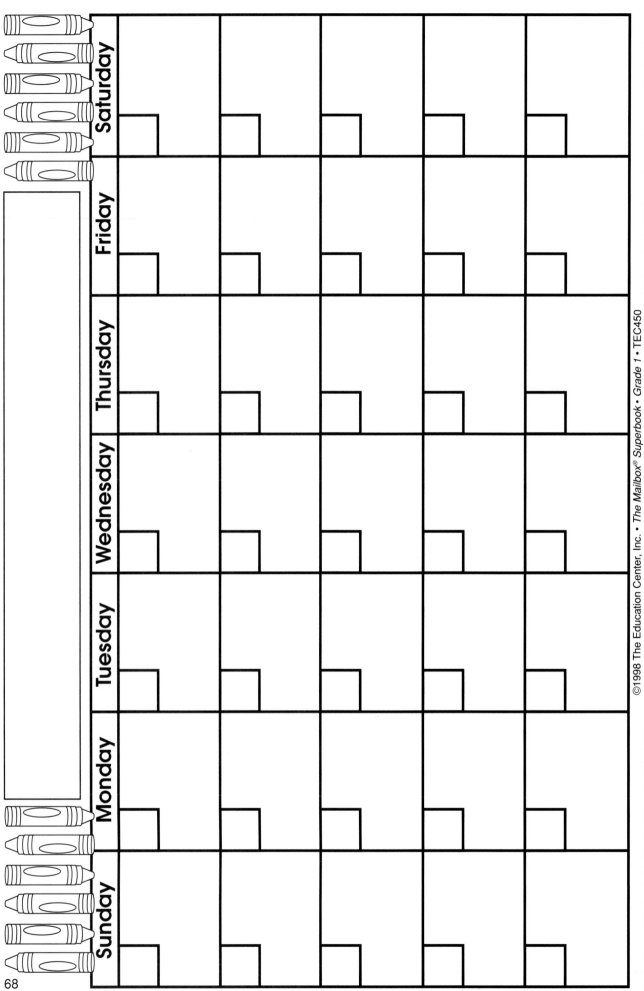

©1998 The Education Center, Inc. • *The Mailbox® Superbook • Grade 1* • TEC450

Note To Teacher: Duplicate one copy of this page, and write the name of the desired month at the top of the calendar. Write the appropriate dates in the smaller squares underneath each day of the week. Use this open calendar for monthly planning or to keep parents informed of classroom activities.

Sunday	Monday	Tuesday	Wednesday	Thursday	Friday	Saturday

BUILDING

STUDENTS' MOTIVATION, SELF-ESTEEM, & CHARACTER

MOTIVATING STUDENTS

This creative assortment of motivational ideas is just what you need to breeze through the year with students who are eager to learn!

Motivational Ideas

Try these ideas to motivate and reward your first graders for good work and behavior:

certificates	ribbons	badges
lunch with you	puzzles	pencils
teach a lesson	stickers	bookmarks
be the line leader	read to you	listen to a tape or record
a round of applause	"No Homework" coupon	play a game with a friend
note to parents	laminate their work	be the teacher's helper
extra P.E. time	snack	have principal sign their work

★You're A Super Student!★

Caught Being Good

Motivate students to be on their best behavior by enlisting students as peer observers. At the beginning of each week, have the students draw each other's names from a can. Instruct each child to keep an eye on her assigned classmate throughout the week, noting any positive behavior. Set aside a few minutes on Friday for students to report their observations. The children will enjoy being complimented by their peers, and you'll appreciate the positive atmosphere this activity generates.

Praise, Praise, And More Praise!

Increase student participation and encourage positive behavior by making it a habit to respond positively to your students. When the class quiets down after being asked, a quick "Thank-you, class" indicates that you appreciate their attention. When a student responds, correctly or incorrectly, to a question, thank him for his good effort. A positive environment is extremely motivational for students.

Auction Tickets

What first grader doesn't love treats? With that in mind, motivate your youngsters by holding an auction each month. To begin, duplicate and cut out a supply of the tickets on page 80. Each afternoon (or each Friday) give a ticket to each student who has exhibited good effort and behavior during the day (or week). Have students store their tickets in personalized envelopes. Then, at the end of each month, hold an auction during which students can spend their tickets on baked goods (donated by parents) and other inexpensive items.

We Earned It!

This cooperative behavior plan encourages students to work together toward positive classroom behavior. In advance program posterboard rectangles and squares with rewards, such as "Ten minutes of free time" or "Bring a favorite toy tomorrow." Wrap each reward with festive gift wrap; then mount each present on a bulletin board labeled "The Reward Board." When the class reaches a predetermined goal, such as everyone having turned in their homework, reward the class by having a student unwrap a present.

The Royal Corner

The opportunity to be the king or queen of the royal corner can entice students to complete their very best work. Place a beanbag, a pillow, several stuffed animals, a crown to wear, and a variety of books in a classroom corner. Reward students who complete satisfactory work with visits to the comfy, royal corner. Students will surely feel as if they are getting the royal treatment!

Seasonal Sticker Strips

Prevent students from turning in carelessly completed work with this motivational idea. Label the narrow side of a sentence strip for each student; then mount the strips on a bulletin board or classroom wall. Explain that each student receives one seasonal sticker for each perfect paper he completes. Encourage students to give their completed assignments a check before turning them in. When the papers are graded and returned, each student sorts through his papers to determine the number of stickers he has earned. He then attaches the stickers to his sentence strip. When a student earns a predetermined number of stickers, he redeems the strip for a free-time privilege or small treat.

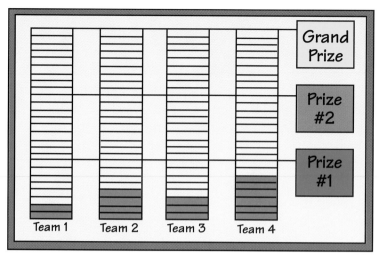

Cooperation Graph

Reinforce group efforts using a cooperation graph. Decorate and label a bulletin board similar to the one shown. To begin, have the students generate ideas about good teamwork. Then divide students into small groups and assign a team number to each group. During the next several cooperative-group activities, reward each team that shows good teamwork by coloring a bar on the graph for that team. When all the teams reach each predetermined mark on the graph, celebrate with a class reward. Consider no-homework passes or free-time privileges for the first two prizes, and a pizza or ice-cream party for the grand prize. If won't be long before students realize that teamwork really pays off!

Marvelous Manners

Encourage good manners in your classroom with weekly marvelous manners awards. Each Monday briefly review classroom rules and polite phrases, such as "Thank you" and "Excuse me." Then, during the week, look for students who demonstrate marvelous manners. Every Friday present each deserving student with a personalized marvelous manners award from page 80. What a polite and peaceful classroom you'll have!

Fishing For Rewards!

Inspire your first graders to excel with a Go Fish program. Cut out several fish-shaped patterns (page 81) and program each pattern with a different reward. Attach a large paper clip to the tail of each fish and place the fish in a bucket. To make a fishing pole, attach a magnet to one end of a string length; then tie the length of string to a ruler. When a student completes a predetermined number of assignments neatly and accurately, she gets to "go fishing" for a reward. To keep motivation high, create new fish with different awards for the bucket. Now, that's a unique way to reel in your youngsters' best work!

10 minutes of free time

Homework Motivator

Encourage all students to complete their homework with this cooperative plan. Decide on a reward treat, such as popcorn or ice cream, and draw a line on the board for each letter in the treat. For each day all students turn in their homework, randomly fill in a letter on the board for the treat. When all the letters are filled in, reward students with the designated treat. For a variation, use this idea to encourage perfect attendance!

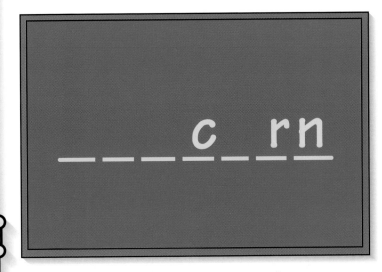

Writing Champs

Most first graders love learning to print the correct way. But once the newness of manuscript writing wears off, the quality of students' penmanship often suffers. To maintain high-quality manuscript writing, use the pencil-shaped punch card on page 81. First give each student a pencil-shaped card and have him personalize it. Each time a student demonstrates high-quality manuscript writing on his assignments, he earns a punch on his card. When his card is completely punched, he redeems it for a small treat, such as a pack of sugarless gum or a free-time coupon. What a great way to maintain high-quality penmanship on daily assignments!

SELF-ESTEEM

Encourage students to appreciate themselves and others with these teacher-tested, self-esteem boosters. It won't be long before your first graders are saying, "Yippee for me!"

Positive People

Get your students drawing for this self-esteem booster. Have each student draw a picture of himself dressed in his favorite clothes and then write his name on the drawing. When completed, each self-portrait is passed around the classroom. Everyone takes turns writing positive comments or words on each classmate's drawing. When all portraits have been circulated around the classroom, they are returned to their owners and read. Students will be thrilled to read what their classmates wrote!

Art Appreciation

Create an appreciation for art in your classroom by having an "Artist Of The Week." Each week display a piece of artwork from a different student. If desired decorate a poster-board frame with glitter and place the artwork in the center. Post a blank piece of paper beside the display. Encourage students to write comments on the paper praising their classmate's artwork. At the end of the week, let the artist take his artwork and his comments home. What a rewarding way to honor your youngsters' creativity!

Artist Of The Week
Chad

Good work, Chad!

You are a good drawer.

I like your picture.

Cool drawing!

Friendship Chain

Build self-esteem and friendship link by link with a friendship chain. Each time a child receives praise or thanks from a classmate, have him write the nice comment on a strip of construction paper. Add the strip to a class friendship chain. As the friendship chain grows, so will your students' self-esteem.

Secret Pals

Enhance positive feelings among students by assigning a classmate to each student in the class. Tell students to keep the identities of their pals secret. Then have each student write her secret pal a letter telling her how special she is. Encourage students to include compliments about their secret pals' unique qualities and talents. Have each student sign her letter anonymously. At the end of the day, collect the letters and read them aloud to the class. After reading each letter, reveal the identities of the secret pals so that everyone has a chance to thank her special friend for the compliments. A short note can go a long way toward building self-esteem!

Dear Cathy,
You are a great friend. Thank you for helping me with my math. You are so good with place value. You are also a great drawer.

Your secret pal

Hidden Notes

Help build students' self-esteem by hiding special notes in unexpected spots. Each day write a quick note of praise, thanks, or encouragement to three students. After students have left for the day, tuck the notes in students' desks, in their daily journals, or in their pockets on a class pocket chart. Imagine your students' faces when they find these special notes!

Achievement Album

Commemorate your students' milestones and achievements by keeping a class scrapbook. Purchase a ready-to-use scrapbook or a photo album. Then, throughout the year, add to the album pictures and announcements of your students' special achievements. Encourage students to decorate index cards on which they write about personal achievements. Students will enjoy perusing the album throughout the year.

All-About-Me Alphabet Books

Encourage reading and build self-esteem with a fun project activity. Read aloud *ABC I Like Me!* by Nancy Carlson. In this delightful alphabet book, friendly characters show readers just how easy it is to feel good about themselves—letter by letter. After sharing the book, have each student write a special quality about herself for each letter of the alphabet. Then, during the next few weeks, have the student write and illustrate each quality in the same manner as the alphabet book. Bind each student's set of completed pages between two construction-paper covers. Have the student personalize and decorate the cover as desired. Invite each youngster to place his book in the classroom library for his classmates to read.

I am a good <u>dancer</u>.

Design-An-Award Center

Shine the spotlight on everyone's positive qualities with a design-an-award center. Stock a center with blank badges, index cards, stickers, yarn, glitter, markers, and other supplies. With your permission, students can visit the center to make awards for their classmates. Encourage students to make awards for classmates who help each other, attain important goals, or work extra hard. Students love the opportunity to be artistic and compliment their classmates at the same time!

Mr. Feel Good

MR. FEEL GOOD

How do you tell your students that they are positively great? Try using an old hand puppet named Mr. Feel Good. To begin, introduce your students to Mr. Feel Good by telling them that he feels good only when he compliments children. Explain to students that Mr. Feel Good likes to see students getting along with each other, trying their best, and helping each other. Place Mr. Feel Good in a prominent location in the classroom and remind students that he will be watching them each day. Then, at the end of each day, use Mr. Feel Good to compliment youngsters who have had a good day. What a fun way to help students feel good about themselves!

Catchy Compliments

Looking for a way to recognize your youngsters' outstanding efforts without just saying "good job"? Then search through this collection of compliments. You're sure to find lots of catchy compliments that will get your youngsters hooked on doing only their best work!

Excellent!
That's the best ever.
Sensational!
Wow!
I knew you could do it!
That's it!
Exactly right.
I'm happy to see you working like that.
You did that very well!
Tremendous!
Good thinking!
You're doing fine!
Superb!
You're on the right track now.
Wonderful!
Congratulations!
Now you have the hang of it!
You outdid yourself!
That's really nice!
That is first-class work.
Way to go!
Keep up the good work!
You are a fast learner.
Right on!
Good for you!
You're doing beautifully!
You are really working hard today!
That's quite an improvement.
I couldn't have done it better myself!

You figured that out fast!
You are a joy!
You've got that down pat!
Fantastic!
Now, that's what I call a fine job!
You are a pleasure to teach.
That's perfect!
Super!
You must have been practicing.
That's how to handle it.
Much better!
You are really learning a lot.
You certainly did well today.
I'm proud of you!
You're getting better every day!
That's coming along nicely.
You are really going to town.
Nothing can stop you now.
Outstanding work!
Look at you go!

CHARACTER EDUCATION

Help your first graders grow into persevering, caring, cooperative, and responsible people with these character-building activities!

WANTED:

Responsible First Graders

Round up responsible buckaroos with this unique bulletin-board activity. Decorate a bulletin board (similar to the one shown) that lists responsible behaviors. Discuss the behaviors with your youngsters; then explain that you will be looking for students each week who exhibit these responsible behaviors. At the end of the week, reward each deserving child with a roundup award from page 81. No doubt, students will turn into responsible wranglers! Yee-ha!

WANTED

WHO: First Graders
WANTED FOR: Being Responsible Students
DESCRIPTION:
1. Completes work on time.
2. Keeps desk and cubby clean.
3. Listens and follows directions.
4. Has proper tools ready to use.
5. Completes homework.
6. Works quietly and neatly.

REWARD BEING OFFERED

Good-News Headlines

Promote kindness among your students with good-news headlines. Each morning write a headline on the chalkboard that briefly describes how a student was kind to a fellow classmate the day before. Then write a sentence or two detailing this act of kindness. Reading this good news at the beginning of the day is sure to inspire positive behavior in your students!

MARK HELPED JASON AT LUNCH YESTERDAY

Jason dropped his tray of food and Mark helped him clean it up.

Yes, I Can

Adopt a "Yes, I Can!" attitude in your classroom with this character-building activity. To begin, read aloud *The Little Engine That Could* by Watty Piper (The Putnam & Grosset Group, 1991). After reading the story aloud, ask students to tell about tasks they mastered after trying again and again. Responses might include learning to ride a two-wheel bike, learning to swim, or memorizing math facts. Provide each student with a copy of the engine pattern on page 82. First instruct the student to draw himself in the window as the engineer. Next have him write "I CAN" on the front of the pattern and then list some of his accomplishments on the back of the pattern.

To follow up this activity, ask parent volunteers to send various canned goodies from home, such as cans of peanuts, potato chips, or fruit cocktail. After sharing the treats with your students, clean the cans and decorate them with construction paper. Label each can "Yes, I Can!" Then, throughout the remainder of the school year, have students record their individual accomplishments on slips of paper and place them in the cans. Periodically read the accomplishments aloud to give your youngsters a pat on the back.

Cooperation Hunt

Promote cooperation and reinforce first-grade skills with a classroom scavenger hunt. In advance create a list of tasks similar to the ones shown. To begin, remind students that cooperation means working together and helping each other in a positive way. Divide students into small groups and distribute a copy of the list to each group. Read the tasks aloud; then challenge each student group to work together to solve and record the tasks on the list. Reward the teams that work together in a positive manner with a treat such as a free-time pass or a coupon good for lunch with the teacher.

1. Write six words that rhyme with *at*.
2. How many chairs are in the classroom?
3. Draw four things in the room that are in the shape of a square.
4. How many boys are in the class?
5. Write three addition problems with the sum of ten.

Auction Tickets

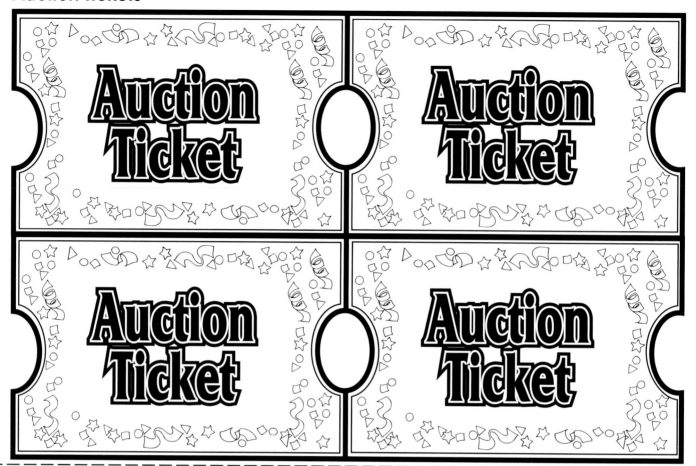

Award

_____
name

has Marvelous Manners!

Please.

Thank-you!

_____
teacher's signature

_____
date

Note To Teacher: Use the tickets with "Auction Tickets" on page 71. Use the award with "Marvelous Manners" on page 72.

Use the pencil pattern with "Writing Champs" on page 73. Use the fish pattern with "Fishing For Rewards" on page 73. Use the award with "Wanted: Responsible First Graders" on page 78.

Pencil Pattern

Name

Fish Pattern

Award

Put 'er here, Pardner!

You have been a responsible wrangler this week!

To: _____

From: _____

Date: _____

©1998 The Education Center, Inc. • *The Mailbox® Superbook* • *Grade 1* • TEC450

Pattern And Award

Use the train pattern with "Yes, I Can" on page 79. Duplicate and personalize the award as needed to reward students.

_____

is a
star student
for

_____

_____ .

_____
Teacher's Signature

PARENT COMMUNICATION

Parent Communication

The Weekly News

This weekly edition of student-reported classroom news is sure to be a parent pleaser! Each afternoon ask a different group of students to determine the most newsworthy events of that day. Have one volunteer from the group dictate the group's summary of the day's news as you record it on a copy of the newsletter form from page 92; then program the newsletter with any additional information. Each Friday send home a copy of the classroom news with each student. Parents will appreciate the opportunity to get the scoop on their child's classroom happenings. Extra! Extra! Read all about it!

Classroom News

Date: March 10, 1998

Teacher: Mrs. Belville

Monday We started new centers today. All the centers have to do with plants, since that's what we are studying.

Tuesday We went on a field trip to a plant nursery.

Wednesday We worked with counting pennies, nickels, and dimes in math.

Thursday We finished working on our class big book called "Plants In Our World."

Friday We had a spelling test. We also had a science quiz on plants.

Looking Ahead
We will continue to study plants for one more week. Next week we will work on telling time in math.

Help Wanted
We need parent volunteers to help us organize our class play.

Superstars
Sarah Whitley was our Student Of The Week.

Reminders
Plant journals are due next Friday.

Classroom Information

Provide important school information to parents with this user-friendly reproducible that lasts throughout the school year. Duplicate a copy of the computer on page 93; then program the blanks with the appropriate information. Next duplicate a class supply on brightly colored paper and, if desired, laminate each one for durability. Encourage each family to post its user-friendly sign in a highly visible place for reference throughout the school year.

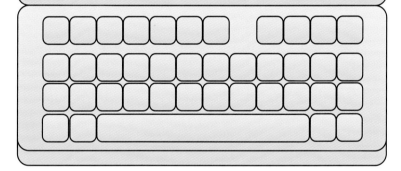

Playground Scrapes

Lots of minor accidents on the playground but no time to jot parents a note about the incidents? Use an injury report to keep parents informed of the bruises or abrasions and the steps that were taken to care for the wounds. Duplicate one copy of the injury report on page 94. Program the report with your school's telephone number and your signature; then duplicate several copies to have on hand. Whenever a child gets hurt on the playground, simply complete the report and send it home with the student. The report takes only a few minutes to complete, and parents will appreciate your concern.

RESOURCE CHECKOUT

Set up an area in the classroom that contains reinforcement materials that may be checked out by parents. Provide flash cards, file-folder games, reproducibles, and reading books. Place a checkout sheet for parents to sign when borrowing games, cards, or books. Be sure to inform parents that if they are unable to visit the school, they may write you a note and you will send the materials home with their children. What a good way to provide parents with appropriate learning materials to use with their children!

Name	Date	Item
Mrs. Chick	10-21	Sight word cards

Weekend Wonder Work

Facilitate a great parent/child dialogue about school with the help of "Wonder Work." Each Friday send home a list of "I wonder" questions for each parent to ask his child. Include school-related items such as happenings in the classroom that week, upcoming projects, or homework. (For example, "I wonder, how did your science experiment on shadows turn out?") Not only will this idea keep parents informed, but students will learn to reflect on their week and evaluate the things they are learning.

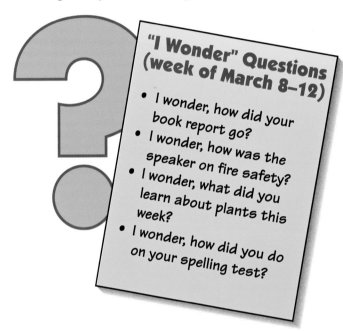

"I Wonder" Questions (week of March 8–12)

- I wonder, how did your book report go?
- I wonder, how was the speaker on fire safety?
- I wonder, what did you learn about plants this week?
- I wonder, how did you do on your spelling test?

Monthly Planners

Keep parents informed by sending home monthly planners. At the end of each month, duplicate a blank calendar (page 68) and program it with the upcoming month's activities. Include items such as field trips, special visitors, library day, due dates for special homework or projects, test dates, assemblies, and class pictures. If desired, write the unit of study at the beginning of each week. Duplicate a copy of the completed calendar for each child to take home. Encourage students and parents to display the planners in a prominent spot. Parents will appreciate the reminders and the daily insight that the planners provide.

WEEKLY UPDATES

Keep parents up-to-date on their children's academic and social progress with this weekly checklist. Personalize a folder for each student. Fill in the grading codes on the weekly report form (page 95) with your own symbols; then staple a copy of the report inside each child's folder. During the week, file corrected papers in the folders. On Friday complete each child's checklist; then send each child home with her folder. Ask students to return their folders and initialed checklists to school on Monday. Use the checklists as references during parent-teacher conferences.

Parents On Tape

Not all parents are able to spend time in their child's classroom during the school year. Provide these parents with an opportunity to be involved in the classroom without having to be present. Take turns sending home a tape recorder and a blank cassette tape to interested parents. Instruct the parent to use the tape to record himself reading a popular children's book, telling his favorite story from childhood, singing a song he learned as a youngster, or reciting a few favorite poems. Students will be thrilled to listen to the new voices in the classroom!

Parents As Pardners

Round 'em up—parents, that is! Parent participation is vital to every teacher's classroom. Be sure to make the most of your year by inviting parents to take an active role in your classroom. Duplicate a class supply of the reproducible on page 96 and send a copy home with each student. Be sure to reward parent volunteers with big smiles!

Parent Of The Week

Put the spotlight on the parents! Each week select a different parent to be the "Parent Of The Week." Invite this parent to visit the classroom during the week and share a hobby, speak about his career, or read a book to the class. (If the parent is unable to visit the classroom, suggest that he write a letter to the class and send some pictures of himself.) Present each parent with a thank-you card or certificate upon leaving. Both parents and students are sure to be delighted with this honoring of parents!

Sharing Class Books

Looking for a way to get students and parents to read together? Try sending home classroom-published books! Each time your students finish making a class book, attach a comment sheet on the inside cover and send the book home with a student. Instruct the child to read the book to a parent, ask his parent to write a note on the comment sheet, and then return the book to school the next day. Route the book to each child until everyone in the class has had a turn to take it home. Not only are parents getting the chance to read with their children, they're seeing what's going on in the classroom, too!

Parent-Child Homework Journal

Provide parents with the opportunity to be involved with their child's homework. At the beginning of the year, ask each child to bring a three-ring binder filled with notebook paper to school. Each Monday write a homework assignment on the board, such as "Look in a magazine or newspaper to find the letters that spell your first and last name. Glue them together to spell your name." Then have students copy the homework assignment in their notebooks. During the week have students work with their parents to complete the assignment. Ask parents to write a comment on the assignment page describing how their child completed the task. When students return their notebooks, read each comment and respond as needed. Hole-punch each student's corrected homework and place it behind her assignment page. At the end of the year, each student will have a portfolio of work to take home.

Open House ...

OPEN HOUSE MURAL

Students will be thrilled to have drawings of themselves to greet them the morning after back-to-school night. In advance cover a bulletin board with light-colored paper and place a supply of crayons and markers within reach. Ask each parent to take a few minutes to draw on the bulletin board a picture of his child doing what he likes best at school. Remind each parent to sign his drawing. If there are some children whose parents were unable to attend, draw a quick picture of them, too, so that everyone will have something to smile about in the morning.

Mrs. Betty Jones

Mr. Thomas Allen

Mr. and Mrs. Justin Douglas

Bushels Of Help

Here's a unique way of asking for supplies at Open House that will "a-peel" to parents! In advance use colored chalk to draw a large tree shape on the chalkboard. Cut out several apple shapes from red, green, or yellow construction paper. Label each apple cutout with the name of a needed supply, such as baby-food jars or cotton balls. If needed, label more than one apple with the same supply. Place a piece of magnetic tape on the back of each cutout, and then place the apples on the tree. Write a note on the board explaining that any parent who is willing to donate an indicated item should take the corresponding apple cutout. Each parent can place the magnetic apple on her refrigerator as a reminder to send in the supply at her convenience.

yarn

felt

lunch bags

craft sticks

glitter

baby-food jars

Parents: If you are able to donate any of these items, please take one of the apple cutouts and send the item to school at your earliest convenience.

Thank you!
Mrs. Beckwith

Tour Guides

Involve students in your back-to-school night by making them tour guides. To distinguish guides, have each guide wear a bright-colored nametag. Station student guides at different areas in the classroom, such as the different centers, reading-group area, and computer. Rehearse a short presentation with each student so he can explain what goes on at his particular station. Students will be thrilled at the chance to familiarize their parents with their first-grade classroom.

A Handy Parent Resource

Here's an informational resource your parents will love! Type up all those things parents will need or want to know about. Include things such as a list of themes and skills for the year, planned field trips, students' names, birthday party guidelines, school vacations, homework and discipline plans, and a class schedule. Collate the pages, hole-punch them, and place them in folders. Then distribute the folders during Open House. Parents will appreciate having this valuable information organized in one place for them.

Parent Portraits

Surprise parents at Open House with student-drawn portraits. Have each child draw a picture of his parent, parents, or guardian. Then assist students in writing short descriptions of these special people. Mount the portraits on a bulletin board or classroom wall for parents to view on the big night.

Find The Footprints

This Open House activity will have parents in step with their children. Several days before Open House, ask each student what his favorite classroom area or learning center is. Have each child trace and cut out a set of his footprints. Encourage him to decorate and personalize his footprints as desired. Then, right before Open House, tape each child's footprints in his favorite classroom area. Also, in each area, display manipulatives, lessons, and activities that would take place there. During Open House, have each parent search the room to find her child's pair of footprints. When the parent finds the footprints, encourage her to peruse the area to try to discover why it is her child's favorite. What a unique way for parents to learn about their child's favorite activities!

Parent-Teacher Conferences

Parent-Conference Schedules

Gather student information from parents and schedule conferences at the same time with this unique idea. Duplicate one copy of the conference note (with questionnaire) on page 97 and sign your name. Next reproduce a class supply of the notes and personalize a copy for each child. Two weeks before conferences, send a note home with each child. As each conference note is returned, send a reminder note (page 94) to be posted at home. Parents will appreciate the reminders, and you will be delighted with the completed questionnaires they bring to the conferences.

Parent-Conference Record Form

Parent-conference record forms can help in presenting important information to your students' parents. Duplicate a class supply of the form on page 98. For each child, record the necessary information on a copy of the form. At each conference, present the form along with samples of the child's work. What a great way to share with parents the needs and accomplishments of their children!

Student-Led Conferences

Add a twist to parent-teacher conferences by inviting your students to facilitate the discussions. In advance, brainstorm a list of questions to ask students concerning their academic and social progress. Use the questions to help create a reproducible similar in format to the one shown; then duplicate a copy of the form for each student. A few days prior to the conferences, meet with each student to discuss the questions on the form and record his response. Set the forms aside to use when meeting with the parents.

At the parent-teacher conference, again ask the student the questions from his completed form. If the child has difficulty answering, refer to his previous response written on the form. After the student responds to each question, add additional praises or concerns. Parents will be amazed at their children's awareness of academic strengths and weaknesses, and students will be proud to be included in this important meeting!

Name: Jordan Manlove   **Date:** Oct. 14, 1998

1. What do you think is your best subject at school? Why?
   Reading. I like to read fun stories.
2. What subject do you think you need to work harder in?
   Math.
3. What can you do to improve in this subject?
   I can pay attention better and practice with flash cards.
4. Do you think you do your neatest work?
   I try to. Some days I'm not as neat.
5. Do you get your assignments turned in on time?
   Most of the time. Sometimes I forget to do all my work.
6. How do you get along with your classmates?
   They are my friends. We have fun playing tag at recess.

Sample Table

Set up a table and chairs in the hall outside your classroom door. Display textbooks, class-made books, and student projects for parents to view while waiting. Also post student artwork in the hall to brighten the waiting time. Parents will appreciate your thoughtfulness!

Report-Card Questions

Questions usually spring to mind as parents look over their child's first-quarter report card. However, many times those questions are forgotten by the time conferences occur. Help open the lines of communication by creating a comment sheet (similar to the one shown) to include in each student's report card. Ask parents to complete the sheet and return it along with the child's signed report card. Review each parent's comments; then set the sheets aside to review with parents during conferences. Now you can be certain that parents' questions and concerns are being answered.

Parent – Teacher Conference Preparation

Mr. and Mrs. O'Neil,
Please record your responses to the items below and bring this sheet to our conference on __Oct. 14__ at __3:30__ a.m./(p.m.)

1. After reviewing my child's report card, I am concerned about_____

2. I am pleased with_____

3. Overall questions I have about first grade are_____

Planning For Successful Conferences

Try these teacher-tested tips to establish a friendly atmosphere and positive attitudes at your next parent-teacher conference:

▷ Place paper and pens at the table for parents to use to take notes if needed.

▷ Reduce the chance of intimidating feelings by making sure your seat and the parents' seats are at equal height.

▷ Cover the table with a tablecloth or brightly colored bulletin-board paper.

▷ Place flowers in the middle of the table.

▷ Provide reproducibles in boxes labeled according to subjects. Parents can choose from these for their children to use as reinforcement at home.

▷ Place photographs of students taken during special events in a photo album for parents to view.

▷ Provide coffee, tea, or water and a plate of cookies for parents to nibble on.

▷ Keep parents up-to-date with current issues in education. Place relevant articles from magazines or newspapers in folders labeled with their topics for parents to refer to as desired.

 # Classroom News

Teacher: _____   Date: _____

Monday _____
_____
_____
_____
_____

Tuesday _____
_____
_____
_____
_____

Wednesday _____
_____
_____
_____
_____

Thursday _____
_____
_____
_____
_____

Friday _____
_____
_____
_____
_____

Looking Ahead

Help Wanted

Superstars

Reminders

Note To Teacher: Use with "The Weekly News" on page 84.

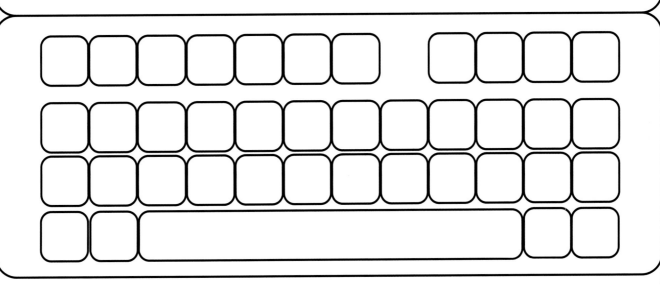

First Grade Is User-Friendly!

School Name: _____

School Address: _____

_____

School Phone Number: _____

Principal: _____

Secretary(ies): _____

Guidance Counselor: _____

Lunch Time: _____:_____ – _____:_____

Price Of Lunch: _____

   Milk Only: _____

Special Classes:

_____   Day: _____

_____   Day: _____

_____   Day: _____

_____   Day: _____

_____   Day: _____

Other Important Information: _____

_____

_____

Note To Teacher: Use with "Classroom Information" on page 84.

Playground Scrape

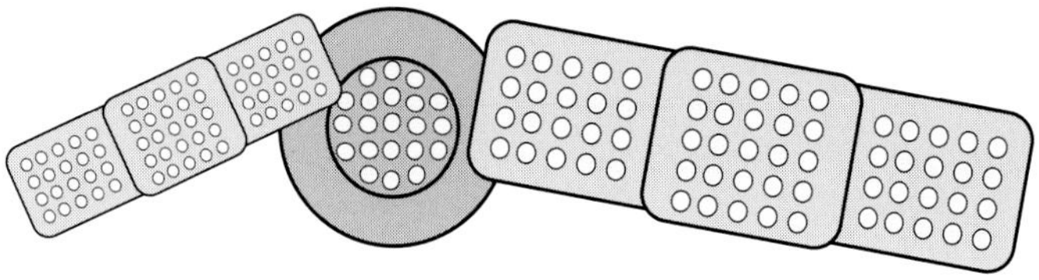

Date: ____________________

______________________________ was injured on the playground
(Child's name)

today. He/she ____

____

____

____.

These steps were taken: ____________________________________

____.

If you have any questions, please call ______________________
(School number)
during school hours. Thank you!

____
(Teacher's signature)

Conference Reminder

Student: ____________________

Teacher: ____________________

Room: ____________________

Date: ____________________

Time: __________ to __________

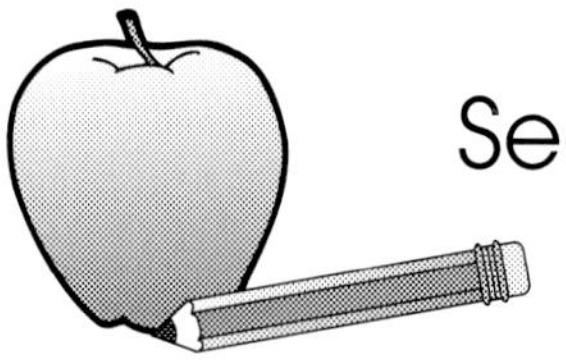

See you then!

Conference Reminder

Student: ____________________

Teacher: ____________________

Room: ____________________

Date: ____________________

Time: __________ to __________

See you then!

©1998 The Education Center, Inc. • *The Mailbox® Superbook* • *Grade 1* • TEC450

Note To Teacher: Use the injury report with "Playground Scrapes" on page 84. Use "Conference Reminder" with "Parent-Conference Schedules" on page 90.

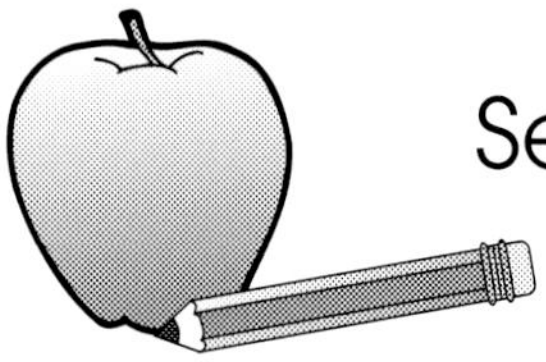

Weekly Update

Name: _____

$\square$ = Outstanding $\square$ = Needs Practice $\square$ = Satisfactory	Week Of:									
Listens Carefully										
Stays On Task										
Follows Directions										
Treats Others With Respect										
Follows Class Rules										
Does His/Her Best Work										
Parent's Initials										

Missed Assignments

_____
date

Dear Parent,

_____ needs to complete

the following assignments:

_____

_____

_____

_____

This work is due by _____.

Your help and support are greatly appreciated.

Sincerely,

Please sign and return.

_____
(Teacher's signature)

_____
(Parent's signature)

Note To Teacher: Use the weekly checklist with "Weekly Updates" on page 86. Duplicate copies of "Missed Assignments" to use as needed.

95

Parent Roundup

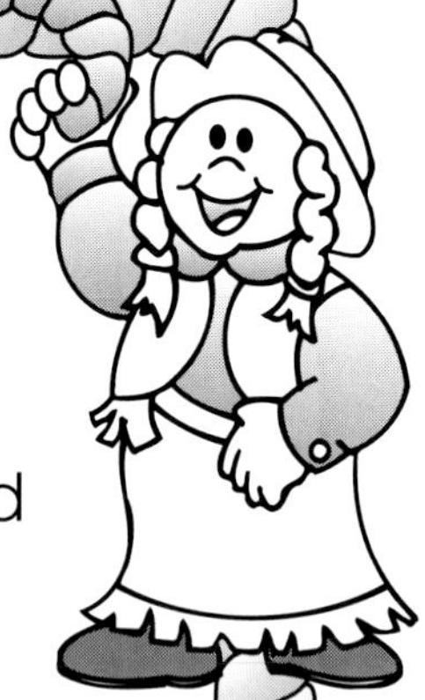

We would like to have you be a part of our classroom and help make our school year a big success. Children need to have good role models and warm, loving adults around to work with them. If you have a little extra time and the desire, your help would be greatly appreciated. If possible, please participate in our roundup by completing this form and returning it with your child to school. I look forward to hearing from you.

____
teacher

I would like to be involved in the following classroom activities:

______ small-group work with students
______ grading papers
______ filing papers
______ duplicating reproducibles
______ constructing bulletin boards
______ other ______________________________

I would like to assist in the following special projects:

______ chaperoning field trips
______ reading program
______ organizing class parties
______ plays
______ telephoning from home
______ fund-raising
______ helping at parties or on special days
______ other ______________________________
______ other ______________________________

______________________________ parent's name

______________________________ child's name

______________________ phone number

Note To Teacher: Use with "Parents As Pardners" on page 86.

Dear Parent,

Your conference for _____ has been scheduled at
                                    child's name

_____ on _____, _____.
      time   day   date

To confirm your conference time, please complete the bottom portion of this form and return it to me as soon as possible.

In preparing for our visit, I would like to know more about your child and your areas of concern. Please answer the questions below and bring the form to our conference. Thank you for your help!

Sincerely,

_____
teacher's signature

My child's strengths are _____

_____

My child's interests are _____

_____

My child's attitude toward school is _____

_____

Topics I am most concerned about include:

_____ work habits at school   _____ self-control

_____ listening/attention   _____ relations with friends

_____ study habits at home   _____ self-esteem

_____ respect for others   _____ other _____

_____ attitude   _____

_____ skill level in _____

Comments: _____

_____

_____

☐ I plan to attend my child's conference at the scheduled time.
☐ I will need to reschedule our conference. Best times for me: _____

_____

_____   _____
      child's name   parent's signature

Parent/Teacher Conference Record Form

Student: _____

Grade: _____

Date: _____

E = Excellent
S = Satisfactory
N = Needs Improvement
U = Unsatisfactory

Work Habits

Listens	
Follows directions	
Works independently	
Works accurately	
Works neatly	
Completes work on time	

Attitude

Gets along with others	
Is courteous and cooperative	
Demonstrates self-control	
Shows respect for others	
Cares for personal property	
Assumes responsibility for actions	

Subjects (Level/Comments)

Reading _____

_____

Math_____

_____

Written Language _____

_____

Science _____

_____

Social Studies_____

_____

Other:_____

_____

Goals ☆

_____

_____

_____

_____

Suggestions

Home _____

_____

_____

School _____

_____

_____

©1998 The Education Center, Inc. • *The Mailbox® Superbook* • Grade 1 • TEC450

98   **Note To Teacher:** Use with "Parent-Conference Record Form" on page 90.

Extra Help Needed

_____
date

Dear Parent,

_____ needs extra help with _____

_____.

Here are some suggestions for how you can help your child at home:

_____

_____

_____

_____

Thank you.

Sincerely,

_____
teacher's signature

Please call

A Note To Let You Know...

Note To Teacher: Duplicate several copies to have on hand. Use as needed.

You're Invited!

Dear Parent,

You are invited to

_____
event

at our school at _____
time

on _____,
day

_____.
date

We hope to see you there!

Sincerely,

_____
teacher's signature

We're Celebrating!

Dear Parent,

We are celebrating _____

_____

at _____ on _____,
time   day

_____. Please help us
date

celebrate by _____

_____

_____

_____

Thank you!   Sincerely,

_____
teacher's signature

Note To Teacher: Duplicate one copy of this page and program the necessary information. Then duplicate copies for your students' parents.

ARTS & CRAFTS

ARTS & CRAFTS

Here We Are!

"Here We Are!" is a unique art project that helps kids get to know one another at the beginning of the school year. Provide each student with a small paper plate on which she draws her face. The student then introduces herself by drawing her hobbies, family, interests, and other favorites on a sheet of paper. To complete the project, she adds construction-paper arms and legs that match what she is wearing. Mount these "students" on your classroom walls for everyone to meet!

Grandparents' Wall Hangings

Photo frames make great gifts for students to give to their grandparents on National Grandparents Day. Begin by providing each student with an 8" x 10" piece of poster board and a 6 1/2" x 8 1/2" piece of drawing paper. Have each student hole-punch two holes at the top of both sides of the poster board. Next have the student draw a picture of his grandparent and himself on the drawing paper, then glue it to the center of the poster board. The student then glues buttons around the illustration to create a frame. Assist each student in threading a length of yarn through the two holes and tying the ends to create a hanger. Any grandparent would be proud to own this special wall hanging!

Fall Foliage Drawings

Enlist your students' help in collecting colorful autumn leaves for this project. To make a fall drawing, have each student glue his leaves in any position onto a 9" x 18" piece of white construction paper. Then have students use crayons or markers to draw a picture incorporating the leaves in a unique way. It's an "autumn-matic" way to stretch your students' imaginations!

"Fan-tastic" Ships

Set sail for "fan-tastic" fun with this art activity for Columbus Day. Have each student fold a sheet of 9" x 6" construction paper accordion-style to create a fan. Next have her pinch and twist one end, then glue or staple the fan to a piece of drawing paper in the position of a sail as shown. Instruct the student to cut out a ship from construction paper and glue the ship under the sail. She then uses crayons or markers to add water and other decorations as desired.

Nina

"Boo-tiful" Ghosts

Delight your youngsters by having them create friendly spooks to add a seasonal touch to the classroom. Provide each student with a 9" x 12" piece of white construction paper. Then, without telling students they are creating ghosts, have each student cut out any closed shape. After students cut out their shapes, have them transform their shapes into ghosts by using cotton balls and construction paper. To make a ghost, the student pulls apart cotton balls and uses glue to attach the cotton to the cutout. The student then adds a construction-paper face and ghostly accessories as desired. What a bunch of shapely spooks!

CANDY-CORN MOSAICS

Let the popular Halloween candy corn turn your Halloween art lesson into a special treat! Play some Halloween music or a story tape as you have youngsters tear orange, yellow, and white construction paper into approximately nickel-size pieces. Next give each student a piece of candy corn and ask him to observe the arrangement of the three colors on the candy. Then have each student create a candy-corn mosaic. Give each student a piece of black construction paper with the outline of a piece of candy corn drawn on it. Have the student spread glue to fill the candy-corn shape, then press each of the three colors of paper pieces on the glue as shown. Adapt this idea to create other Halloween mosaics, such as jack-o'-lanterns, spiders, ghosts, or witches.

Indian Corn

Harvest a bumper crop of colorful Indian corn with this tissue-paper activity. Have each student wad brown, orange, yellow, and black squares of tissue paper, then glue them onto a tagboard cob cutout (page 116) to resemble Indian corn. Then have each student trace his cob cutout onto a brown paper lunch sack and cut on the outline (through both layers). Next have him slightly crumple the two resulting cornhusk shapes.

To assemble the project, place the ear of corn between the two cornhusks. Hold the lower edges of the cutouts together as you fan the tops slightly. When the desired look is achieved, staple the lower edges in place. If desired fashion a bow from raffia, and glue it to the project as shown.

Recycled Christmas Ornaments

Turn Styrofoam® meat trays into colorful Christmas ornaments! In advance cut holiday shapes from white Styrofoam® meat trays. Provide each student with a holiday shape and have her use permanent markers to decorate both sides. After she decorates the resulting ornament, have the student punch a hole at the top of the ornament and add a piece of yarn for hanging. Now that's a dazzling, yet earth-friendly ornament!

Sandpaper Gingerbread Ornaments

These gingerbread ornaments look good enough to eat—but don't! They are for festive decoration purposes only. In advance create several gingerbread-bear templates using the pattern on page 117. To make a gingerbread ornament, have each student use a template to trace the gingerbread bear onto a 5 1/2" x 8" piece of sandpaper. After she cuts out the shape, have each student paint her gingerbread-bear ornament with tempera or fabric paints. After the paint dries, invite her to use a fine-tipped permanent marker to draw on other features—such as a nose, a mouth, eyes, and buttons. Hole-punch the top of the ornament; then thread a length of ribbon through the hole for hanging. Display the gingerbread ornaments in the classroom; then send them home to become treasured family keepsakes!

Sparkling Menorahs

Light up the Hanukkah season with these dazzling menorahs!

Materials for each student:
1 paper plate
two 8" pieces of aluminum foil
one 12" x 18" piece of black construction paper
eight 3/4" x 5" strips of blue construction paper
one 3/4" x 6" strip of blue construction paper
nine 1" squares of yellow construction paper
glue
scissors

Steps:

1. Fold the paper plate in half; then open it up and cut it in half on the crease.
2. Cover the bottom of each paper-plate half with an aluminum-foil piece.
3. To create the base of the menorah, glue the covered paper-plate halves onto the black paper so the curved edges meet as shown.
4. Glue the blue construction-paper strips to the black paper to create candles as shown.
5. Cut a flame from each yellow square.
6. Glue a flame to the end of each candle.

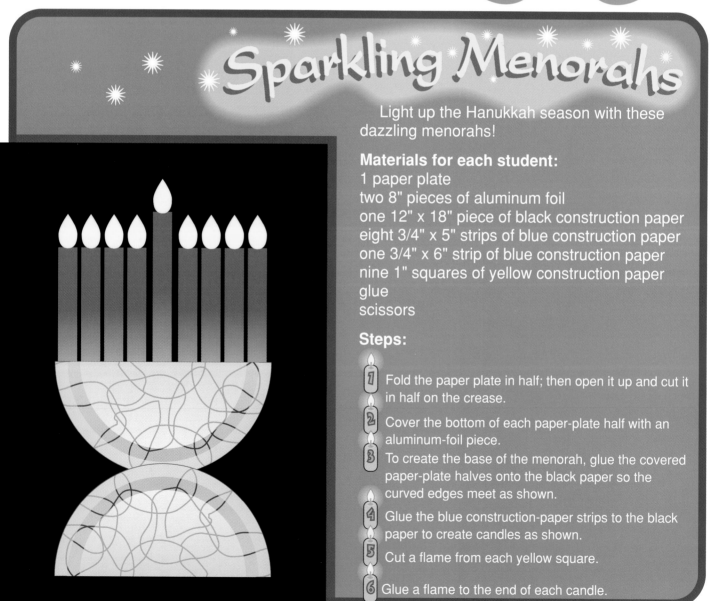

Enlighten your students as to the traditions of Kwanzaa with this festive kinara (candleholder) and the mishumaa saba (seven candles) that are traditionally lit during the seven-day Kwanzaa celebration.

Materials for each student:

7 clothespins
red, green, and black paints
paintbrush
one 9" x 12" sheet of
   brown construction paper

seven 1" x 2" pieces of
   yellow construction paper
scissors
glue

Steps:

1. Fold the sheet of brown construction paper into thirds lengthwise to form three narrow columns.
2. Open up the paper and make a one-inch fold on each of the long edges.
3. Glue these two folds together to make a flat, triangular base for the kinara.
4. Paint three clothespins red, three clothespins green, and one clothespin black. Set them aside to dry.
5. Cut a flame shape from each of the seven pieces of yellow construction paper.
6. Glue each flame cutout to the handheld end of a painted clothespin.
7. Clip each clothespin to the kinara base as shown.

A Star-Studded New Year

Ring in the new year with this star-studded display. Duplicate a copy of the star pattern on page 117 for each student. Then enlarge a copy of the star pattern and duplicate a class supply onto yellow construction paper. To begin give each student one white and one yellow star. The student cuts out both stars and then writes a personal goal for the new year on the white star. She accordion-folds a 1" x 3" strip of yellow construction paper, then glues one end of the strip to the center of the yellow star, and the other end to the back of the white star. To complete the project, have each student add glitter or sequins around the border of the larger star.

SPARKLING SNOWFLAKES

Sparkle away those winter blahs with these glittering snowflakes. To make a snowflake, a student glues an even number of cotton swabs to a three-inch tagboard circle as shown. Next he spreads glue on the tagboard circle and sprinkles glitter on the glue. Pin these glistening snowflakes to winter bulletin boards or attach them to your classroom walls to create a classroom blizzard.

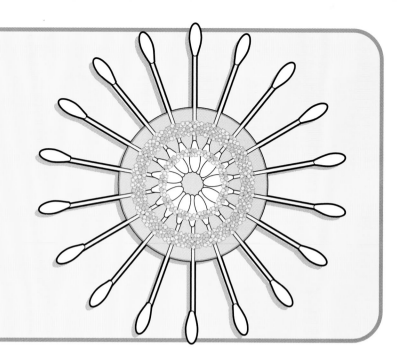

Snowfall Scenes

Welcome winter with this tasty winter art activity. To begin, a student cuts construction-paper scraps and glues them onto a piece of dark blue or black construction paper to create a wintry scene. Next fill a large paper grocery bag with air-popped popcorn; then add a small amount of white tempera paint. Close the bag and shake it to mix the paint with the popcorn. To create the appearance of snow falling, the student places his paper in the bag, closes it, and shakes. After shaking the bag for approximately one minute, he removes the paper and sets it aside to dry. What a winter wonderland!

Heart Critters

If your students are wild about animals, February is the perfect time to create a bunch of wild-and-crazy critters. Provide students with various colors of construction paper, several sizes of heart-shaped templates, glue, crayons, and scissors. Have each student decide on an animal to make out of hearts; then have her trace and cut out one or more hearts. After cutting out the heart(s), have each student glue it (them) to a piece of contrasting construction paper. Then have the student use crayons to convert the heart(s) into a wild animal. These critters may be wild, but they'll have a lot of heart!

VALENTINE BAGS

These adorable heart creatures double as Valentine's Day mailboxes. Each student will need one white paper lunch bag, a four-inch red construction-paper square, two 1" x 5" strips of red construction paper, and two 1" x 8" strips of red construction paper. To begin, a student cuts out one construction-paper heart, decorates it to resemble a head, and glues it to the top of the bag as shown. Next he accordion-folds the four construction-paper strips. He then glues the two shorter strips to the side of the bag for arms, and the two longer strips to the bottom of the bag for legs. Encourage students to add smaller construction-paper hearts as hands and feet, and then use crayons to decorate and personalize their bags. These bags are a sweet treat even before they are filled with cards and candy!

Cherry Tree Pencil Holders

Celebrate George Washington's birthday with these eye-catching pencil holders. In advance gather a class supply of toilet-paper tubes and cut six 1/2-inch slits on each end of each tube. To make a pencil holder, a student paints the outside of a toilet-paper tube brown, then sets it aside to dry. As the tube dries, he cuts a treetop shape from each of three 3" x 4" pieces of green construction paper. Next the student hole-punches several cherries from a small piece of red construction paper and glues them onto the treetop cutouts. After the toilet-paper tube has dried, the student folds the tabs out on one end of the tube to create roots. On the other end of the tube, the student slides each treetop cutout between two slits as shown. Tape each student's tree to his desk by its roots. There's sure to be no chopping down of these cherry trees!

Shamrock Masterpieces

Invite the luck of the Irish with these lovely shamrock works of art. Provide students with two-inch, eight-inch, and ten-inch shamrock templates. Have each student trace the eight-inch template onto a piece of white paper and the ten-inch template onto a piece of green paper. Then, using a two-inch template and a green crayon, the student traces shamrock shapes onto the white paper. After tracing several shamrocks, she decorates each shamrock with a different design. To complete the project, she glues the white paper shamrock to the green one. Display these green masterpieces in your classroom to add a touch of St. Patrick's Day spirit!

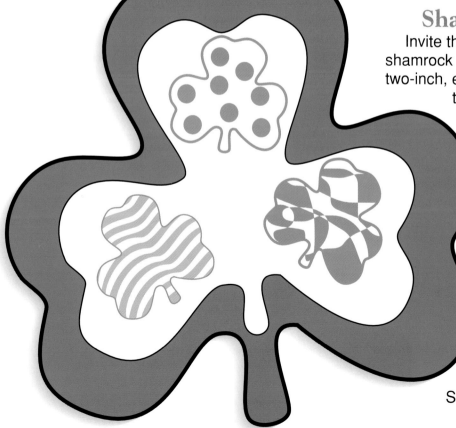

A "Hand-some" Bouquet

Your classroom will bloom with these spring flowers. Have each child place the palms of her hands in green paint, and then on a piece of construction paper as shown. (Be sure to add a squirt of dishwashing liquid to the paint to make cleanup easier.) When the paint is dry, have the student cut out ten construction-paper flowers and glue one flower to each finger. Voila, a floral masterpiece!

Gina's Floral Bouquet

"Eggs-ellent" Spring Greetings

Hatch an Easter bunny with this card-making project.

Materials for each student:
2 egg patterns (page 118) duplicated onto colorful construction paper
two 4" construction-paper circles
scrap construction paper in various colors
glue
scissors

Steps to make the egg:
1. Cut out two egg patterns of the same color construction paper.
2. Cut one egg in half along a zigzag line to create a cracked egg.
3. Glue the edges of the cracked egg's lower half to the uncut egg pattern to create a pocket.
4. Glue the top edge of the cracked egg's top half to the uncut egg pattern to create a flap.

Steps to make the bunny:
1. Cut one construction-paper circle in half to create ears.
2. Glue the resulting ear cutouts to the top of the other circle.
3. Add construction-paper features to the bunny's face.

Steps to assemble the card:
1. Lift the top flap and slip the bunny into the pocket of the egg.
2. Personalize the front of the egg as desired.
3. Write an Easter message on the back of the egg; then deliver the egg to someone special!

Mother's Day Surprise

Moms are definitely going to get attached to these magnetic refrigerator frames that highlight students' work! Purchase a precut mat, or cut a mat from poster board for each student. To decorate a frame, a student tears pieces of colorful construction paper and glues them onto the frame in a mosaic pattern. Then he attaches self-adhesive magnetic strips to the back of the frame to complete the project. Mothers will be pleased to receive these frames on Mother's Day!

✔+   Jason

Spelling

1. cat
2. dog
3. pig
4. sun
5. see
6. hot
7. top
8. cap
9. hat
10. ham

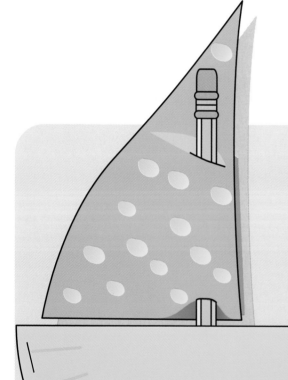

Sail Into Second Grade

Making this end-of-the-year art project is a breeze! To make a hull of a sailboat, have each student paint the bottom side of a paper plate. When the paint is dry, have him fold the plate in half (with the painted side out) and use a hole puncher to punch a hole in the center of the folded edge. To create a mast, the student places a pencil through this hole and tapes it to the inside of the plate. Next he decorates a diagonally cut piece of paper for a sail; then he punches two holes in it and inserts the pencil through the holes as shown. To complete the project, the student staples along the open edge of the paper plate and personalizes it as shown. What a great way to assure students of smooth sailing ahead in second grade!

Initial Art

This simple yet fun art project is sure to stretch your students' imaginations! Provide each student with a bulletin-board letter of his first initial. Have him trace the letter on construction paper, cut it out, and then glue it in any position onto a contrasting color of construction paper. Challenge each student to use crayons to draw a picture incorporating the letter in some distinctive way. Now, that's creative artwork!

Felt Lollipops

These sweet treats have taste appeal! Cut various colors of felt into 3/4-inch-wide strips, and distribute two different-colored strips to each student. To make a lollipop, a student glues the strips together—one atop the other—and then rolls them together to resemble a striped lollipop. Next she glues the loose end down and glues a lollipop stick (or a cotton swab with one end cut off) to the back of the rolled felt. When the glue is dry, assist the student in wrapping a piece of plastic wrap around the lollipop and tying a colorful bow at its base. Top off the project with the *real thing*—lollipops, that is!

Nifty Notebooks

These composition-style notebooks are just what you need to liven up writing projects that you plan to display on a bulletin board. To make the notebook, a student sponge-paints a 12" x 18" sheet of black construction paper with white paint. When the paint has dried, the student folds the paper in half, writes her name on a self-stick label, and attaches the label to the front of the resulting notebook. The student then staples her writing assignment in the opened notebook. Mount the completed notebooks for everyone to see!

Susan

A New View Of Drawing

This unique art activity will have your students on the floor—literally! In advance tape a sheet of white construction paper under each student's desk. To begin, ask students if they have ever been anywhere that has had its ceiling painted. After allowing students to share any experiences, ask students to brainstorm the problems they might encounter if they were painting the ceiling of their classroom. Then have each student lie on his back under his desk. Challenge each student to draw a design that would be suitable for the classroom ceiling. After students complete their drawings, tape them together, and mount them on your ceiling or a bulletin board if desired.

Art Recipes

Use the following recipes to expand your classroom palette.

Edible Peanut-Butter Clay

(Serves 18 students)
2 cups peanut butter
1 cup honey
1 teaspoon oil
3 cups instant dry milk

Mix peanut butter with honey. (Swirl oil in the measuring cup before measuring to avoid sticking.) Add instant dry milk, a little at a time, until stiff. Mix with hands. Refrigerate overnight. The next day, provide each child with a piece of waxed paper and some peanut-butter clay. Have students wash their hands and then model their clay into different shapes. When finished, let the students eat their tasty creations.

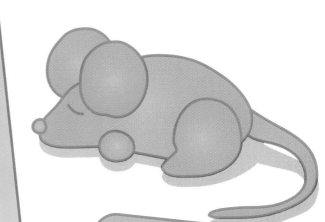

Papier-Mâché

liquid starch
cold water
newspaper strips

Mix equal parts of liquid starch and cold water. Dip newspaper strips in the mixture before applying to a form of chicken wire or rolled newspaper.

Magic Putty

2 parts regular white Elmer's® Glue
    (not Elmer's® School Glue)
1 part liquid starch

Mix ingredients. Let dry in air. Have students experiment with it and write down their observations: it bounces, it stretches, it lifts pictures from newspapers. Store the putty in an airtight container.

No-Cook Modeling Dough

2 cups flour
1 cup salt
water
food coloring or tempera paint
2 tablespoons vegetable oil (optional)

Mix the ingredients using enough water to create the desired consistency. If desired, add oil to keep the dough from hardening; then store it in an airtight container after each use.

Pattern

Use with "Indian Corn" on page 105.

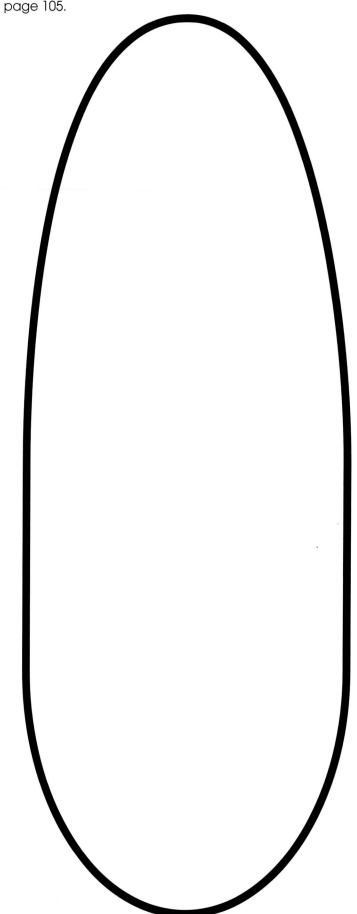

Patterns

Use the gingerbread bear with "Sandpaper Gingerbread Ornaments" on page 106.

Use the star with "A Star-Studded New Year" on page 107.

Pattern
Use the egg with " `Eggs-ellent'
Spring Greetings" on page 111.

CENTERS

CENTERS

Materials List For Making Centers

USING CENTERS

Centers are instructional stations that are set up away from students' regular work seats. They provide students with the opportunity to work individually; to be responsible for completing assignments on their own; and in some classrooms, to make choices about what they do. Some teachers use centers as enrichment activities. In that case, students work at centers whenever they finish a given assignment. Other teachers might choose to have students work at centers at an assigned time during the week.

The activities set up in centers need to be designed so that students are able to complete them with little or no assistance from an adult. Centers can be set up on almost any subject. Most teachers use centers to reinforce a skill or topic the class is currently studying.

REMINDERS FOR SETTING UP CENTERS

1. Decorate centers so that they are appealing to students.

2. Use words and symbolic pictures to write directions to centers. Be sure to also orally explain the center directions.

3. Schedule a time for each student or group of students to visit each center once a week. See the ideas described in "Where Is Everybody?" (page 121) for suggestions.

4. Determine a plan for students to record completed centers. (See page 127 for a center recording sheet.)

5. Place all materials at the center that students will need to complete the work. File folders and small boxes are helpful for storing center supplies.

6. Determine the maximum number of students that may go to each center.

7. If possible, design a method for students to check their own center work.

- scissors
- glue
- construction paper
- paint
- game markers
- math manipulatives
- file folders
- crayons
- newspapers
- magazines
- envelopes
- resealable plastic bags
- writing paper
- story paper
- drawing paper

A COLLECTION OF CENTERS

Listening Center: Provide students with headphones to listen to a set of taped directions or recorded stories. Drawing activities, writing assignments, or skill sheets can accompany each recording.

Writing Center: Activities might include writing journals, reports, letters, or stories. Place a variety of writing materials—such as stationery, story paper, and dictionaries—at the center.

Math Center: Provide hands-on activities that reinforce a current math skill.

Language Arts Center: Provide games and activities to reinforce basic skills.

Reading Center: Place reading materials—such as children's magazines and encyclopedias, picture books, poetry selections, and newspapers—at the center. Consider spotlighting fiction and nonfiction books on specific topics or authors.

Art Center: Use seasonal themes, curriculum tie-ins, and materials in many different mediums for students to use in creative expression.

Science Center: Provide students with the opportunity to use microscopes, hand lenses, scales, and other equipment as they conduct experiments and make observations.

Social Studies Center: Encourage students to play games or complete activities that reinforce the basic skills in this curriculum area.

Games: Keep a supply of purchased games, puzzles, critical-thinking activities, and word searches at the center to help students develop problem-solving strategies.

WHERE IS EVERYBODY?

Try these easy ideas to keep tabs on which students have visited a center.

- Each week create a simple chart similar to the one shown for students to refer to daily. Reprogram the chart each week or at the beginning of the center rotation cycle.

Center Schedule	Mary, Sue Paul, Mike	Amy, Jane, Harry, John	Gina, Rachel, Bob, David	Wendy, Joe, Rose, Roger
Monday	math	writing	spelling	language
Tuesday	writing	language	art	spelling
Wednesday	language	art	math	writing
Thursday	art	spelling	writing	math
Friday	spelling	math	language	art

- To allow students independence in choosing their centers, use a pocket chart and personalized cards to create a chart similar to the one shown. When it is time for centers, have each student place his card in the column of the center he would like to attend. Be sure to set a limit on the number of students allowed at each center.

Math	Listening	Writing	Art	Science
Mark	Jenny	Alex	Martin	Carlos
Beth	Karen	Jon	Angie	Keisha
Owen	Justin	Brandi	Tia	Ryan
Ruben	Seth	Alan	Cassie	Zach

CENTERS, CENTERS, EVERYWHERE!

Need more room for your classroom centers?
Then try these ideas for making the most of unused space.

Use chalkboard paint, available from most craft stores, to paint the surfaces of old cabinets. After the paint has dried, students may use chalk to write on the cabinets just like on a chalkboard. Keep chalkboard erasers handy to clean the boards.

Place a chart stand between two desks as shown. On each side of the chart stand, suspend a poster labeled with directions. Students can sit on either side of the chart stand and complete a center activity. Changing the centers is as simple as changing the posters.

Place a strip of magnetic tape on the back of a learning center; then stick the center onto the side of your file cabinet.

Convert a discarded paint easel to divide a room. Suspend a center task on the easel.

Cut off one side of a large box to create a center area inside. Desks can also be placed around the outside of the box for additional centers.

Divide the top of a table with cardboard to create four work areas. Cut two long pieces of cardboard, each the length of the table. Mark the middle of each piece and make a partial slit. Turn the pieces so they intersect each other and slide the cut portions together. Use masking tape to hold the divider in place on the table.

Language Arts Center

Write the spelling words in ABC order.

Math Center
• Find 5 objects in the room that are shorter than 6 inches.

THE WRITING CENTER

CENTER DIRECTIONS

Help students identify key words in their center directions with the help of this unique poster. To make the poster, cover a sturdy piece of cardboard with bright-colored Con-Tact® paper. Then use a hot glue gun to attach an empty bottle of glue, a lightweight pair of scissors, a crayon, a sharpened pencil, and a small paperback book to the cardboard. Label each item as shown and add the title "Direction Words"; then display the poster where everyone can see it. Now when your students have trouble reading a direction word, they can refer to the poster instead of having to ask you.

TASTY GAME MARKERS

Treat your students to edible game markers. Provide students with candy corn in the fall, green and red M&M's® in December, conversation hearts in February, and jelly beans in the spring. Upon completion of a game, have students leave the edible markers with the game; then provide them with a handful of fresh pieces of candy to eat. What a tasty addition to any game!

A CHEER FOR CHECKERS

Create a multitude of learning centers with this nifty idea for a checkerboard. Place a white self-sticking label on each black square of a checkerboard (except the squares on the two starting rows) as shown; then cover the board with clear Con-Tact® paper. Choose a math or vocabulary skill; then use a wipe-off marker to write a word or math fact in each square two times (as shown) so that it can be read by either player. To play the game, a player chooses a square and reads the word or answers the math fact. If he is correct, he may move to that space on the board. If he is incorrect, he loses his turn. Players continue in the same manner as a game of checkers. To reuse the board, simply use a damp cloth to wipe the board, and then program it with a different skill. The possibilities are endless!

OPEN-ENDED GAMEBOARD

Make your own board games for students with this nifty idea. Duplicate the gameboard pattern (page 128) onto tagboard. Add a clever title to the front of the gameboard and the directions with a skill to practice on the back. Program the spaces with vocabulary words, math facts, or curriculum-focused questions; then laminate the board for durability. Place the gameboard, a die, and game markers at a center for student use.

BEACH READING

Add excitement to your reading center by placing a small children's wading pool in the area. Include a basket of beach towels, a beach umbrella, and a tape recording of ocean sounds. Invite students to take off their shoes and sit in the pool as they read books from the center.

SHOWER-CURTAIN GAMEBOARDS

Plastic shower-curtain liners paired with beanbags make great manipulative centers! Use a permanent marker to visually divide a liner into equal-size sections; then program each section with a math fact, vocabulary word, or any other skill. Then have students take turns tossing a beanbag onto the gameboard and determining the answer. Students will enjoy the games, and you will love them because they are versatile, easy to program, and a cinch to store!

$1 + 2 =$	$5 - 3 =$	$2 + 4 =$	$1 + 3 =$	$4 - 1 =$
$3 + 3 =$	$2 - 1 =$	$6 + 1 =$	$3 + 4 =$	$5 - 2 =$

PICTURE-PERFECT WRITING

If you enjoy taking photographs, here's an easy way to provide your budding authors with loads of writing inspiration! Each time you develop a roll of school-related snapshots, request double prints. Mount your extra set of prints on individual pieces of bright-colored construction paper; then exhibit five or six photos from the set at a center. (Save the rest of the mounted photos for later use.) Have each student write a story about her favorite snapshot or create a dialogue between the members of the picture. Encourage students to share their writings with the class. When desired, just replace the existing photos at the center and you have a brand-new writing center!

FAIRY-TALE MAGIC

Whisk your students off to the land of fairy tales by creating a fairy-tale center. Each month choose a different fairy tale to feature at the center. Obtain several different versions of the story and place them at the center. Then, each week, plan a different activity relating to the current fairy tale for students to complete. Consider activities such as illustrating a favorite scene, writing a letter to a character, rewriting the ending, or creating a character out of play dough. By varying the fairy tales and the activities throughout the year, you're sure to have a center that everyone will enjoy!

ALPHABET SOUP

Warm up to beginning sounds with a bowl of alphabet soup. To make the center, cut 26 elbow noodle shapes from tan construction paper. Program each cutout with a different letter of the alphabet; then laminate for durability. Attach an adhesive-backed magnet strip to the back of each noodle; then store the noodles in a bowl. Place the bowl, a metal spoon, and a supply of duplicated response sheets, like the one shown, at a center.

To use this center, a child places a spoon in the bowl to attract a magnetized noodle. He reads the letter on the noodle and then writes four words on his recording sheet that begin with the letter. The student continues in this manner until he has written four words for five different letters. Soup's on!

A SHOPPING SPREE

There's plenty of shopping to be done at this center! Cut pictures of kid-pleasing items from discarded magazines. Glue the pictures to the inside of a file folder. Label the pictures with prices; then decorate the front of the folder. Laminate the folder and place it at a center with a supply of plastic or paper coins. A student counts out and places a matching amount of coins on each item. Check student work or provide an answer key listing possible coin combinations for each item.

A HANDFUL OF ESTIMATION

Reinforce estimating and counting skills at this hands-on center. To begin, fill or partially fill each of ten disposable bowls with a different item that is suitable for estimating and counting. Label each bowl; then place the bowls at a center along with a supply of duplicated response sheets like the one shown. A student chooses a bowl; then he estimates the number of items he could pick up in a handful and records his estimate. Next he takes a handful of the items and counts them. After recording his count, he places the items back in the bowl. The student repeats this procedure for each of the remaining bowls. When all students have completed the center, simply empty the bowls; then refill the bowls as desired and relabel them accordingly. Place a new supply of response sheets in the center, and the center's ready to use again!

beans

counters

bears

Name *Alex*

Item	Estimate	Count
beans	20	15
bears	13	17

Fish Measurement

This colorful center can easily be tailored to meet your youngsters' measurement needs. Cut out an assortment of premeasured fish in various colors and lengths. Number each fish; then program an index card with desired student directions. For self-checking, program the back of the index card with an answer key. Laminate all pieces and place them in a large, resealable plastic bag. A student measures each of the fish lengths and records his answers on a sheet of paper. Then he checks his work using the answer key on the back of the index card. Since making this center is a cinch, it can easily be adapted for each of several different units of measurement.

Center Recording Sheet

Name: _____ Date: _____

Center	Completed	Center	Completed
1. **Math** $2 + 6 =$		2. **Language Arts** A C B	
3. **Science**		4. **Social Studies**	
5. **Arts And Crafts**		6. **Reading**	
7.		8.	
9.		10.	

Note To Teacher: Duplicate one copy of this page and program any additional centers. Duplicate copies for your students. Check off or stamp the marked squares as each child completes the centers.

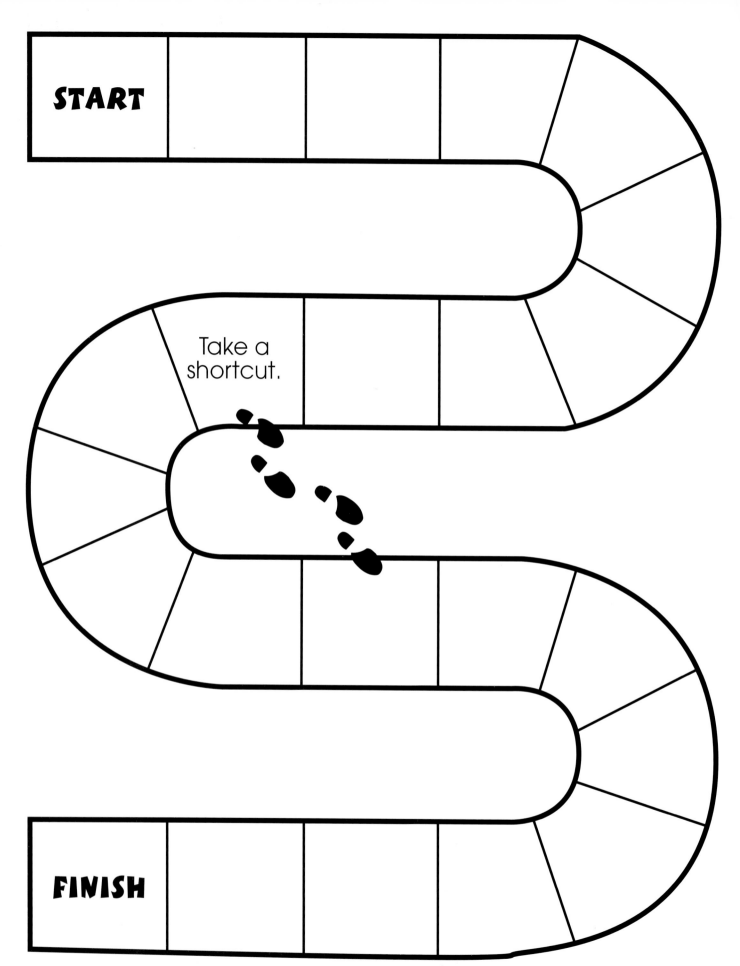

START

Take a
shortcut.

FINISH

Note To Teacher: Use with "Open-Ended Gameboard" on page 124.

GAMES

GAMES GALORE

Looking for a quick classroom pick-me-up? Games are a great way to boost students' motivation, fill a rainy-day lull, or educate during those short spans between lessons. Try one of these game suggestions the next time you find yourself in need of a fun change in your daily routine.

INDOOR GAMES

PEEP, CHICKEN, PEEP

Rainy weather got you cooped up indoors? Then gather your chickens for this simple game. Choose one student to be It; have him wait in the hall while you choose a student to be the "chicken." Ask all the students in the classroom to hide their mouths with their hands; then invite It to return to the classroom. Have It say, "Peep, chicken." At his command, the "chicken" peeps one time. Allow It three guesses to determine who the "chicken" is. Whether or not the guess is correct, have the "chicken" reveal himself. "Chicken" becomes It for the next round of play.

GUESS WHO?

Tap students' deductive reasoning skills by engaging them in this fun-filled version of a favorite game. Choose a student to be the detective, and have her leave the room while you select a helper. Ask the helper to stand at the front of the classroom and choose one student to be the suspect. Have all students stand; then call the detective back into the room. To play the game, the detective asks a yes-or-no question such as, "Is the suspect a boy?" The helper answers the question. Then the detective asks students to sit down if he feels they don't qualify as the suspect. After several questions have been asked, and all but one student is eliminated, the helper reveals the correct suspect. You'll know your detective has sharp reasoning skills if the student left standing is the suspect.

Anywhere Scavenger Hunt

If you find yourself with a few extra minutes, engage your students in a scavenger hunt. Divide your class into groups; then assign each group a search category. For example, you might ask a group to find items that begin with *m*, or things that are cube-shaped. Set a timer, and let students begin searching. As each item is found, have a team member write it in a list, or draw a picture of it. When time is up, count the number of items each group found. The group with the most items wins!

1. flag
2. fruit
3. funnel
4. faucet
5. fan

VARIATIONS ON DOTS

This familiar game can be given new life with curriculum-related variations. Create a grid of 25 dots as shown and duplicate a class supply. According to traditional rules, pair students and give each pair a grid. Have each child in a pair use a different-colored pencil to play. Instruct students to take turns drawing a line to connect two dots. Each time a line is drawn that completes a square, the student can claim the square by writing a spelling word, vocabulary word, math problem, or science term in the box instead of his initials. With this curriculum enhancement, you will encourage your students to play this game time and time again.

GUESSING GAME

Your students can enjoy this fun observation game anytime, since it requires no preparation or supplies. Arrange students in a circle; then ask one student to leave the room. After the student is out of sight, tap another student as a silent signal to hide in a predetermined location in the classroom. Invite the first student, or guesser, back into the classroom and give him three chances to determine which child is missing. If the student doesn't guess correctly by the third try, have him say, "I know you're hiding; say 'Hello!', but don't come out till we tell you so." The hiding player says, "Hello!" from his hiding spot, and the first player guesses again. Regardless of the final guess, the hidden student then becomes the guesser and leaves the room, while the original guesser rejoins the circle.

TAKING A TRIP

Your students will stretch their imaginations when they play this alphabet game. Have your students sit on their desks, or in a circle on the floor. Provide one student with a beanbag, and ask that student to name a location and an item beginning with the letter *a*. For example, "I'm taking a trip to Africa and I'm bringing an apple." The student then tosses the beanbag to another child, who creates a phrase using a location and an item beginning with *b*. Students will have fun tossing around ideas from *a* to *z*!

> I'm taking a trip to the beach and I'm bringing a book.

What's Missing?

Sharpen students' visual memories while reviewing content-area words. Write the words you want students to review on separate cards; then tape them to the chalkboard. Have students study the words. Then ask students to close their eyes, put their heads on their desks, and count to ten while you remove a card. When a student identifies the missing word, challenge him to spell it and/or give the definition. Continue the game by removing a different card each time.

dog	cat
bird	pet
food	water
fish	puppy

H-O-W-D-Y

Students are sure to enjoy this variation of bingo. Duplicate a blank bingo grid for each student. Have students gather signatures from classmates until their grids are full, then cover names with markers as they are called out. When a student covers a row vertically, horizontally, or diagonally, he calls out, "Howdy." Then ask the child to read aloud the names he has covered. If he correctly reads them, he wins!

H	O	W	D	Y
Tracey	Meg	Kara	Noah	Joey
Jose	Christa	Josie	Steve	Mako
Justin	Scot	Jordan	Adam	Kara
Amy	Rachel	Juan	Kelly	Mario
Rob	Jess	Tia	Kim	Hope

MY CLASSMATES ARE GREAT!

Get your students up and moving with this fast-paced game. Have all students but one form a large circle with their chairs. The extra student sits in the middle and is It. It says, "My classmates are great, especially those [wearing red, with March birthdays, with blond hair]." Those having what It has said must scramble to find different chairs while It tries to steal an empty chair. The person left in the middle becomes It and play continues.

Team Challenge

Review addition and subtraction facts with a quick game of Team Challenge. Divide the class into two teams. Have a student from each team come to the chalkboard. Write an addition or a subtraction problem on the board for each student. Set a time limit during which the two players try to solve their problems. If a player solves his problem correctly, his team scores one point. If solved incorrectly, his opponent can try to correct the problem. If he does, that player scores an extra point for his team. Continue in this same manner until each student has had a turn. The team with the most points at the end of the game wins.

ADDITION TIC-TAC-TOE

Tic-tac-toe your way to reinforcing addition skills. Draw a large tic-tac-toe grid on the chalkboard. Divide the class into an *X* team and an *O* team; then give each team a pair of dice. To play, have each team, in turn, roll both dice and add the numbers together. The team with the highest answer gets to place its *X* or *O* on the tic-tac-toe grid. The first team to complete a tic-tac-toe wins!

STOPWATCH FUN

Keep a stopwatch handy for a multitude of activities that can be played at a moment's notice. Time students to determine how fast they can perform activities, such as tying their shoes, counting to 100, or finding a word in the dictionary. For added fun, invite students to submit activities to be timed. Students are sure to enjoy the activity, and they'll be gaining a better knowledge of time, too!

MOVE IT OUTDOORS

Some games are just meant for bigger places. So when the weather's calling for you and your students to get outdoors, try one of these fun games that require more space.

Bow Tag

Students will enjoy the new twist on this familiar game. Acquire a large package bow that has sticky backing (or attach tape to the back). Designate a child to be It, and challenge him to try to stick the bow to another player. The player who gets the bow then becomes It. Try this fun game to wrap up a birthday celebration. Or exchange the bow for a holiday shape cut from construction paper—such as a heart, snowflake, or shamrock—to liven up any holiday party.

STOP-AND-SPELL TAG

Engage your students in this lively version of tag and incorporate spelling skills at the same time. Choose a student to be It. To avoid being tagged by It, each student may quickly squat down and spell a word that has at least four letters. If the speller isn't fast enough and gets tagged, she stays down. To be freed, another player must spell a word while touching her. Change the skill practice by requiring students to call out math facts instead of words.

Distraction

Your students will really come alive with this fun team game. Divide your class into two teams. Have one team form a circle and join hands, while members of the other team stand scattered outside of the circle. Have the team that's scattered send one member inside the circle; then let the game begin. Students on the outside must try to distract the joined team using any method except touch. While his teammates create distractions, the student in the middle tries to escape the circle. If he successfully escapes, have the teams switch roles and play another round. To make the game more interesting, periodically call out, "Turn!"; then students forming the circle must let go of hands, turn to face the other direction, and rejoin hands before the captured student escapes. Watching students' creative distractions will put a smile on your face and on theirs.

5-MINUTE FILLERS

Making The Most Of Every Minute

Got a few extra minutes? Make the most of them with these classroom-tested ideas!

State Your Knowledge

Students demonstrate their knowledge of the 50 states with this brainstorming activity. Display a large map of the United States. Invite one student to come to the map, close his eyes, and randomly point to a state. Write the name of the chosen state on the chalkboard. Then ask students to brainstorm all the things they know about the state. Record their responses on the chalkboard. Students enjoy sharing their knowledge and travel experiences, and it also provides great geography practice!

Florida
sunny
warm
oranges
Disney World
lots of beaches

Good News!

Put a smile on everyone's face with a few minutes of good news each day! Write each child's name on a craft stick; then place the sticks in a decorated coffee can. Whenever you have a few extra minutes, randomly pull a stick from the jar, read the child's name, and ask her for some good news. The student may choose to announce something that has happened to herself, her family, or a friend. Place the child's stick aside and continue removing sticks from the can, one at a time, as time permits. Be sure to continue the activity the next day, beginning with the students whose sticks are still in the can. Students will look forward to hearing good news day after day!

Problem Solvers

Students can be great problem solvers when given the chance. Choose a problem in the school, such as trash on the playground or a noisy cafeteria. Ask students to brainstorm solutions to the problem, and record their responses on chart paper. Next discuss the advantages and disadvantages of each solution; then challenge students to determine the best solution from the list. Write the chosen solution on a piece of paper and present it to the principal. Surprisingly enough, your youngsters may think of more creative solutions than you or your co-workers.

At the grocery store, you can buy a <u>c</u>arrot.

A Shopping Spree

Take your students on an imaginary shopping spree for lots of productive learning fun! First decide with the help of your students what kind of store you'll be shopping in today. Will it be a pet store, a grocery store, or a toy store? Then, beginning with the letter *A,* have youngsters work their way through the alphabet, naming things you can buy in the selected store that begin with the appropriate letter. It's an instant activity that hones students' phonetic skills!

What's The Rule?

Sharpen your youngsters' observation skills with a game called What's The Rule? One by one, physically sort students into groups. Challenge students to determine the rule that you are using to sort them. For example, your rule for sorting might be as simple as students who have shoes that tie and those who don't. The first student to guess the rule makes up the rule for the next sorting game.

News For Today!

This time-filling activity encourages students to discuss current events in the world, state, and local area. Keep a current copy of the daily newspaper in your classroom. When you find yourself with a few moments to spare, read aloud an article from the paper, and invite students to share their views on the subject. You're sure to evoke some great conversation!

What's In Your Name?

In turn, call each child to the chalkboard and write her name in large capital letters. Ask her classmates to find hidden words in the child's name. Record students' responses on the chalkboard. Students will be eager to tell parents just how special their names are.

ELIZABETH

bet

lit

hit

bat

at

Animal Challenge

Have a few minutes to spare? No sweat! Play a quick game of Animal Challenge. Begin by deciding on an animal. Once you've decided, call on students in turn to guess the animal by asking questions that can be answered with a yes or a no. If desired invite the student who guesses the correct animal to whisper an animal for the next game. Students quickly realize the importance of listening to their classmates' responses, as well as which questions are the most effective.

Does the animal have fur?

Does the animal live in a cold place?

5 10 15 20 25 30 35 40 45 50

SOUND OFF!

Whenever you have a bit of extra time, you can use it to improve your youngsters' skip-counting skills. Begin by announcing a counting pattern such as tens, fives, or twos; then point to a student to start the counting. After the child announces the starting number, quickly point to another student to say the next number in the pattern. Continue in this same manner until students reach a predetermined number. Not only will this activity keep students on their toes, but they'll learn to skip-count faster, too!

Time For A Rhyme?

Use extra minutes throughout the day to enrich your youngsters' rhyming skills. Create a list of incomplete rhyming couplets (see the list for suggestions). Whenever you have a few minutes, read a couplet and challenge students to supply the last word. It won't be long before students are making up their own couplets for their classmates to complete.

My lemonade is pink.
Would you like a _____?

I met a handsome fellow,
Dressed in a suit of _____.

Oh, what do I do?
I can't tie my _____.

We drove very far.

Ready To Laugh?

Here's a fun way to fill a few extra minutes. In advance cut jokes from the newspaper or worn-out joke books. Place them in a small decorated box labeled "The Joke Box." Whenever you have time, draw a joke from the box and read it to your students. If desired give the used jokes to your students, or place them in a secure spot to use next year. Not only will students look forward to hearing the jokes, but they'll also enjoy adding their own jokes to the box.

What do you get when you shake a cow?

A milkshake

Spot The Mistakes

When your lesson takes less time than you had planned, fill the extra minutes with this simple activity. Write a sentence on the chalkboard, deliberately including spelling, capitalization, and punctuation errors. Have each student correct the sentence and write it on a piece of paper. Then ask a student volunteer to correct the sentence on the chalkboard. Students will be thrilled at the chance to correct *your* work!

We're going on a field trip today?

The Picture Box

If some of your youngsters find themselves with time to spare, suggest they go to the picture box. Keep a box filled with a variety of laminated magazine pictures. When a youngster has some time on his hands, he may select a picture from the box and write something about it. Children who want to share their writings can be given an opportunity to do so during a daily sharing time.

"What If...?"

This five-minute filler enhances your students' thinking skills. Present a what-if situation to your students and challenge them to brainstorm the pros and cons of the situation. Consider situations such as "What if we went to school only on the weekends?" or "What if Christmas were in July?" Be sure to allow each child a chance to add his thoughts about the topic.

I do not think hamburgers are the best fast food. I like pizza because...

In My Opinion

This partner activity improves communication skills and requires no planning. To play, pair students; then announce a statement such as "Hamburgers are the best fast food" or "Soccer is a hard sport to play." Each partner then has one minute to express a personal opinion about the statement. Be sure to remind students that there is no wrong opinion. Ready? Start talking!

Categories

Sharpen students' listening skills with the game Categories. Ask each child to stand beside his desk. Announce a category, such as food or things to do outside, and set a time limit of five seconds for students to contribute a word to the stated category. If a student gives a wrong answer or can't think of an answer, he must sit down. Play continues until one student remains standing.

Ask The Expert

Give students a chance to shine with this unique sharing activity. Whenever you have a few extra minutes, choose a student volunteer to be the expert on a topic of his choice. Invite the other students to ask him questions about the chosen topic. Students will look forward to their chance to be the expert in the class!

There are several kinds of horses. One kind of horse is...

Poem Of The Week

Each week choose a poem to correlate with whatever subject or theme your students are studying. Write the poem on chart paper or an overhead transparency. Whenever time allows, use the poem for handwriting practice, illustrate it as an art activity, chorally read and role-play it, or sing it (if appropriate). Students will love this unique break from their regular activities.

SUBSTITUTE TEACHER TIPS

Substitute Lifesavers

Help keep your substitute afloat with the following ideas and reproducibles.

Welcome Banner

Have students work in small groups to make welcome banners for upcoming substitutes. Provide each group with markers and a piece of bulletin-board paper. Then have each group draw pictures on its banner. Next ask each student in the class to sign his name on each group's banner. Store the banners in a handy spot. Assign two students to be in charge of choosing a banner and displaying it whenever there is a substitute teacher. What a great way to welcome the substitute teacher!

Good-News Report

Here's a management tip that's sure to help substitutes. At the beginning of the day, have the substitute post a large sheet of paper on the board labeled "Good-News Report." Then, throughout the day, have her record students' positive behaviors and good deeds. Ask her to leave the report on your desk. Since students will be eager to be added to the list, they'll be on their best behavior!

Putting Names With Faces

Make your substitute's day easier by adding this timely addition to your substitute folder. Simply obtain a photo of each of your students and tape the pictures to a piece of light-colored construction paper. If desired, photographs can be arranged to resemble a pictorial seating chart. Then write the name of each student under his photo. Duplicate this page and include the copy with the substitute's other materials. Using this aid, your substitute can begin immediately to develop positive rapport by calling each child by name.

Crystal

Substitute-Teacher Folder

A substitute-teacher folder is just what your substitute needs to carry out the day. Duplicate and complete a copy of the reproducibles on pages 143–146. Place the completed reproducibles in a folder labeled "Substitute Lifesavers." Then, whenever you're going to be absent, simply place your lesson plans in the folder and leave it on your desk. Your substitute is sure to agree that this packet is a lifesaver!

Substitute Lifesavers

Substitute Lifesavers
(Substitute-Teacher Information)

Faculty Information:

Principal:

_____

Secretary:

_____

Custodian:

_____

Aide:

_____

Helpful Teachers:

_____

_____

Procedures For:

Start Of Day: _____

_____

_____

Attendance: _____

_____

_____

Fire Drill: _____

_____

Recess: _____

_____

Lunch: _____

_____

_____

Behavior Policy: _____

_____

_____

Other: _____

_____

Children With Special Needs:

Health: _____

_____

_____

_____

_____

Supervision: _____

_____

_____

_____

Learning: _____

_____

_____

_____

**Student Pull-Outs
For Special Programs:**

Name   Class   Day/Time

_____

_____

_____

_____

Helpful Students: _____

_____

Class Information

_____   _____
teacher   grade

Student Name	Bus No.	Parent's Name	Daytime Phone No.	Special Needs

Daily Schedule

Time	Monday	Tuesday	Wednesday	Thursday	Friday

Free-Time Activities: _____

_____

_____

_____

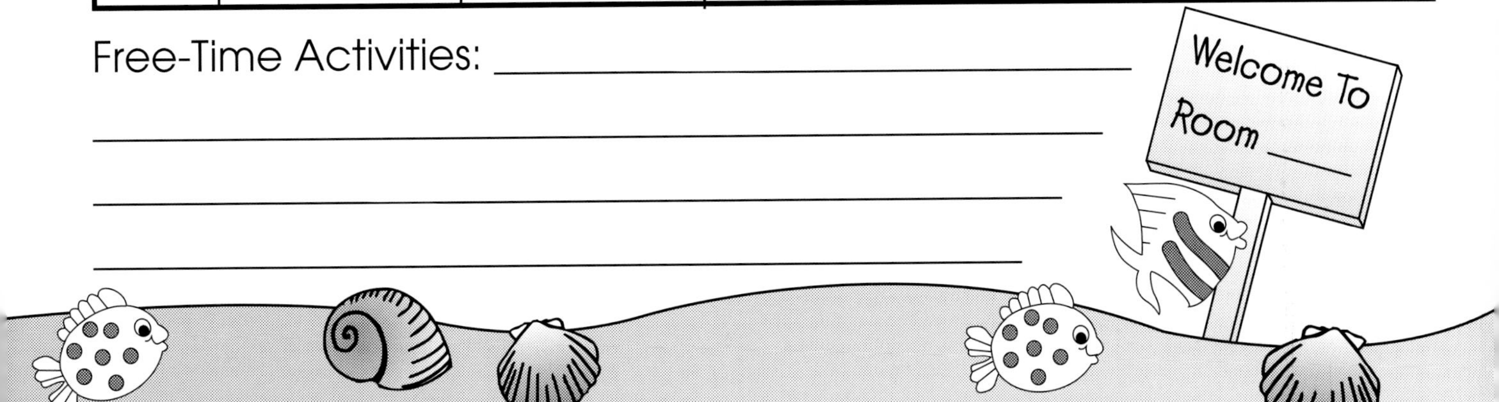

Welcome To Room ____

Reading	
Language	
Math	
Science	
Social Studies	
Other	

LANGUAGE ARTS

WORD SKILLS

MAGNETIC Spelling

Attract student interest in spelling practice with this nifty alternative! For an individual or a partner activity, place two small magnetic boards (or cookie sheets), a supply of magnetic alphabet letters, and a spelling word list at a center. Each student uses the magnetic letters to spell the words from the list. If two students are working together, they can trade magnetic boards and check each other's spelling. Now, that's an attractive idea!

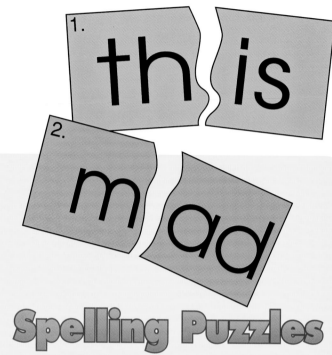

Spelling Puzzles

Students piece together their weekly spelling words by completing this center activity. Program a blank card for each weekly spelling word. Number each word; then cut each card to create a two-piece puzzle. Laminate the puzzle pieces for durability before storing them in a resealable plastic bag. A student assembles each card and then copies the words on her paper in numerical order. She then checks her spelling of the words against a provided answer key.

"SPELLING-GO-ROUND"

This unique variation of the traditional spelling bee allows all players to participate throughout the game! Have students stand in a circle. Call out a spelling word, and then have one student begin by announcing the first letter of the called word. The student to the beginning player's right announces the second letter of the word, and so on until the entire word has been spelled. If a student gives an incorrect letter, he must sit down, and the next player in the circle tries to supply the correct letter. A player who is seated continues to play, and may stand once he supplies a correct letter. Now, that's a spelling bee worth buzzing about!

Sight-Word Lotto

Reinforce listening skills and provide basic sight-word practice with this lotto-type game. Write any 30 sight words on the chalkboard. Provide each child with a blank lotto board. Instruct her to randomly program each of the 16 squares with a different word from the chalkboard. As students are programming their boards, write the 30 posted words on small pieces of paper and place the papers facedown in a container. Also distribute 16 game markers to each child. To play the game, draw a word from the container and announce it. If a student has the announced word on her board, she covers it. The first student to cover four words in a row announces, "I know my sight words!" To win the game, she must read aloud the words on her board for verification. If desired, the declared winner of the game becomes the caller for the next game.

I	is	yes	no
we	◯	he	to
the	that	cat	red
big	they	◯	can

Stuck On Spelling

Use the versatile contract form on page 171 to help your first graders improve spelling study habits. Duplicate student copies. Have each student write his spelling words on the lines and then color a bee every day he studies his words. If desired, ask each student to attach the list to his family's refrigerator. You can count on other family members seeing the list and being tempted to quiz the youngster on his spelling words, too.

Name _Hank_
Spelling contract

Stuck On Spelling
Write your spelling words on the lines.
Color a bee each day you study your words.

1. cat — Monday
2. hat
3. pat — Tuesday
4. rat
5. sat
6. that — Wednesday
7. mat
8. fat
9. bat — Thursday
10.
11.
12.
13. — Friday
14.
15.

TACTILE SPELLING

"Bee-dazzle" your first graders with these activities, which will give them a real feel for spelling.

 Pair students and distribute a spelling word list to each pair. Have each student take turns "writing" spelling words on her partner's back with her fingers. The partner being written on must identify the word.

 Place clean paintbrushes, cups of water, and individual chalkboards at a center. A student paints the letters of each spelling word on a chalkboard. As the water dries, the words disappear.

 Partially fill a shallow box with sand, flour, or cornmeal. Place the box and the weekly spelling words at a center. A student reads a word from the list and uses his fingertip to write the word in the box. After he checks his spelling against the provided list, he uses his hand to smooth out the writing surface; then he repeats the activity with a different spelling word.

 Place pretzel sticks, O-shaped cereal, and the weekly spelling words at a center. A student uses the snacks to spell each word on the list.

 Place letter cutouts needed to spell the words on the weekly spelling list in individual containers. Number the containers. A student first numbers her paper to match the numbered containers. She then manipulates the letters in each container to spell a word and writes the word on her paper by its corresponding number.

Word Aerobics

This aerobic spelling review is sure to receive rave student reviews! In the school gym or on the playground, display a list of the weekly spelling words. Have students spread out; then encourage students to copy your aerobic movements as you spell each word. For example, hop up and down or perform jumping jacks for each letter of a word. After kinesthetically spelling each word, invite student volunteers to decide movements as the class spells the words again. Students will love exercising their way to spelling success!

SIGHT-WORD FISHING

Two players will be fishing for matching sight words (or vocabulary words) with this adapted version of Go Fish. Program each of 12 index cards with a different sight word, and then make a duplicate set. Laminate the cards for durability; then place the cards in a resealable plastic bag at a center. To begin, one student deals seven cards each to himself and the other player; then he places the remaining cards facedown to form a draw pile. Each player places all his matching pairs of sight words on the table. Player One begins by asking Player Two for a sight word to match one that he is holding. If he receives the match from Player Two, he places the pair on the table and takes another turn. If Player Two does not have the card Player One requested, Player Two says, "Go Fish," and Player One draws a card from the pile. If he draws the card he requested, he may lay down the pair and take another turn. If he does not draw a match, he keeps the card and Player Two takes a turn. Any time a player lays his last card on the table, he takes one card from the draw pile. When the draw pile is gone, the game ends. The player with the most pairs wins the game!

Vocabulary Keepers

Help students keep track of vocabulary words they need to learn with these nifty holders. Gather a class supply of empty margarine tubs with lids. Have each student use permanent markers to personalize her tub as desired. Then, after introducing a new vocabulary list, distribute a copy of the list (in the style shown) to each student. A student cuts the words on the dotted lines and places them in her vocabulary keeper. She may study the words at school with a partner or take them home to learn. After demonstrating knowledge of the words, the student may glue the words into a personal dictionary. If she needs additional practice learning a word, she places it back in her vocabulary keeper.

cat	pet
dog	vet
sheep	cow
horse	deer
frog	rabbit

Shape Up! Vocabulary

Watch students' vocabularies and knowledge of beginning sounds take shape when you use this nifty idea. For each letter of the alphabet, cut a large sheet of colored construction paper into a design that begins with the letter. For example, if the letter of the day is *a*, cut the paper into an apple shape. Enlist students' help in writing words on the cutout that begin with an *a*; then mount the cutout on a classroom wall. A student can glance quickly at the displays and find words to help him complete an independent writing activity.

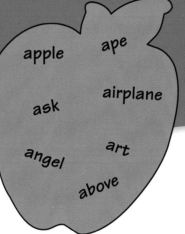

apple ape
ask airplane
angel art
above

Remember That Word

Challenge your students' reading of vocabulary words and their visual memory skills by having them play a game of Concentration. To prepare, write each vocabulary word twice on separate index cards to make a matching set. Then place the cards at a center. A student shuffles the cards and places them facedown on a table. To begin, he flips over two cards. If the cards match, he must read the word to keep the cards. If the cards are not a match, the student returns them facedown to the table. The other players take their turns in the same manner, continuing the game until all the matches are found.

Words-We-Know Challenge

Show your beginning readers how much they can already read with the Words-We-Know Challenge. To begin, tape a large piece of bulletin-board paper to a table. Place a supply of letter manipulatives and several markers at the table. Then, in turn, invite a small group of students to the table. Each student manipulates the letters to spell words she knows. After a student spells a word correctly and reads it back to you, she records the word on the paper. It won't take long for students to fill the paper and boost their self-esteem!

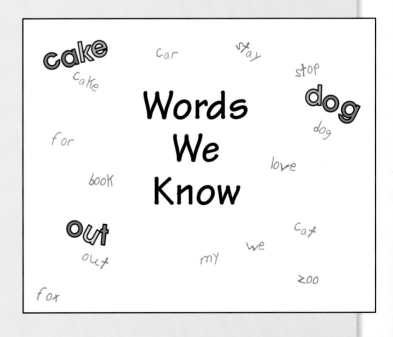

LEARNING LETTER SOUNDS

With this nifty activity, learning alphabet sounds is a cinch! After studying a particular letter of the alphabet, ask each student to bring to school three objects that begin with the designated letter. Have each student share and name the items she brought. Write the name of each object on the chalkboard. Then, if desired, have each student write the names of the objects in a personal dictionary.

PHONICS POCKETS

Students can show off their phonics skills using these individual display pockets. To make a pocket, position a 4 1/2" x 9" piece of construction paper horizontally. Create a pocket along the lower edge by folding approximately 1 1/2 inches of the paper upward. Staple the folded edges in place. Next program the top third of a 1 1/2" x 3 1/2" construction-paper rectangle for each letter of the alphabet. Place the letter cards and the pocket in a resealable plastic bag. To practice phonics skills, have each child remove the letter cards and the pocket from her bag. Announce a word that reflects your students' spelling abilities (without duplicating letters). Each child forms the word by placing the correct letter cards in her pocket. Have each student display her pocket before she clears it and you announce another word. At the end of the activity, have students store their letter cards and pockets in the bags.

A To Z Treasure Chest

Practice initial-consonant sounds with this idea for a class book. Program a craft stick for each letter of the alphabet; then place the sticks in a container. Have each student draw a stick and then think of five objects beginning with the letter that he would like to find in a treasure chest. Next the student draws and labels the objects on a sheet of drawing paper. As students are completing their projects, create a story introduction similar to the one shown. Place the introduction atop students' completed work; then bind the compiled pages between two construction-paper covers. This treasure of a story is sure to be a popular addition to your classroom library.

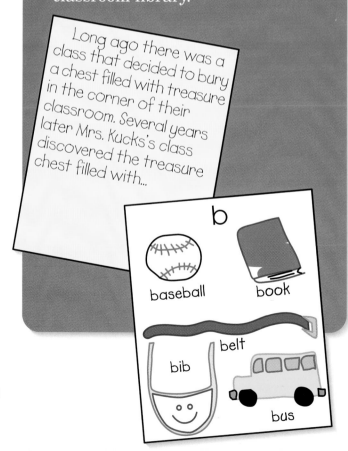

Long ago there was a class that decided to bury a chest filled with treasure in the corner of their classroom. Several years later Mrs. Kucks's class discovered the treasure chest filled with...

b

baseball   book

belt

bib

bus

Vowel Munchers

These gobbling guys provide a novel way to reinforce vowel sounds. Duplicate, color, and cut out ten monsters using the pattern on page 172. Label each monster with a different long or short vowel before laminating them for durability. Post the monsters at the top of a chart. To begin, decide whether the vowel-eating monsters want short or long vowels to eat. Next announce a word that contains a short-vowel (or long-vowel) sound and ask a student volunteer to name the vowel. If the student is correct, he writes the word on a construction-paper card. Then he "feeds" the card to the corresponding monster by taping the card under it.

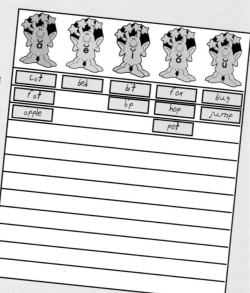

THUMBS-UP!

Good vowel-sound discrimination will pop up everywhere with this quiet activity. Specify a vowel sound for students to listen for; then announce a word. If a student hears the sound, he puts his thumb up. If not, he puts his thumb down. After announcing several words, invite student volunteers to take turns announcing words.

See the Ready Reference on page 167 for 100 short- and 100 long-vowel words.

A Scoop Of Blends

Give your youngsters the scoop on blends with this cooperative-group activity. Before beginning the lesson, duplicate four or five ice-cream cones onto light brown construction paper and a large supply of ice-cream scoops onto various colors of construction paper. (Patterns on page 172.) Cut out the patterns. Next write a blend on each cone and mount them in a location that is accessible to your students. Divide students into groups; then assign a cone to each group. Challenge each group to list on scrap paper as many words as it can that begin with the blend on its cone. When time is up, check each group's list. Have students rewrite the correct words on separate ice-cream scoops. Then, in turn, have the members of each group read their words for the class before they attach the scoops to their cones.

See the Ready Reference on page 168 for a list of blends and digraphs.

Word Families Houses

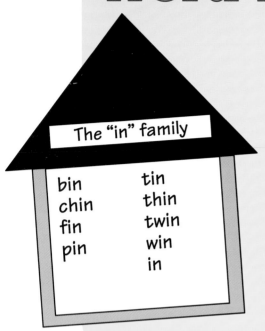

The "in" family

bin	tin
chin	thin
fin	twin
pin	win
	in

Introduce your youngsters to word families with construction-paper houses. For each word family being introduced, glue a white sheet of paper to a slightly larger sheet of colored construction paper; then glue a construction-paper roof atop the house as shown. Label the roof of each house with a word family or *rime* (the part of a single syllable word from the vowel onward) before laminating it for durability. Then, as you introduce a word family or rime, use a wipe-off marker to write a student-generated list of words that "live" in the house. Post the houses in a prominent location for students to refer to in their independent writing. Before long, students will know each family very well!

RHYMING BOX

The timing for rhyming is now! Collect old game pieces and small toys that are rhyming pairs. Store the rhyming pairs in a box. Next gather students in a circle. Invite a student volunteer to choose an item from the box. Then ask another to try to find an item from the box that rhymes with the first one. Have students continue in this manner until all the rhyming pairs have been discovered. Happy hunting!

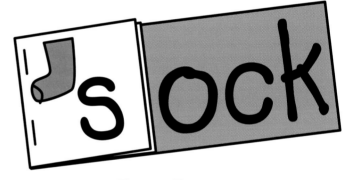

FLIP BOOKS

These unique books will have students flipping over word families! To make a book, a student staples a desired number of two-inch squares of white paper to the left edge of a 2" x 5" construction-paper rectangle. Next she writes the word family or rime on the construction paper as shown. Then, on each white paper square, the student writes a letter that makes a word when joined with the rime. To read the flip book, the student flips each paper square and reads the word. No doubt students will be eager to flip through their classmates' books, too!

Everyone moves and everyone learns with this rhyming activity. Divide your students into two teams and have them line up in two lines. Choose one team to begin; then announce a word family or rime such as *in.* The student at the front of Team One states a word in the featured family and then moves to the end of the line. The first player on Team Two repeats this process with a different rhyming word. Alternating from Team One to Team Two, repeatedly ask each student to say a different rhyming word until one team is unable to think of another one. Award the last team to say a rhyming word a point. To continue the game, announce a new word family and begin where play left off. The team with the most points at the end of the designated game time wins!

LOOK! A Book!

Students will be full of giggles after making this hilarious rhyming book. To begin, have your students name sets of three rhyming words—one set of words per student. Write their responses on the chalkboard. Next have each student select one set of words. On a sheet of story paper, the student writes and illustrates a sentence that includes his three words. Encourage each student to share his completed project; then bind the papers into a class book and place it the library for all to enjoy!

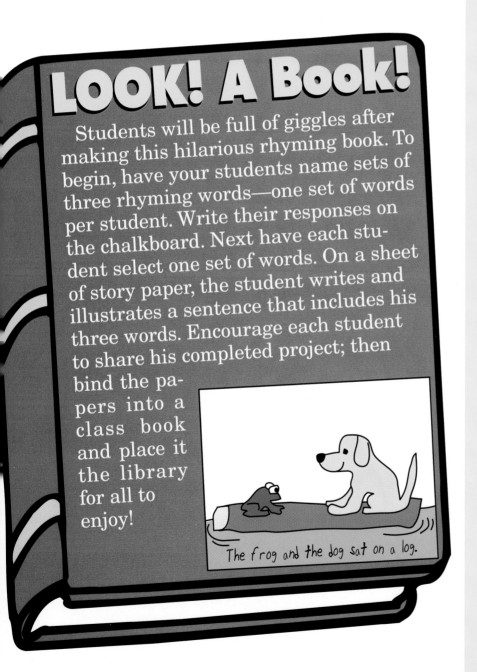

The frog and the dog sat on a log.

Night House, Bright House

Monica Wellington's *Night House, Bright House* (Dutton Children's Books, 1997) is a wonderfully appealing and motivating literature selection to complement your rhyming activities. In this book full of rhymes, all the objects in a house wake up and cause an uproar in the middle of the night. Each object says something that rhymes with its name. (For example, " 'What's that noise?' said the toys.") After sharing this delightful book with your youngsters, ask each child to list on a piece of scrap paper three objects found in her bedroom. Next have her imagine that each object can talk. Using the same dialogue form as the book, each student then writes and illustrates a rhyme for each object, stating what it would say. Bind students' completed work together between decorated construction-paper covers. Then invite each child to read her rhymes to the class.

Olivia

 "Is it red?" said the bed.

 "Did you look?" said the book.

 "Where is my robe?" said the globe.

Building Compound Words

Use plastic or wooden building blocks to help students build compound words! Attach a piece of masking tape to one side of several blocks. Program each block with a word that could be used to make a compound word. Place the blocks, some pencils, and a supply of writing paper at a center. A student arranges the blocks to create compound words and records them on a piece of paper. (Be sure to inform students that not all word combinations will make compound words.) If desired, include an answer key of all the possible combinations. What a fun way for students to build their knowledge of compound words!

snow man ball

See the Ready Reference on page 169 for a list of compound words.

Picture These Compound Words!

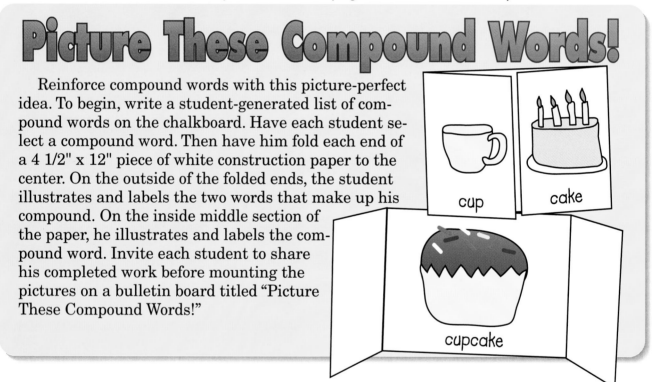

Reinforce compound words with this picture-perfect idea. To begin, write a student-generated list of compound words on the chalkboard. Have each student select a compound word. Then have him fold each end of a 4 1/2" x 12" piece of white construction paper to the center. On the outside of the folded ends, the student illustrates and labels the two words that make up his compound. On the inside middle section of the paper, he illustrates and labels the compound word. Invite each student to share his completed work before mounting the pictures on a bulletin board titled "Picture These Compound Words!"

cup   cake

cupcake

MAKING CONTRACTIONS

Help students develop a better understanding of contractions with this hands-on activity. Write each letter needed to make two words (that can be made into a contraction) such as *is not* on a separate 9" x 12" sheet of construction paper. Also program another construction-paper sheet with an apostrophe. To begin, give each of five students a letter card needed to spell *is not.* Have the students arrange themselves so that they spell the two words correctly, leaving a space between the words and holding the letter cards so they are visible to their classmates. Next write the contraction *isn't* on the chalkboard. Give the apostrophe card to a student volunteer and have him take the place of the student holding the *o* card. The remaining students holding letter cards close the space to spell *isn't.* Continue in this same manner with additional contractions until students have a good understanding of what happens when a contraction is formed.

CONTRACTIOIN SUPERSLEUTHS

Get your supersleuths hunting for contractions with this nifty idea. Have each student cut out as many contractions as he can find from discarded magazines. While students are hunting for contractions, label a piece of poster board with the categories shown. Read the headings and ask each student to group his contractions based on the categories. Next announce a category and have students, in turn, glue their contractions in its column and write the two words that make up the contraction beside it. Continue in this same manner for the remaining categories. Display the completed project for students to use in independent writing assignments.

Contractions

am	are
I'm I am	we're we are
	you're you are
has	have
he's he is	
is	bit
us	will
	would

See the Ready Reference on page 170 for a list of contractions.

Opposite Posters

Now, here's a cooperative-group activity that reinforces opposites. For each of several pairs of opposites, divide and label a sheet of poster board as shown. (Consider using pairs such as *big* and *little, hot* and *cold, living* and *non-living, boy* and *girl.*) Then divide students into as many groups as there are labeled

posters. Distribute a poster to each group and have students cut pictures from discarded magazines to illustrate their pair of opposites. The students then glue their pictures to the corresponding side of the poster board. Ask a student from each group to share his group's poster. Then display the completed projects on a classroom wall for everyone to view.

Mix-And-Match Opposites

Further reinforce opposites with this interactive activity. Secretly assign each student a different concept such as *short, long, quiet, loud, rough,* or *smooth.* Ask each student to cut a picture from a magazine or draw a picture that represents her given concept. Then have each child share her item, being sure to use her given concept word. As she shares, encourage her classmates to see if they think they might have an opposite match. If a child thinks he has an opposite match, have that child stand and share about his item. If they are opposite matches, have the students be seated together.

See the Ready Reference on page 169 for a list of antonyms.

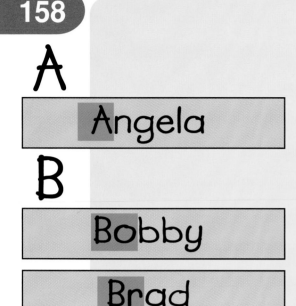

Easy As ABC!

What better way to teach alphabetical order than by using your youngsters' first names? Have each student write her first name on a construction-paper strip and then use a highlighter to highlight the first letter. To begin, slowly recite the alphabet, stopping after each letter to ask students to stand if their names begin with the announced letter. Tape the strips in alphabetical order on a classroom wall. When more than one student has a name that begins with the same letter, have those students highlight the second and possibly third letters in their names before continuing to alphabetize. The final result will be an eye-catching and alphabetized list of truly important words—students' own names!

ABC ORDER IN THE CLASSROOM

Students will take stock of your classroom with this alphabetizing activity. Use a red marker to program a sheet of chart paper with each letter of the alphabet; then post it on the chalkboard. For each letter, use a black marker to write a student-generated word naming an item in the classroom that begins with that sound. Encourage students to think of variations in naming items, such as a binder instead of a notebook. After completing the list, add the title "ABCs In [teacher's name]'s Classroom," and post it in the hallway for everyone to see.

ABC's In Mrs. Aikman's Classroom

Art easel	Notebook
Book	Overhead projector
Clock	Pencil
Desk	Quilt
Eraser	Rug
Flag	Sink
Globe	Table
Heater	Umbrella
Ink pad	Videos
Journal	Window
Knapsack	Xerox® paper
Lamp	Yardstick
Manipulatives	Zipper

Quick And Easy Alphabetizing

These alphabetizing activities are just what you need to reinforce this important skill.

- Have each student select five crayons from her crayon box. (If desired, tell students not to select more than one crayon that begins with the same letter.) Have her arrange the crayons in alphabetical order. Then have a partner check her work before the student returns the crayons to the box.

- Instruct each student to think of five toys that have different beginning sounds. Next have him draw a picture of each toy on a separate index card. Then have each student arrange his cards alphabetically on his desk. Check each student's work; then have each student paper-clip his cards together. Collect the card sets and redistribute them for different students to alphabetize.

Punctuation & Capitalization

Stop-Sign Periods

Your students will find that learning to use periods is a breeze with the help of stop signs. To prepare, cut several two-inch octagons from red construction paper and write "STOP" on each cutout with a white correction pen. Explain to your students that a period is similar to a stop sign. A stop sign tells a driver to stop. A period tells a reader to stop. A period signals the end of a complete thought and tells the reader to stop briefly before continuing. If a period is missing, the reader will not know to stop, and the words in one sentence will "crash" into another sentence.

After sharing this information with your students, write a short story on chart paper without using any periods. Read the story as a class, and challenge students to determine where the periods belong. Ask student volunteers to tape the stop-sign cutouts where the periods should be. Then invite students to join in as you reread the story, this time pausing where the stop signs have been placed.

One day my dog and I went for a walk STOP We saw birds and cats STOP We also saw a big brown dog STOP He scared us, so we went home STOP

TASTY PUNCTUATION

Try using 3-D punctuation marks in your classroom to reinforce students' punctuation skills. In advance, write several sentences that end with periods, question marks, and exclamation points on a sheet of poster board; but instead of writing the punctuation, glue the following items after each sentence: period = a piece of Kix® cereal, question mark = a piece of elbow macaroni and a piece of Kix® cereal, exclamation point = broken piece of fettuccini and a piece of Kix® cereal. Discuss the chart with your students; then give students a writing assignment. Have each student refer to the chart and use glue and the appropriate pieces of pasta and cereal to punctuate sentences in the assignment.

I see a cat

Do you see it

I love it

MAGNETIC CAPITALIZATION

You're sure to attract students to this capitalization activity! Each morning write several sentences on a magnetic chalkboard, omitting all capitalization. Challenge student volunteers to correct the sentences by positioning magnetic capital letters atop the appropriate lowercase letters. What an easy way to improve students' capitalization skills!

Is It Complete?

Looking for a unique way to introduce your first graders to complete sentences? Then try this idea! Tell your students to "Turn to page…" or "Write a story about…." Ask students if they understand the directions. Discuss the importance of stating a complete thought to communicate ideas. Next pair students and give each pair a picture from a discarded magazine. Instruct each group to write complete sentences about its picture. After a designated amount of time, invite each group to share its complete sentences with classmates.

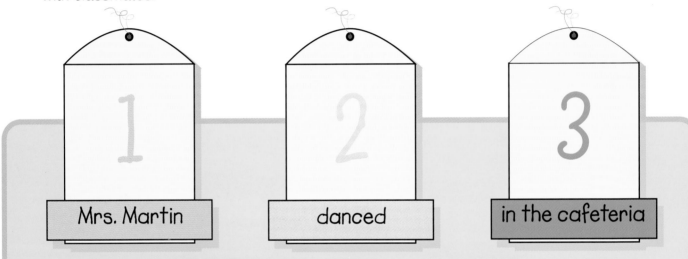

MAKING SENTENCES

Perfect for reviewing sentence structure, this center activity will have your students full of giggles! Program ten strips of colored construction paper with a variety of subjects, another set in a different color with a variety of predicates, and another different-colored set with a variety of prepositional phrases. Store each set of colored strips in a string-tie envelope. Arrange the envelopes at the center with the subject folder on the left, predicate folder in the middle, and prepositional envelope on the right; then use a marker in the same color as the strips to number each folder sequentially as shown. The student chooses one strip from each envelope and arranges the strips to create a silly sentence. He then copies the sentence on writing paper before returning the strips to their correct envelopes. The student continues in this same manner until he has written ten silly sentences. For added enjoyment, include names and areas from your school on the strips.

Logan
1. Mr. Adams jumped in the library.
2. Mrs. Martin danced in the cafeteria.

Plurals Practice

This hands-on activity provides your first graders with practice using singular and plural forms of words. Have each student visually divide a sheet of paper in half, then label one half of the paper "singular" and the other half "plural." Give each student several stickers of the same design. A student glues her stickers on her paper to show the meaning of *singular* and *plural.* Then she labels the resulting pictures with the appropriate singular and plural word forms. If desired, have the student illustrate a background scene.

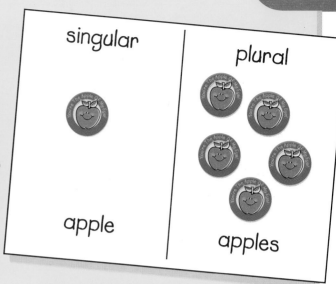

singular plural

apple apples

Practice With Possessives

For a fun introduction to possessives, have each student illustrate something she owns on a sheet of story paper. Then have her write a sentence that declares her ownership. Invite each child to share her completed work before displaying the projects on a classroom wall.

Morgan

This is Morgan's teddy bear.

COMPLETE-SENTENCE CHALLENGE

Reinforce the concept of complete sentences with this whole-group activity. Gather students in a circle and announce a word such as "We" or "I" that could start a sentence. Then choose a student to say another word that could come after the first word in a sentence. The child then "passes" the phrase to the student on his left to continue. Students continue in this same manner until a complete sentence is formed. Then write the completed sentence on the chalkboard for everyone to see. Using a new beginning word each time, repeat this activity until each student has had a turn to contribute to a sentence.

DESCRIPTIVE STUFFED ANIMALS

Your first graders might be too young to learn the word *adjective,* but they'll certainly be ready to describe their stuffed animals. In advance send a note home asking each student to bring a stuffed animal to school. On the day of the lesson, have each student share his stuffed animal. On a sheet of writing paper, write a student-generated list of adjectives that could describe the animal. Repeat this procedure for each student's animal. Then place each student's stuffed animal and sheet of describing words on a table for everyone to view.

READING

ORAL-READING POINTERS

Encourage emergent readers to improve one-to-one correspondence when reading with the help of smart sticks. To make a smart stick, spread glue on one end of a craft stick; then sprinkle glitter over the glue. When oral-reading practice is scheduled, distribute the smart sticks to your youngsters. Students use the sticks to follow along as their classmates read orally. Now, that's a smart idea!

READING STRATEGIES

Reinforce reading strategies by having students correct your deliberate oral-reading mistakes. Before beginning the activity with a reading group, tell students that you are going to make some mistakes in the sentences you will be reading. Then have students follow along as you read several sentences, deliberately making mistakes as you read. Ask students to name the words you mispronounced. Then have students describe reading strategies you could have used to determine each unfamiliar word. Strategies might include using picture clues, chunking the word into parts, sounding out each letter, or listening to yourself read. After students have explained several reading strategies, reread the sentence correctly. Continue in this same manner in various parts of the story. Your youngsters will be pleased with your reading progress and more than eager to try these strategies in their own reading.

STUDENTS AS THE AUTHORS

Heighten student interest in your current literature with this prediction activity. Read aloud a story to your students, stopping before the conclusion. On a piece of story paper, have each student write and illustrate a prediction of what will happen next. Encourage students to share their predictions with their classmates; then read aloud the conclusion of the book. If desired, bind your students' predictions into a book and place it and the actual book in your reading area for students to compare.

Main-Idea Sandwich

Help your students better understand the main idea of a story with this appetizing analogy. On a sheet of poster board, draw a large sandwich as shown. While explaining the parts of a story, label the sandwich as follows:

—top slice of bread: introduction of the story
—meat: main idea
—lettuce, tomato, cheese: details
—bottom slice of bread: conclusion of the story

Provide practice by reading a short story to your students. Then have students identify the parts of the story as you write their responses on another sandwich drawing.

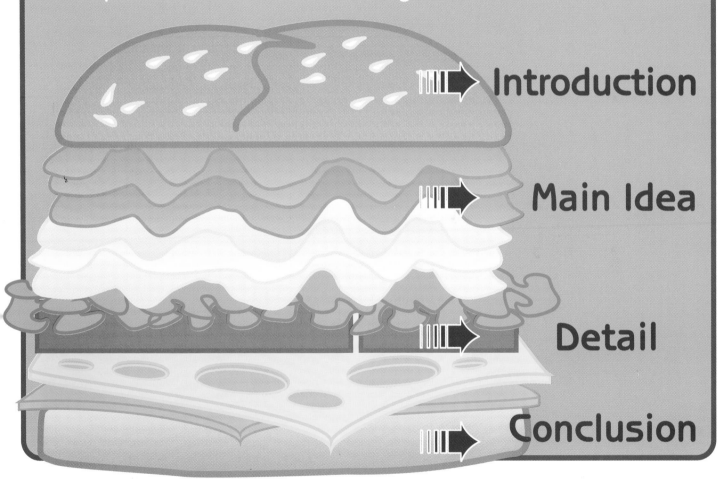

Introduction

Main Idea

Detail

Conclusion

BOOK TITLES

This is a job for the main-idea sleuths! Without telling your students the title, read aloud a book that they probably have not heard before. After reading the book, ask students to reflect on the events of the story and create a title for the book. Before revealing the book's title, encourage students to share the titles they chose.

PICTURE THE MAIN IDEA

You will get an enthusiastic response from this main-idea activity. Pair students and provide each pair with a picture (cut from a discarded magazine) that depicts an event or interesting situation. Have each pair discuss its picture and tell the main idea. For added practice have the pairs exchange their pictures.

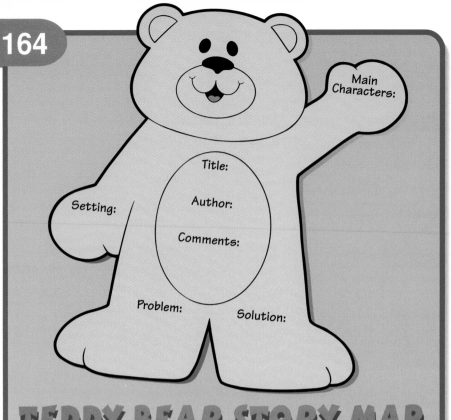

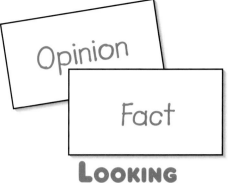

Opinion

Fact

LOOKING FOR THE FACTS

Review fact and opinion with this daily activity. Have each student use a crayon to program one side of an index card "Fact" and the other side "Opinion." Have students store their cards in their desks. Each day secretly record five student-generated statements—some facts, some opinions. Then, at the end of the day, read a statement from the list. If a student thinks the statement is a fact, she displays the fact side of her card. If she thinks the statement is an opinion, she shows the opinion side of her card. Continue in this manner until all the statements have been read. Next reread each statement and reveal its answer. Students can't help but be amazed at the interesting statements they say throughout the day!

TEDDY BEAR STORY MAP

This unique idea is a "bear" essential when it comes to assessing your students' reading comprehension. On light brown bulletin-board paper, draw and label a large bear cutout as shown. Laminate the cutout for durability before mounting it in a prominent location. After reading a story aloud, use a wipe-off marker to write the story's title and author at the top of the bear's tummy. Next write student-generated responses to the four story parts listed on the bear's limbs. Then ask students to share their comments and opinions about the book. Record students' responses below the author's name. When it's time to review another book, simply wipe away the programming, and the story map is ready to use again!

LISTEN UP!

Strengthen your youngsters' listening skills with this humorous activity. To begin, read or tell your students the story of *Goldilocks And The Three Bears.* Next ask student volunteers to recount Goldilocks's actions from the beginning of the story until the end. Then retell the fairy tale using different events. For example, Goldilocks may flip the channels on the Bears' big-screen television, make herself a peanut butter and sauerkraut sandwich, and take a bath in their hot tub. Now challenge students to retell this new version of the story. The first student to correctly retell the story gets to create the next version. Continue in this manner for a predetermined amount of time. Now, that's listening at its silliest!

SIMPLE STORY SEQUENCING

Improve students' reading comprehension skills with this nifty sequencing activity. Gather several books that you have recently read to your students. For each book select five story events that clearly show the sequence of the story line. Cover the page numbers and duplicate each page; then number the backs of the pages for self-checking. Laminate the sets of pages for durability and store each set in an envelope labeled with the title and author of the corresponding book. Place the envelopes and the books at a center. A student sequences the pages from each envelope, referring to the book as needed. Then she flips the pages to check her work.

Reality vs. Fantasy

Could Be	Could Not Be
• Cinderella has two mean stepsisters.	• Cinderella has a fairy godmother.
• Cinderella has to do all the chores.	• A pumpkin turns into a coach.
• She loses her slipper.	• The mice turn into horses.
• The prince finds her slipper.	• Cinderella's torn dress turns into a beautiful gown.

What better way to introduce your students to the difference between fantasy and reality than with the current literature selection? Label one half of a sheet of chart paper "Could Be" and the other half "Could Not Be." Then mount the chart in a prominent location. After reading a story aloud, have students name examples of story events that are fantasy and some that could be reality. List students' responses under the correct heading on the chart. For a fun follow-up, have students replace the fictional parts of the story with things that could happen in reality. Or have students try turning the nonfiction parts of the story into fantasy.

Inference Bags

Here's a fun yet simple way to provide your youngsters with practice making inferences. Have each student secretly place an object or a magazine picture of an object in a paper lunch bag. Each student then writes three clues about his item on an index card, folds his bag, and tapes the card on the outside. In turn invite each student to read his clues to the class and call on a volunteer to infer the bag's contents.

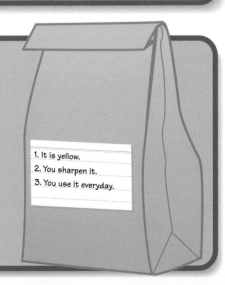

1. It is yellow.
2. You sharpen it.
3. You use it everyday.

RESEARCH SKILLS

PERSONAL DICTIONARIES

Familiarize your first graders with the dictionary by having each student keep a yearlong alphabet notebook. Before the school year begins, alphabetize the pages of a spiral notebook for each student. Then, during the first week of school, present each youngster with a notebook to personalize. Throughout the year, encourage students to enter a variety of words, such as number words, classmates' names, color words, and vocabulary words. Also suggest that youngsters refer to their notebooks when they are writing independently. At the end of the school year, your students' notebooks will be bursting with words!

A

Allen
apple
ask
are

TABLE OF CONTENTS

Here's a fun way for students to learn how to use a table of contents. For each child, place a copy similar to the reproducible shown atop ten blank pages; then staple them between two slightly larger construction-paper covers. To begin, remind students that a *table of contents* shows the divisions of a book (units, chapters, or topics). Show students several books that contain tables of contents. Then distribute a writing journal to each student. For each of the next ten school days, a student enters a writing topic in his book's table of contents before writing about the topic in his journal. After each student has completed ten entries, have students share their tables of contents with their classmates. Encourage students to place their journals in the classroom library if desired.

Table Of Contents
1. My Dog, Buddy
2. Pizza
3.
4.
5.
6.
7.
8.
9.
10.

FICTION OR NONFICTION?

Help your students distinguish a fiction book from a nonfiction one with this nifty idea. Gather a class supply of easy-to-read books, half fiction and half nonfiction, and display them in a prominent location. Remind students that *fiction books* are make-believe. These books have their own place in the library and are usually found in alphabetical order by the author's last name. Then remind students that *nonfiction books* tell true stories and give facts. These books are put on the shelves in number order according to their subjects.

After sharing this information with your students, distribute a displayed book to each student. Instruct each student to look at the title and pictures in her book to decide if it is a fiction or nonfiction book. Ask each student to share her decision with the class.

100 Short Vowels

Short *A* Words	Short *E* Words	Short *I* Words	Short *O* Words	Short *U* Words
add	bed	big	box	bug
bad	beg	bill	cot	bus
bag	desk	crib	dog	cub
bat	egg	dish	drop	cup
cab	fed	fib	fog	drum
cap	fence	grin	fox	fun
dad	get	hill	hop	gum
fan	help	in	hot	hut
fat	jet	king	jot	jug
ham	leg	lid	knob	luck
hat	met	milk	lock	mud
jam	nest	pig	mom	mug
man	pet	rip	mop	nut
map	red	ship	not	pup
nap	sent	six	on	rug
pan	ten	this	pot	run
rag	test	tin	rock	sun
ran	vet	whip	song	tub
sad	web	win	top	umbrella
tag	yes	zip	toss	up

100 Long Vowels

Long *A* Words	Long *E* Words	Long *I* Words	Long *O* Words	Long *U* Words
ape	bee	bite	bone	cube
bake	cheese	bride	close	cute
cape	deep	fire	cone	dude
cave	feet	five	dose	duke
date	free	hive	froze	dune
face	he	ice	globe	flute
flame	heat	kite	hole	fume
gate	key	life	home	fuse
grape	knee	line	joke	huge
hate	lead	mice	lobe	mule
lake	meet	mine	mole	music
make	pea	nice	nose	mute
name	please	nine	note	prune
page	read	pine	pole	pure
plane	see	ripe	robe	rule
rake	she	size	rope	spruce
same	three	smile	stove	tube
skate	tree	time	tote	tulip
take	we	vine	vote	tune
tape	week	wide	woke	yule

Ready Reference

Consonant Blends And Digraphs

bl
black
blame
blank
blast
bleed
blend
blind
blink
block
blow
blue
blush

br
brag
brain
brake
brand
brave
breeze
brick
bring
broke
broom
brother
brown
brush

ch
chain
chair
chalk
chance
change
chase
chat
check
cheek
chest
chick
chin
choose
chop

cl
clam
clap

class
claw
clay
clean
climb
clock
close
clown

cr
crab
crack
crash
creep
crib
crime
crop
cross
crow

dr
drag
draw
dream
dress
drip
drum
dry

fl
flag
flake
flame
flap
flash
flat
flip
float
flow
fly

fr
frame
free
freeze
fresh
friend
frog

from
front
fry

gl
glad
glass
glove
glow
glue

gr
grab
grape
grass
green
grin
grip
grow

pl
place
plan
plane
plate
play
please
plot
plug
plus

pr
press
price
pride
prince
prize

sh
shade
share
shark
she
sheep
sheet
shell
shine
ship

shirt
shop
shot
should
show
shut

sl
slam
sled
sleep
slid
slip
slow

sm
small
smart
smell
smile
smoke

st
stand
step
sting
stop
store
street

th
that
the
then
these
they
thin
think
this
thumb

wh
whale
what
when
where
white
why

Compound Words

airplane	downstairs	mailbox	seahorse
barnyard	fingernail	newspaper	sidewalk
baseball	firecracker	nobody	skateboard
bathtub	flashlight	notebook	snowflake
bedroom	football	outside	snowman
beehive	goldfish	paintbrush	somebody
birdbath	grandparents	pancake	something
birdhouse	grasshopper	patchwork	strawberry
butterfly	groundhog	peanut	suitcase
chalkboard	hairbrush	playground	sunlight
cowboy	haircut	policeman	sunshine
cupcake	handshake	popcorn	teamwork
daydream	homework	railroad	teapot
daylight	indoor	rainbow	toothbrush
doghouse	keyboard	sailboat	underline
dollhouse	ladybug	sandpaper	watermelon
doorbell	lighthouse	scarecrow	weekend

Antonyms

above—below	cold—hot	forget—remember	on—off
alike—different	crooked—straight	give—take	polite—rude
always—never	dark—light	happy—sad	pull—push
asleep—awake	day—night	hard—soft	rich—poor
attack—defend	deep—shallow	healthy—sick	rough—smooth
back—front	difficult—easy	heavy—light	save—spend
beautiful—ugly	down—up	high—low	short—tall
before—after	dry—wet	kind—mean	start—stop
begin—end	early—late	large—small	strong—weak
best—worst	easy—hard	leave—stay	tame—wild
big—little	empty—full	long—short	thick—thin
bottom—top	evil—good	loose—tight	true—false
bright—dull	far—near	lose—win	wide—narrow
clean—dirty	fast—slow	many—few	yes—no
close—open	first—last	noisy—quiet	

Ready Reference

Contractions

A contraction is a shortened form of a single word or word pair. An apostrophe is used to show where a letter or letters have been omitted to create the shortened form.

word with "am"

I am	I'm

words with "are"

they are	they're
we are	we're
you are	you're

words with "has"

he has	he's
it has	it's
she has	she's
what has	what's
where has	where's
who has	who's

words with "have"

I have	I've
they have	they've
we have	we've
you have	you've

words with "is"

he is	he's
it is	it's
she is	she's
that is	that's
there is	there's
what is	what's
where is	where's
who is	who's

words with "not"

are not	aren't
cannot	can't
could not	couldn't
did not	didn't
do not	don't
does not	doesn't
had not	hadn't
has not	hasn't
have not	haven't
is not	isn't
must not	mustn't
should not	shouldn't
was not	wasn't
were not	weren't
will not	won't
would not	wouldn't
we would	we'd

word with "us"

let us	let's

words with "will"

he will	he'll
I will	I'll
she will	she'll
they will	they'll
we will	we'll
you will	you'll

words with "would"

he would	he'd
I would	I'd
she would	she'd
they would	they'd
who would	who'd
you would	you'd

Stuck On Spelling

Write your spelling words on the lines.
Color a bee each day you study your words.

1. _____

2. _____

3. _____

4. _____

5. _____

Monday

6. _____

Tuesday

7. _____

8. _____

9. _____

Wednesday

10. _____

11. _____

12. _____

Thursday

13. _____

14. _____

15. _____

Friday

Note To Teacher: Use with "Stuck On Spelling" on page 149.

Patterns

Use the monster pattern with "Vowel Munchers" on page 153.

Use the ice-cream cone and scoop with "A Scoop Of Blends" on page 153.

Roll up your sleeves and build students' writing skills with these easy-to-follow blueprints. You'll find ideas for handwriting, the writing process, creative and journal writing, poetry, letters, and much more. So what are you waiting for? Start building!

Handwriting

Handwriting Made Simple

Prepare your students for a handwriting lesson with this nifty idea. Teach handwriting placement as though letters lived outside. Refer to the area above a dotted line as the sky, below a dotted line as the grass, and below a bottom solid line as the ground. Students will easily recognize and remember correct placement with this method.

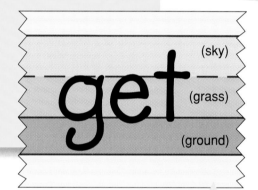

(sky)

get (grass)

(ground)

Space Sticks

Help students remember to put space between their words with "space sticks." Give each student a craft stick and encourage him to personalize and decorate it as desired. To use the stick, the student places it on his paper to hold a space after each word. Before long you'll begin to notice neatly spaced papers!

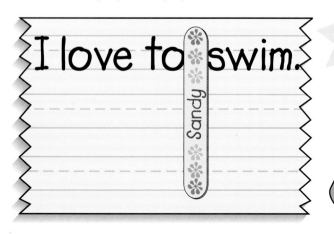

I love to swim.

Sandy

Spotlight On Handwriting

Reinforce neat handwriting with this radiant activity. Provide your youngsters with highlighter markers. At the end of a handwriting practice session, ask each student to highlight the best letters or words on his practice paper. Students are sure to feel proud of their bright accomplishments!

The Writing Process

Planning	First Draft	Revision	Edit	Final Draft
Cara	Mike	Lisa	Penny	
Mary	Lori	Jerry		
Baron	Eugene			
	Calvin			

Managing Classroom Editing

Try this simple technique to keep track of where each student is in the writing process. Write each child's name on a piece of animal-shaped paper, laminate it, and attach a piece of magnetic tape to the back. Then divide the chalkboard into five columns: planning, first draft, revision, edit, final draft. Each student begins a writing assignment with his name under the planning column and moves his marker as he progresses through the writing process. When the student reaches the editing phase, meet with him individually. Now you will no longer have a line of students at your desk waiting for help.

Literature Links

- In *From Pictures To Words: A Book About Making A Book* by Janet Stevens (Holiday House, Inc.; 1995), the author tells how she came to write her first story and turn it into this very book. Students will enjoy watching as she decides on her story's setting and plot, lays it out on a storyboard, and sends the final version to her editor.
- In *Arthur Writes A Story* by Marc Brown (Little, Brown And Company; 1996), Arthur's teacher asks him to write a story with a beginning, a middle, and an end; to use details; and to be creative. But every time Arthur tries his tale out on friends and family, they give him different editorial advice. Students will enjoy the chance to see Arthur writing just like them!

Editing Checklist

Even young writers can benefit from a writer's checklist such as the one on page 190. Duplicate and distribute student copies, instructing students to check off each guideline as they evaluate their writing. By adding this writing step to the editing (proofreading) step, students are sure to eliminate careless mistakes.

Proofing Buddies

Have students work as editing partners. After a student has edited his partner's work, have him share at least one positive comment about the writing and one writing suggestion. Also encourage students to work together to correct spelling and punctuation errors.

Writing Log

Individual writing logs are a great way for students to keep track of where they are in the writing process. Staple a copy of the writing log (page 189) inside each student's writing folder. For each story a student writes, he records the date he starts writing and the title. He then checks off each step in the writing process as he completes it. Now, that's a handy organizational tool!

Be sure to also check the Ready Reference on page 186 for additional information on the writing process.

Creative Writing

Treasure Basket

A basket of toys is a terrific way to evoke creative thoughts and writing from your students. Encourage students to help fill a basket with small toys obtained from fast-food restaurants. At designated times have a child choose an item from the basket. Display the item in a prominent location. Challenge students to write stories that are related in some way to the displayed object. Now, that's writing to treasure!

STICKER SCENE STORIES

If you use stickers as incentives, this creative-writing idea is for you! Each time a student exhibits behavior worthy of a sticker, make a tally mark beside her name on a chart. At the end of each week, count the number of tally marks each child has and award her with that number of motivational stickers. Have the student use the stickers in place of words as she writes and illustrates a story. Students will be stuck on these fun-to-write sticker stories!

One day when the ☀ was shining very bright, I saw a 🦋 flying around some 🌸s, and I started following it. It led me through a COOL! forest and to a lake full of 🐟. In the forest I saw big fat 🐻 and big lizards that looked almost like 🦎s. I was amazed and scared at first, but the animals were all very friendly.

Picture-Perfect Writing

My name is Katie the cat. I love to play with yarn. One day I got so tangled in a ball of yarn that I had to lie on the floor until my owner came in the room and used scissors to cut me free. That was very funny, and I still play with yarn.

Trigger creativity and writing enthusiasm with students' school photographs. In advance duplicate each student's school photo. Trim each child's face from her photocopy; then distribute the copy of the child's face and a piece of story paper to her. Each child chooses an animal or a story character she would like to be. She then writes a story as if she were the animal or person. After completing the story, the child glues the photocopy of her face to her paper. She illustrates the rest of herself using her face as the face of the animal or person. Mount each child's completed story on a slightly larger sheet of construction paper before displaying it on a bulletin board for all to see and enjoy.

I turned my triangle into a parrot because I wish I had one. My parrot has wings and feathers made of hearts.

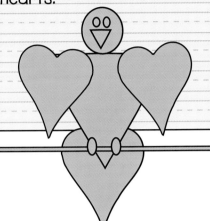

Shapely Stories

Your students' writing will really take shape with this creative-writing activity! Provide each student with a sheet of colorful construction paper and instruct him to cut out any large shape. Next have the student use construction-paper scraps to transform his shape into a person, animal, or object. Challenge each student to write a story about his creation. After they complete their stories, invite your young authors to share their stories with their classmates.

Animals	Action words	Naming words
cow	played	park
dog	jumped	school
cat	swam	pool
bunny	skated	beach
lion	talked	phone
bear	jogged	pencil
elephant	sang	shower
tiger	climbed	bed
giraffe	ate	book
horse	rode	car

Story Starters

Spark the imaginations of your youngsters with story titles written on craft sticks. Write story titles such as "The Day A Dragon Came To School" or "Winnie The Talking Bear" on several craft sticks; then place the craft sticks in a decorated can. Invite students to choose starter titles from the can whenever they have difficulty deciding on a writing topic.

(See the Ready Reference on page 187 for more story titles.)

Silly Animal Antics

Create extraordinary writing enthusiasm with this sentence-building activity. To begin, enlist students' help in making lists on the chalkboard of animals, action words (in the past tense), and naming words. After writing at least ten words in each list, provide each child with a piece of story paper. Instruct each student to choose one word from each list, then use the words and any needed prepositions to create a sentence. Remind students to use the words in the order they appear on the chalkboard: animals, action words, naming words. After all students have written and illustrated their sentences, compile the pages between two construction-paper covers. Add the title "Silly Animal Sentences" and display the book in your classroom library.

The cow sang in the shower.

One day my parents took me to the beach. We had a fun time. We swam in the ocean, looked for seashells, and built a sand castle. I even saw a dolphin. I can't wait to go again!

Sunshine Isle

Picture Collection

Don't toss out discarded calendars and postcards! Use the pictures as unique story starters. Clip pictures from discarded magazines, calendars, and postcards. Mount and laminate each picture on a slightly larger sheet of construction paper. Display a picture from the collection and ask students to share their thoughts about it. Write students' ideas on the chalkboard. Then have each student use the ideas to help write a story about the picture. After students have completed their stories, stack the pages and staple them together along the top margin. If desired send the stories and the picture home in a large envelope for students to share with their parents.

Fantasy Or Reality?

Reinforce the concepts of *fantasy* and *reality* with this delightful writing activity. After reading aloud a fantasy book, have students name the parts of the story that are fantasy, or could not happen in real life. Write students' responses on the chalkboard. Then enlist students' help in turning the book into reality. Ask students to share ideas for changing the fantasy parts of the story into reality. Use their ideas to write a reality version of the story. Or, if desired, have students use the ideas on the board to write their own reality versions of the story.

Cinderella

<u>Fantasy</u>
- a pumpkin turned into a coach
- mice turned into her drivers
- a fairy *godmother*

Seasonal Word Banks

Keep first graders motivated and independently writing creative stories with seasonal word banks. Each month have students brainstorm seasonal words. Write the words on a large seasonal cutout, and display it in a prominent location. When students are ready to write, they can refer to the word bank for help with writing topics and spelling.

winter
mittens
snow
sled
snowman
ice
snowball
hat
scarf
gloves
hot chocolate
cold

Special Storybook Visitors

Stimulate young writers by incorporating storybook characters into their writing. Share several classics with your students, such as *Cinderella, Snow White And The Seven Dwarfs,* and *Little Red Riding Hood.* After completing each story, ask students to imagine how the characters from these stories would act if they visited the classroom. Then challenge students to choose one of the characters and write a story about the character's visit to the classroom. When the stories are complete, compile and bind stories about similar characters together and place them in your classroom library.

STORY SANDWICHES

How are a sandwich and a story alike? They each have three parts! In advance prepare a peanut-butter sandwich to use in a demonstration. To begin, remind students that a good story has a *beginning,* a *middle,* and an *ending.* As you present these three story parts, refer to the top piece of bread as the beginning, the peanut butter as the middle, and the bottom piece of bread as the ending. Ask each student to keep this image in mind as he plans and writes an original story. If desired invite students to make their own peanut-butter sandwiches after they successfully complete the activity.

Newsworthy Journals

If your students have difficulty deciding what to write in their daily journals, try this approach. Near the end of each day, have students summarize the day's events as you write them on the chalkboard. Then have each student choose one of the events to write about in his journal. At the end of the school year, each student will have a keepsake journal that highlights some of the year's events.

Today we:
- went to the library
- wrote a story about our class bear, Homer
- practiced our play
- worked on our subtraction facts
- read to our reading buddies

Limitless Literature

If you're searching for journal topics, try using literature as a creative stimulus. Choose a particularly imaginative read-aloud—such as *Where The Wild Things Are* by Maurice Sendak—to share with your youngsters. Afterward brainstorm possible rewritten versions or story extensions. Then set youngsters loose with their journals to write and illustrate their own ideas. When the momentum on one particular story subsides, introduce another new, imaginative book. The possibilities are endless!

MONDAY-MORNING JOURNAL

Madison

Monday-Morning Journals

Establish this book-related journal routine to foster your youngsters' love for literature and encourage parental involvement. Have each child decorate a cover for her journal; then bind a supply of blank pages into each child's journal. Each Friday have students check out books from your classroom library. Encourage children to read the books with their parents, then bring the books back to school on Monday morning. On a page of her Monday-Morning Journal, have each child write anything she would like that is related to the book, such as a description of her favorite character or part of the story. What a great way to see how many books students have read throughout the year!

Stuck On Journal Writing

Everyone in class earns a sticker with this journal-writing activity! Give each child a sticker that has a character on it. The student attaches the sticker to his paper and writes a story about the character. Each story's setting and plot must be related to the sticker. The child can include other characters in the story as well. What a great way to inspire students' writing!

> Beatrice The Bunny loved carrots! She loved them so much that she would leave her home and hop over to Farmer Fred's yard to eat his carrots. One day Farmer Fred saw her eating the carrots. He told her to stop and chased her out of his carrot patch. Beatrice hid in the bushes until he went back inside, and then she hopped

Journal Topic Joggers

Inspire creative journal writing by having students bring in items to serve as writing topics. Encourage students to submit objects such as magazine pictures, ticket stubs, postcards, stickers, gift wrap, greeting cards, and other small objects as journal-writing topics. Review each submission and place the approved objects in a container on your desk. Return the unapproved objects to students to take home. When a student can't think of anything to write about in his journal, have him draw an object from the container and use it as his writing topic. To keep student interest high, encourage students to periodically replace the items in the box.

Journal Topic Joggers

Bright Ideas

The Magic Bean · Space · If I was in a book · My favorite holiday · When I grow up . . . · If I was invisible · I heard a bump! · I can fly

Bright Ideas For Journal Writing

For writing motivation have students brainstorm writing topics. In advance laminate and cut out a large sun shape (with rays) from yellow poster board. Then use a wipe-off marker to write a journal topic on each of the sun's rays. To change the journal topics, simply wipe off the old topics with a damp cloth and reprogram the rays with new topics. What a bright way to encourage positive journal-writing experiences in your class!

POETRY

Haunted house
Apples for bobbing
Looking silly
Looking scary
Owl overhead
Witches, too
Eeeek!
Exciting
Nice night!

Seasonal Acrostic Poems

Put your young poets to work writing seasonal acrostic poems! To begin, write a student-generated list of words associated with the current season or holiday on the chalkboard. After making the list, write the season or holiday vertically in all capital letters. Then have students use the list to write an acrostic poem about the topic. Invite students to illustrate and share their poetry with their classmates.

Poetry Puzzle

Motivate your first graders to read poetry with this unique idea. Each week write a favorite poem on a piece of poster board; then add decorations around the border. Cut the poster board into large puzzle pieces. Place the pieces in a large envelope labeled with the title of the poem. Place the puzzle at a center and challenge students to put the puzzle together and read the poem. What a great twist to reading poetry!

SWEET SIMILES

Entice your first graders to write a class simile poem with the help of chocolate-chip cookies. To begin, give each student a cookie. Ask students to name words that describe their cookies. Write students' descriptions on a piece of chart paper. Next reread the first word on the list, and have students think of an object that has a similar feature. Write that word beside the descriptive word; then add the needed words ("as") to create a simile. Continue in this manner with the other descriptive words on the list. To complete the poem, simply add the title "Chocolate-Chip Cookie." Invite students to munch on their cookies as you read the completed poem. Now, that's sweet success with poetry!

Poetry Selections

Capture the hearts of your youngsters with poems from the following poetry collections.
Falling Up by Shel Silverstein (HarperCollins Publishers, Inc.; 1996)
A Pizza The Size Of The Sun by Jack Prelutsky (Greenwillow Books, 1996)
Lunch Money And Other Poems About School by Carol Diggory Shields (Dutton Children's Books, 1995)

Chocolate-Chip Cookie

As sweet as a piece of candy,
As delicious as a birthday cake,
As brown as a camel,
As round as the sun.

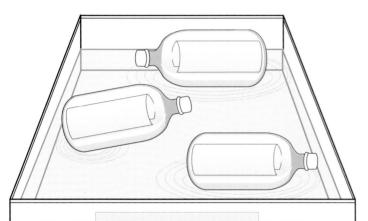

Please take a container.
Read the letter and write
back to its author.
Deliver to Mrs. Speckman's
room (8). Thank you.

Letter-Writing Center

Motivate your first graders to become independent letter writers with these center ideas. They're guaranteed to deliver letter-writing fun!

- Provide greeting cards, leftover stationery pages, and postcards for students to use.
- Provide art supplies—such as markers, glitter, rubber stamps, stamp pads, and envelopes—for students to use in creating their own stationery.
- Purchase a premade mailbox center (or make one from shoeboxes), and label a mailbox for each student and yourself. Encourage students to write letters to their classmates and then deliver the letters to their classmates' mailboxes. Be sure to remind students to respond to the letters they receive!
- Collect free offers from magazines and highlight the addresses. Place the offers at the center and encourage students to write letters asking the companies to send their free products. Assist students in addressing the envelopes. If desired ask parents to donate stamps to use in mailing the letters. Students are sure to be delighted when they receive these free products in the mail!

Message In A Bottle

Keep your youngsters' letter-writing skills afloat with this schoolwide activity. In advance collect a class supply of airtight plastic containers and place a partially filled water table (or plastic tub) in your school's lobby. To begin, have each student write a letter telling about himself to an unnamed pen pal; then have him insert his letter in a container and float it in the water table. Post a sign near the water table encouraging staff, parents, and fellow students to take a container, read its contents, write a response to the author, and deliver the letter to your classroom. Students will be thrilled to receive letters, and long-term pen pals may develop, too!

Fairy-Tale Mail

Heighten student interest in letter writing with the help of fairy-tale characters. For writing inspirations read aloud *The Jolly Postman Or Other People's Letters* by Janet & Allan Ahlberg. Then have each student write a letter to his favorite fairy-tale character telling the character why he or she is his favorite. After he completes the letter, have each student illustrate his chosen character. Post the letters and the illustrations on a bulletin board for everyone to see.

I have a dog named Hobbes.
He loves to go for walks.
He sleeps at the foot of my bed.
He barks at strangers.
He is the best dog in the world.

Flip Books

Provide students with easy-to-make flip books to use in publishing their work. To make a booklet, stack three 8 1/2" x 11" sheets of white paper and hold the pages vertically in front of you. Slide the top sheet upward one inch; then repeat the process for the second sheet. Next fold the paper thicknesses forward to create six graduated layers or pages (see the illustration). Staple close to the fold. A student writes the title of his story and his name on the cover, then writes sentences on the bottoms of the booklet pages as shown. Next have the student illustrate the sentence on each page. Students will be flipping over this publishing method!

Pop-Up Cards

Students will enjoy illustrating their stories in pop-up cards. Have each student publish his favorite story in a self-made pop-up card.

To make a pop-up card:

1. Fold in half a 9" x 12" sheet of white construction paper.
2. Cut two 2-inch slits in the center of the fold about 1 1/2 inches apart. Open the card and write a short story near the bottom of it.
3. Illustrate the main character in the story on a three-inch square of white construction paper. Cut out the illustration.
4. Pull the narrow strip in the center of the opened card forward and crease it in the opposite direction from the fold. Glue the cutout to the lower half of the strip; then illustrate the inside of the card as desired.
5. Close the card, making sure the strip stays inside.
6. To complete the project, write the title of the story on the outside of the card.

One day I was walking in the forest when I met a bear named Bessie. We became friends. I took her food and taught her to read.

PAPER-PLATE BOOKS

With this method of publishing, students can easily share their favorite literary pieces. Provide each student with two paper plates, lined paper to fit inside the paper plates, and various art materials—such as construction paper, wiggle eyes, pipe cleaners, glue, and scissors. To make a plate book, a student decorates one paper plate as desired, then staples the lined paper between the front cover and the back cover. The student then writes her story on the lined paper. What a great way to get students wild about writing!

Sturdy Class Books

If your class books do not hold up to heavy use, try this tip. Purchase clear, plastic sheet protectors from an office-supply store. Place the protectors in a three-ring binder. Insert pages for a class book in the protectors back-to-back. If you have a binder with a clear pocket on the cover, just slip your book cover inside. These sturdy class books will hold up for the entire year. At the end of the year, simply pull out each child's pages and return them. Then reuse the binder and sheet protectors next year.

Plastic Class Books

Make classroom-published books more durable with gallon-sized, resealable plastic bags. To make a book using this method, have each child insert his page into a resealable plastic bag. Staple all of the bags together along the sealed end. Cover that end with colored tape and you've got a bound book that will stand up to your youngsters' hands.

Author Photos

This tip makes it easier for students to identify which of his classmates created a specific page in a class-made book. Photocopy a picture of each of your students. To each page in the book, glue a photocopied picture of the student who created it. Then youngsters can tell at a glance which page belongs to which student.

Easy Book Binders

Looking for alternatives to metal ring binders? Then try these tips!

- Use plastic shower-curtain rings to bind your classroom-published books instead. Not only do they come in a variety of colors, but they're also less expensive and easier to open and close.
- Use a hole puncher to make holes in each book; then insert a twist-tie through each hole and twist the ends of the ties together. Wow, book making has never been so easy!

Grocery-Bag Books

Recycle your paper grocery bags to make big books. To make the pages and covers of the book, cut the front and back panels from several large paper grocery bags. Have students use markers to illustrate and write on each page; then laminate the pages and covers if desired. Punch two holes along the left-hand side of each page; then use heavy string to bind the pages between the covers.

The Writing Process

There are five steps to the writing process.

1. **Plan**
   - Think of subjects to write about.
   - Choose the best one.
   - List ideas about your subject.

2. **Write**
   - Write about your subject.
   - Be sure to include a beginning, a middle, and an ending to your story.
   - This step is considered the first draft.

3. **Revise**
   - Read over your writing and/or have someone else read it.
   - Change parts to make them better.
   - This step is often when the teacher has a conference with the student about the writing.

4. **Check (Proofread)**
   - Check spelling, capital letters, and punctuation.

5. **Publish**
   - Write a neat copy to share.

Story Titles

Lost At Sea
The Magical Mirror
The Vanishing Footprints
Race Against The Clock
Visitor From Another Planet
Stranded On A Desert Island
The Big Escape
The Ice-Cream Gang
Monster On The Loose
The Secret Formula
The Empty Cage
The Case Of The Stolen Key
My Day As A Giraffe
The Perfect Birthday Party
The Runaway Sled
Stuck In The Snow
Magical Mittens
A Visit From The Snow Fairy
The Valentine Surprise
Bang! The Race Began!
Whispers In The Forest
The Runaway Bus

Footsteps In The Mud
The Talking Bear
The Mystery In The Schoolroom
Surprise!
Freddie The Frog
The Giggling Gorilla
The Puppy In Trouble
The Mountain Rescue
Trapped!
The Day The Sun Disappeared
The Talking Cloud
The Pig That Kept Growing
The Lost Penguin
The Magical Wizard
The Surprise Package
The Secret Of Candy Cave
The Winning Goal
A Field Trip To Mars
Danny Dinosaur Saves The Day
The Perfect School Playground
The Day A Monster Ate My Homework
The Camping Trip

Poetry

In an **acrostic poem (or name poem),** the title or topic is printed vertically, letter by letter. Each letter is used to begin a phrase or sentence that describes the topic.

Cute
Helpful
Right-handed
Intelligent
Shares

A **diamante** is a form of unrhymed poetry that follows a specific format and resembles a diamond.

topic
two describing words
three action words
a four-word phrase capturing some feeling about the topic
three action words
two describing words
ending word

A **couplet** is a verse composed of two lines that usually rhyme.

There once was a girl named Jane
Who liked to dance in the rain.

In an **alphabet poem,** the letters of the alphabet are used as a framework. Each letter is used to begin a word about a particular topic. The poem may be a list or a description of a topic.

Winter

Arctic Air
Brrr
Cold
Delightful
Exciting
Frosty

Friendly Letters

A friendly letter has five parts. The parts are marked in the letter below.

Date September 16, 1998

Greeting Dear Aunt Alice,

Body
    How are you? I'm fine. I lost my first tooth yesterday. I was eating my snack at school. The tooth fairy left me $1.00. I can't wait for my new tooth to grow in.
    I'm so excited about visiting you at Thanksgiving. Will Uncle Bob take me to the park with the tall slide again? I hope so!
    I love you.

Closing Love,

Signature Sharon

Writing Log

Write the date you start each piece of writing.
Make checks in the boxes after you complete
each step in the writing process.

Date	Story Title	Pre-writing	First Draft	Teacher Edit	Revision	Editing	Final Copy

Note To Teacher: Use with "Writing Log" on page 175.

Did You Reach The Finish Line?

Check each box as you read your story.

- ☐ My name is on my paper.

- ☐ My story has a title.

- ☐ My story has a beginning, a middle, and an ending.

- ☐ I used complete sentences.

- ☐ Each sentence begins with a capital letter.

- ☐ Each sentence ends with a **.** or **?** or **!**.

- ☐ I used my neatest handwriting.

If you checked each box, color the bear.
Congratulations! You reached the finish line!

LITERATURE

READING MOTIVATION

Looking for practical and easy-to-manage ideas to motivate your youngsters to read? Then try this fresh collection of teacher-tested ideas. A good time will be had by all, and a love for literature will most certainly be nurtured.

LIFE-SIZE LIBRARY FIGURES

Invite your youngsters to enter the world of books by enlarging library-book characters onto 45-inch poster board. Color, cut out, and laminate each figure. Display the characters in your classroom or in the hallway. Then add conversation bubbles encouraging students to read.

ALL ABOARD!

All aboard for this reading-incentive program! Mount a construction-paper engine on a classroom wall. Provide each student with several colored copies of the boxcar pattern on page 203 to take home. Each time the student reads a book at home, have her complete the information on the boxcar, cut it out, and return it to school. Mount the boxcars on the wall to create a train. As the train grows throughout the year, so will your students' reading abilities!

Name Deanna
Title IF I Ran The Zoo
Author Dr Seuss
Rating ★★★★☆

Name Keith
Title Whistle For Willie
Author Ezra Jack Keats
Rating ★★★☆☆

Name Seth
Title Nana Upstairs And Nana D
Author Tomie dePaola
Rating ★★☆☆

THE GROWING CATERPILLAR

Motivate students to read independently by challenging them to achieve a group reading goal. To create this display, cut a supply of large construction-paper circles. Add pom-pom eyes, a yarn mouth, and pipe-cleaner antennae to one circle to resemble a caterpillar's head. Mount the caterpillar's head on a classroom wall. Tell students that for every book a student reads, a segment will be added to the caterpillar. The student must write his name, the author's name, and the title of the book on a construction-paper circle, then have a teacher or parent initial the circle to indicate that he told them about the book. Reward the students with a special party in their honor upon completion of their goal. Your students will be amazed at how fast the bookworm grows!

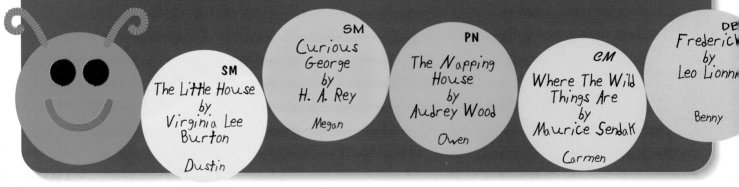

SM
The Little House
by
Virginia Lee Burton
Dustin

SM
Curious George
by
H. A. Rey
Megan

PN
The Napping House
by
Audrey Wood
Owen

CM
Where The Wild Things Are
by
Maurice Sendak
Carmen

DB
Frederick
by
Leo Lionni
Benny

TIME TO READ

This motivational activity will encourage your students to take time to read every night. Duplicate a copy of the recording clock on page 203 for each student to take home. Instruct students to color five-minute intervals on their clocks to show how long they read each night. After a student reads for one hour, have him ask his parent to sign the clock before returning it to school for a new one. Enlist the help of a parent volunteer to keep track of how many hours each student has read. Then periodically have students calculate the number of hours the whole class has read. When the class has read a predetermined number of hours, such as 100, celebrate with an ice-cream party!

PERSONALIZED READING

Students will fall in love with reading when you use this personalized approach. Ask each student to tell you her favorite hobby or interest. Record each student's response in a small journal. Then, periodically throughout the year, check out books from the library that feature a student's hobby. Have the honored student choose one of the books for you to read to the class; then have her take the other books home to read and return the next week. By the end of the year, each student will have had a chance to learn more about her favorite hobby. What a great way to promote reading and share students' special interests!

WILD ABOUT READING

Students are sure to stick their necks out for this reading-motivation display. Draw the outline of a large giraffe onto white bulletin-board paper. Cut out the giraffe and mount it on a classroom wall. Then cut out several patches for the giraffe from tan construction paper. Place the patches and several black, thin-tipped markers at a table near the display. For each night a child reads a book with a family member, have him write his name, the title of the book, and the date on a patch. Then have the student tape the patch to the giraffe. It won't be long before the giraffe has plenty of patches!

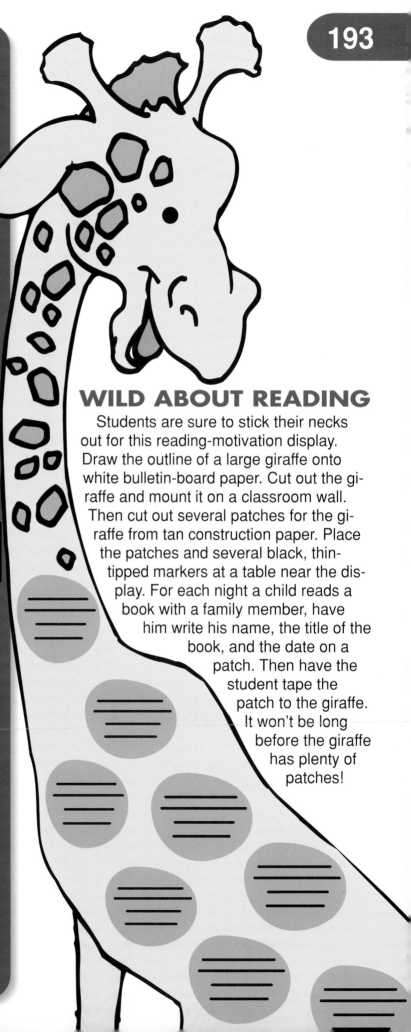

SEASONAL READING

Try these seasonal displays to motivate your youngsters to read! Each month mount the designated character (or object) on a classroom wall. Then have students add titles of books they've read on the smaller designated cutouts. Mount the cutouts on the wall along with the title.

 September—tree, apples, "A Bushel Of Good Books"

 October—scarecrow, pumpkins, "Reading At The Pumpkin Patch"

 November—turkey, feathers, "Books To Gobble About"

 December—Christmas tree, ornaments, " 'Tis The Season To Read"

 January—Martin Luther King, hands, "Reading For Peace"

 February—cupid, hearts, "We Love To Read"

March—leprechaun, shamrocks, "Get Lucky And Read"

April—rabbit, eggs, "Hop Into These Great Books"

May—cowboy, horses, "Rounding Up A Great Year Of Reading"

READ-IN

Boost students' interest in reading by hosting a daylong read-in. Ask each student to bring magazines and books, a pillow, a sleeping bag or towel, and a nutritious snack for the event. Schedule times for independent reading, a read-aloud session with follow-up activities, and other organized reading events such as partner, small group, and choral readings. What a fun change of pace for everyone involved!

BOOK BUDDIES

Motivate your youngsters to read with this lovable idea. Place a basket of stuffed animals at your reading center. Encourage students to keep these animals "healthy" by reading to them each day. Students will enjoy the chance to practice reading to a book buddy before reading to a friend or to you. Not only will students be more eager to read, their reading confidence is sure to improve, too!

CAUGHT READING!

Challenge your first graders to catch their family and friends reading. For one day have each student record on a piece of paper whom she sees reading, what they are reading, and where they are reading. Explain to students that any type of reading counts—shopping lists, menus, street signs, books, magazines, or newspapers. Have each student share some of her responses. Record different responses on chart paper; then facilitate a discussion of *why* people read. Students will be intrigued to discover the many reasons people read each and every day.

READING RECORDS

This reading-motivation idea doubles as a great organizational tool for you! Create a reading record form similar to the one shown. Duplicate several copies and staple one inside a personalized folder for each student. Have students store their folders in their desks. Then, after a student does any independent reading, have her record the book's title, the pages read, and the date in her folder. When a student completes one reading record form, simply staple a new one on top of the old. Students will be motivated to add to their reading records, and you'll have plenty of documentation for student portfolios and parent conferences.

Name Troy D.

Book Title	Pgs. Read	Date
The Teeny-Tiny Woman	4	Sept. 7
	2	Sept. 8
	1	Sept. 10
	2	Sept. 11

Troy D.

A SAFARI ADVENTURE

Entice readers to your book corner by turning it into a safari adventure! Place two small lounge chairs in a quiet corner of the classroom along with several pillows and a collection of books in a net. Add some stuffed safari animals, such as a lion, an elephant, and a leopard. Invite students to visit the center and travel on a safari to the wonderful world of reading!

Better Than A BOOK REPORT

This collection of kid-pleasing ideas is just what you need to provide your students with new and exciting literature activities throughout the year.

A BIG BOOK OF REVIEWS

Turn students' book reviews into a big book. First ask each student to bring her favorite book to class. Have the student choose a favorite page from her book; then make a photocopy of that page. Next provide each student with a 12" x 18" sheet of construction paper that has been folded in half. Have each student unfold her paper and glue her photocopy onto one of the halves. Then have her add a review of her book on the other half of the paper, answering such questions as: "What is special about the page you selected? Why is this book your favorite? What is the book about?" Put all the completed pages together to make a big book. Display the book in the classroom library so students can use it as a source of reading suggestions.

IT COULD HAVE HAPPENED THIS WAY

Here's a fun way to extend a literature lesson into a language experience activity. When you reach the end of a story, have students brainstorm other possible endings for it. Instruct each student to write and illustrate another ending for the story. Then invite each student to share his ending with his classmates. You're sure to see bunches of creativity with this activity!

BOOK CUBES

Build student interest in literature with book cubes. After he reads a story, have each student use the information in the story to make a cube. Duplicate the pattern on page 204 for each student. Direct him to fill in each section of the cube with information about the story. Help students assemble their cubes; then create a display by arranging the cubes on a bookshelf.

Sharon

My favorite book is Hansel And Gretel. It is about a brother and a sister who meet a mean witch. My favorite page is of the witch inviting the brother and sister to eat dinner.

"Let's run, Hansel!" cried Gretel. The old woman crooked her long bony finger and squeaked, "Don't be afraid, little ones. I won't harm you! Come in, come in. Have some dinner with me." The dinner set on her table smelled so tempting that Hansel and Gretel stepped inside.

Book Cube by Candi

What I Liked Best About This Book: I liked the clues in the borders.

Book Title: The Mitten

Author: Jan Brett

LIGHTS! CAMERAS! ACTION!

The promise of being videotaped adds to the excitement of this reading activity. Ask each student to choose a book and practice saying its title and author, followed by a brief summary. Encourage students to share the main characters, the setting, and the plot of the book. When a student feels prepared, videotape him giving his report. After all your students have been videotaped, play the tape for them. Briefly discuss each book presented and encourage students to look for these book titles in the library. The tape can then be lent to neighboring classrooms or taken home by students and viewed with family members.

IT'S IN THE BAG

This reading homework assignment is sure to bring squeals of delight! Ask each student to find an object at home that somehow reminds him of a designated story that was recently read in class. Have students bring their mystery objects to school in paper bags. On the following day, have each student give clues to the contents of his bag while his classmates try to guess his mystery object. When a student reveals his object, have him explain why the object reminded him of the story. What a great way to expand each student's understanding of the story!

BOOK SHARING

Here's a fun book-sharing activity that can be presented to the entire class or placed in a listening center. You will need one blank cassette tape for every student. In advance copy the list of questions shown onto a piece of poster board; then display the poster in a prominent location. After each student reads a favorite book, have him practice reading it aloud and answering the questions on the list. When each student is prepared, assist him as he records himself reading aloud his chosen story. Record an auditory signal each time the student turns a page of his book. After he reads the book aloud, assist the student in recording a book report. Read the questions from the list and allow time for the student to answer each one. A student can present his favorite book to his classmates by playing the tape. Or he can place the tape and a copy of the book in a listening center for all to enjoy.

- What is the title, and who is the author of the book?
- Who are the characters?
- What problem did the main character have?
- How was the problem solved?
- Which part of the book did you like best?
- Why should your friends read this book?

AUTHOR QUILTS

Looking for a way to familiarize your students with several books by the same author? Then have your youngsters make an author quilt. After sharing several stories written by a selected author, ask students to illustrate their favorite scenes from the stories. Provide each student with a sheet of drawing paper and an assortment of art materials such as markers, construction paper, fabric scraps, and glitter. Have the storybooks handy for students to refer to as they draw. Arrange the completed illustrations on a bulletin board to resemble blocks on a quilting pattern. Use a marker to add stitch marks around each square. Just imagine the variety of quilts you'll see by the end of the school year!

CHARACTER PIE GRAPH

Your youngsters are sure to love this pie-graphing activity! In advance use yarn to create a circle on the floor; then use four yarn lengths to divide the circle into quarters. After reading aloud a story that has four main characters, label a sheet of construction paper for each of the four story characters and place each sheet in a different quadrant of the circle. Next ask each student to choose his favorite character from the story. Announce one character's name, and ask the students who chose this character as their favorite to sit side by side along the perimeter of the corresponding circle quadrant. Adjust the yarn lengths so that the section of the circle is proportional to the number of seated students. Repeat the same procedure for each character, making necessary adjustments to the yarn sectors. Examine the resulting pie graph. To create a permanent pie graph, have each child return to his desk and illustrate his favorite character on a provided card. Assist the students in gluing their illustrations to a large, black-paper circle. Use chalk to draw the sectors; then display the resulting pie graph for all to see.

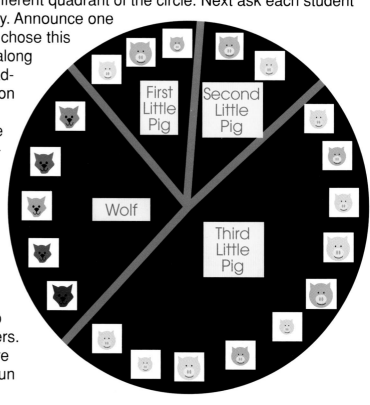

Character pie graphs may also be used to graph stories that have two or three characters. Simply use as many yarn lengths as there are characters when dividing the circle. What a fun and easy way to extend almost any story!

LITERATURE QUESTION AND ANSWER

This question-and-answer game is a great follow-up to any story. Decide on three categories relating to books, such as characters, plots, and settings. Write each category on a strip of construction paper and mount the categories on a bulletin board as shown. Next brainstorm ten questions for each category about books you have shared with your students. Write each question on the front of a 4" x 6" index card, and the answer on the back of the card. Next fold in half thirty 9" x 12" pieces of construction paper and staple each to form a pocket on the bulletin board as shown; then place each question card in a pocket with the questions facing forward.

To play the game, divide students into two groups. Have one player on Team One choose a category and then touch a pocket under that category. Read the question aloud. If the player correctly answers the question, award the team one point and remove that pocket from the board. If the player incorrectly answers the question, place the card back in the pocket. Play alternates between the two teams until all the pockets have been removed. The team with the most points wins the game.

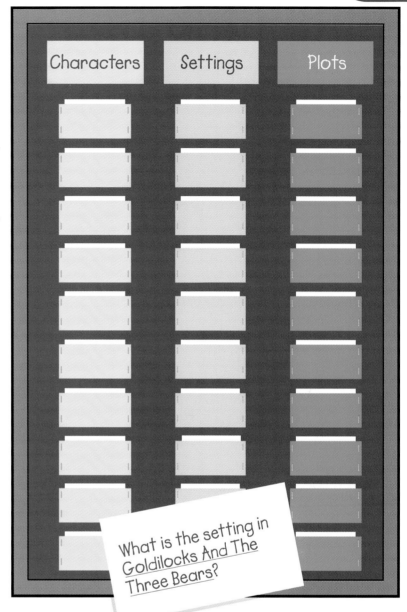

What is the setting in Goldilocks And The Three Bears?

READING CELEBRATION

This literature event will be talked about for weeks! In preparation for the party, enlist your students' help in creating invitations for their families. Also have each student choose a book and practice reading it. During the party have each student read his book aloud, then tell about his favorite part. Plan to serve refreshments if desired. Conclude the party by presenting each child with a personalized reading certificate. Parents will be thrilled to see their children's reading progress!

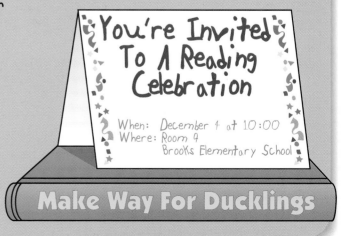

You're Invited To A Reading Celebration

When: December 4 at 10:00
Where: Room 4
Brooks Elementary School

Make Way For Ducklings

HONORARY BOOK AWARDS

Students are sure to pour their creativity into making book awards to honor books they've read. Have each student select a book to read. Then have him create an award to honor a certain aspect of his book, such as best character, best setting, best plot, or best ending. Encourage students to use a variety of materials, such as construction paper and markers, in constructing his award. If desired have each student fill out an accompanying certificate explaining why the award was presented to the book. This project is sure to create lots of excitement for reading in your classroom!

1st **FIRST PLACE**

Title: Clifford

Author: Norman Bridwell

Best Animal Character:

I liked Clifford because he tries to be helpful.

Best Animal Character

READING SCAVENGER HUNT

Send your supersleuths on the trail of reading fun with a scavenger hunt. After reading a picture book together, enlist students' help in making a list of objects in the book. Record students' responses on a sheet of paper; then duplicate several copies. Divide students into small groups and provide each group with a list of the items. Then have students search in the classroom and at home, if necessary, to find the items. What a great project to wind up a literature-based unit!

READING SCAVENGER HUNT

- [ ] basketball
- [ ] eyeglasses
- [ ] kite
- [ ] penny

FILMSTRIP FUN

Creating filmstrips is a fun way for students to write story summaries. Duplicate the filmstrip reproducible on page 205 for each student and yourself. Assign each student a page from a recently read book. Instruct each student to draw a picture illustrating that page of the book; then, if desired, have the student write a short summary of the page. While students are completing their pictures, write the title, the author, and the characters' names on a copy of the reproducible. After students have completed their illustrations, tape the pages together to form an entire filmstrip. Post the filmstrip along a hallway wall for everyone to view!

ARTHUR GOES TO CAMP
by
Marc Brown

CHARACTERS:
Arthur, Arthur's father, Buster, Francine, Rocky, Muffy, Becky

Popular Children's Authors

Aardema, Verna

Adler, David A.

Aliki

Allard, Harry

Andersen, Hans Christian

Barrett, Judi

Bemelmans, Ludwig

Berenstain, Stan and Jan

Brett, Jan

Bridwell, Norman

Brown, Marc

Carle, Eric

Cohen, Miriam

Cole, Joanna

Crews, Donald

dePaola, Tomie

Dr. Seuss

Eastman, P. D.

Freeman, Don

Gibbons, Gail

Henkes, Kevin

Hoban, Lillian and Russell

Howe, James

Keats, Ezra Jack

Kellogg, Steven

Lionni, Leo

Lobel, Arnold

Marshall, James

Martin Jr., Bill

Mayer, Mercer

McCloskey, Robert

Minarik, Else Holmelund

Noble, Trinka Hakes

Numeroff, Laura Joffe

Parish, Peggy

Peet, Bill

Polacco, Patricia

Rey, H. A. and Margret

Rylant, Cynthia

Sendak, Maurice

Silverstein, Shel

Steig, William

Stevenson, James

Van Allsburg, Chris

Viorst, Judith

Wells, Rosemary

Wood, Don and Audrey

Yolen, Jane

Caldecott Award And Honor Books, 1993–1997

1997 Medal Winner: *Golem* written and illustrated by David Wisniewski (Houghton Mifflin Company, 1996)

Honor Books:

Hush! A Thai Lullaby written by Minfong Ho and illustrated by Holly Meade (Orchard Books, 1996)

The Graphic Alphabet written by David Pelletier (Orchard Books, 1996)

The Paperboy written and illustrated by Dav Pilkey (Orchard Books, 1996)

Starry Messenger written and illustrated by Peter Sis (Frances Foster Books, 1996)

1996 Medal Winner: *Officer Buckle And Gloria* written and illustrated by Peggy Rathman (G. P. Putman's Sons, 1995)

Honor Books:

Alphabet City written and illustrated by Stephen T. Johnson (Viking Penguin, 1995)

Zin! Zin! Zin! A Violin written by Lloyd Moss and illustrated by Marjorie Priceman (Simon & Schuster Books For Young Readers, 1995)

The Faithful Friend written by Robert D. San Souci and illustrated by Brian Pinkney (Simon & Schuster Books For Young Readers, 1995)

Tops & Bottoms written and illustrated by Janet Stevens (Harcourt Brace & Company, 1995)

1995 Medal Winner: *Smoky Night* written by Eve Bunting and illustrated by David Diaz (Harcourt Brace & Company, 1994)

Honor Books:

John Henry written by Julius Lester and illustrated by Jerry Pinkney (Dial Books For Young Readers, 1994)

Swamp Angel written by Anne Isaacs and illustrated by Paul O. Zelinsky (Dutton Children's Books, 1994)

Time Flies written and llustrated by Eric Rohmann (Crown Books For Young Readers, 1994)

1994 Medal Winner: *Grandfather's Journey* written and illustrated by Allen Say (Houghton Mifflin Company, 1993)

Honor Books:

Peppe The Lamplighter written by Elisa Bartone and illustrated by Ted Lewin (Lothrop, Lee, & Shepard Books; 1993)

In The Small, Small Pond written and illustrated by Denise Fleming (Henry Holt And Company, Inc.; 1993)

Raven: A Trickster Tale From The Pacific Northwest written and illustrated by Gerald McDermott (Harcourt Brace & Company, 1993)

Owen written and illustrated by Kevin Henkes (Greenwillow Books, 1993)

Yo! Yes? written and illustrated by Chris Raschka (Orchard Books, 1993)

1993 Medal Winner: *Mirette On The High Wire* written and illustrated by Emily Arnold McCully (G. P. Putnam's Sons, 1992)

Honor Books:

The Stinky Cheese Man And Other Fairly Stupid Tales written by Jon Scieszka and illustrated by Lane Smith (Viking Children's Books, 1992)

Seven Blind Mice written and illustrated by Ed Young (Philomel Books, 1992)

Working Cotton written by Shirley Anne Williams and illustrated by Carole Byard (Harcourt Brace & Company, 1992)

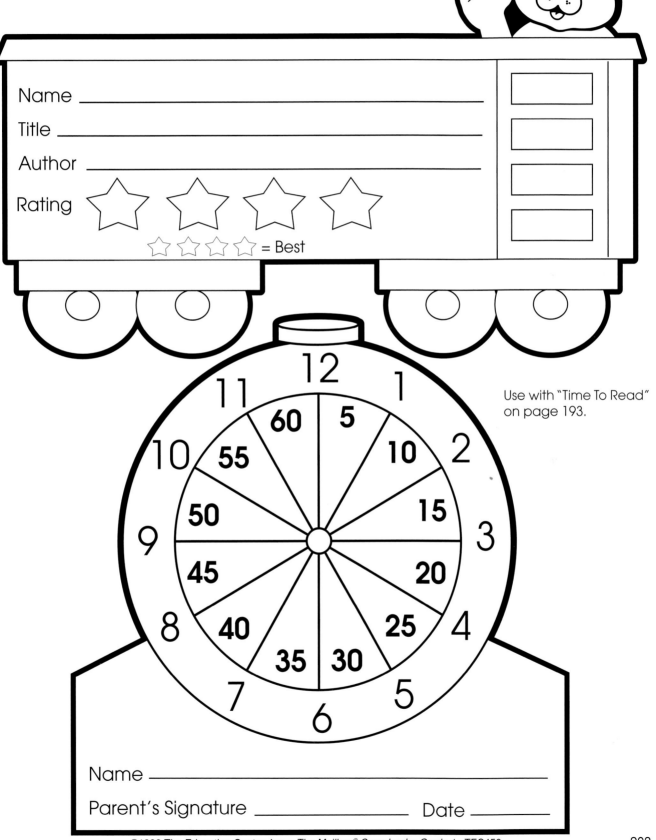

Name _____

Title _____

Author _____

Rating ☆ ☆ ☆ ☆

☆☆☆☆ = Best

Use with "Time To Read" on page 193.

Name _____

Parent's Signature _____ Date _____

Book-Cube Pattern

Use with "Book Cubes" on page 196.

Glue here.

Glue here.

Main Characters:

What I Liked Best About This Book:

Book Cube
by

©1998 The Education Center, Inc.

What I Liked Least About This Book:

Book Title:

Author:

Glue here.

Glue here.

Setting:

Glue here.

Glue here.

Glue here.

©1998 The Education Center, Inc. • *The Mailbox® Superbook* • *Grade 1* • TEC450

Read All About

_____
book title

Written by reporter _____ Date _____

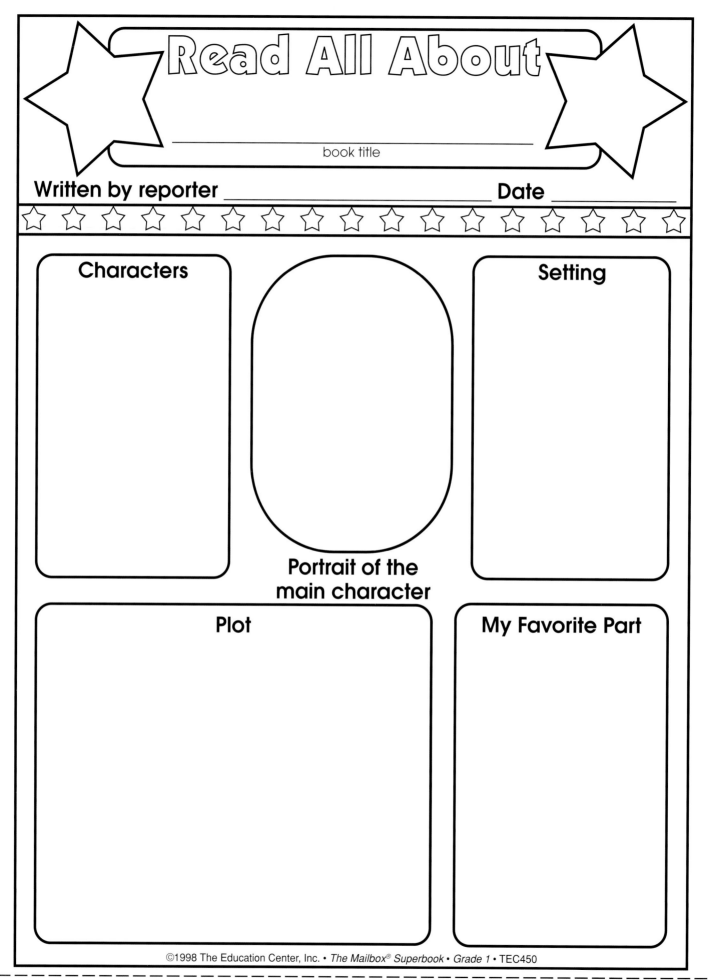

Characters

Setting

Portrait of the
main character

Plot

My Favorite Part

Note To Teacher: Duplicate student copies. Use as a follow-up to a class read-aloud or to an individually read book.

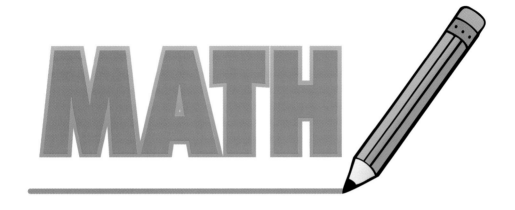

NUMBER SENSE

TALLY-MARK MATCH

Do your students have difficulty making the connection between tally marks and numerals? If so, try this activity. Make tally-mark index cards for half of your class and matching numeral index cards for the other half. At your signal, encourage each student to find the classmate who is holding his card's match. Have each pair of students sit down after determining their match. To repeat the activity, simply have students exchange index cards with a classmate.

That's The Number!

Looking for ways to help students recognize, write, and read numbers? Then peruse the following ideas for some great suggestions.

❋ Have your youngsters practice writing numerals using fingerpaints, instant pudding, shaving cream, or sand.

❋ Have a number of the day to reinforce number awareness. For example, when working with the number three, have students work in trios, bring three small items from home, or write their names three times on their papers.

❋ Play a recording of some lively music with a steady beat. As the music is playing, announce directions, such as "Tap your head eight times" or "Hop up and down ten times." Have students count out loud as they follow the directions.

❋ Divide a piece of poster board into nine squares; then write a numeral in each square. In turn, have students toss a beanbag, name the numeral the beanbag lands on, and clap that number of times.

Ordinal Numbers

Write the ordinal numbers *first* through *tenth* on the chalkboard, and direct one student to stand beneath each number. In turn, have each seated person give another seated person a direction to follow, such as "John, please tap the fourth person on the head." When each seated student has had a turn to follow a direction, replace the students standing for students sitting and repeat the activity. It's a great way to reinforce the concept of ordinal numbers!

More Or Less?

This hands-on activity will help students identify more or less with numbers. Pair students; then place 19 counters between each student pair. Instruct each student to take from one to ten counters from the pile, making sure they each have a different amount. Next flip a coin. If the coin lands on heads, the student in each pair with more counters wins. If the coin lands on tails, the student in each pair who has fewer counters wins. Players then return all the counters to the pile and play begins again. More isn't always better!

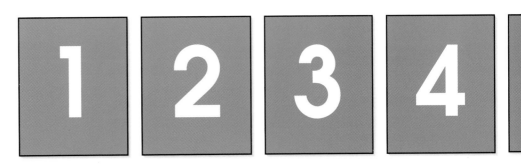

Order, Please!

This daily activity will get students' sequencing skills in order. Label an 8 1/2" x 11" piece of paper with a numeral for each student. (Start with one and do not skip any numerals.) Give each student a labeled piece of paper and have him read his numeral. As a class determine which students have the highest and the lowest numerals. Have these two students hold their numerals as they stand facing their classmates at the front of the room. Position one student to the far right and the other to the far left. Then, on your command, the remainder (or a designated group) of the students line up in sequential order based on the numerals on their pieces of paper. Sequencing numerals has never been more fun!

Even Or Odd?

Here's a hands-on approach to identifying even and odd numbers. Give each student pair a plastic bag of manipulatives, such as dry cereal, counters, or dried beans. Name a number; then have the student pairs count a corresponding number of manipulatives. To determine if the number is even or odd, have the students attempt to share their manipulatives by dividing their counted manipulatives into two equal groups. If the groups are equal in number, the number is even. If the groups are not equal in number, the number is odd. Repeat the activity several times, using a different number of manipulatives each time.

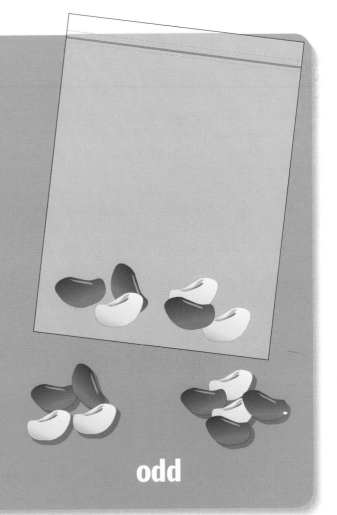

odd

COMMUTATIVE PROPERTY

$4 + 2 = 6$

$2 + 4 = 6$

Clothes hangers and several clip clothespins are perfect manipulatives for demonstrating the commutative property of addition. Provide each child with a clothes hanger and ten clothespins. Display a number sentence. Have each student clip clothespins to his hanger to match the sentence. Without removing the clothespins, have students flip the hangers to show the inverse of the original number sentence. Discuss the fact that the sums are equal, illustrating the commutative property of addition.

Roll 'Em!

Here's a fun way for students to improve recall of math facts without creating competition between classmates. Create a class supply of the recording sheet shown; then duplicate and distribute a recording sheet and a pair of dice to each student. Before students begin the activity, designate the operation (addition or subtraction). Have each student roll the dice and either add or subtract the two numbers. Then, starting at the bottom of the recording sheet, have the student color in the correct box depicting the sum or difference rolled. Have students continue in this same manner until each one reaches the top of one column. Ask each student to announce which of his numbers reached the top first.

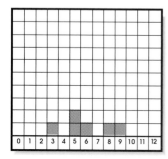

$5 + 1 = 6$

Domino Addition

Dominoes are great manipulatives for teaching the commutative property of addition. Distribute a copy of page 228 and a domino to each student. Instruct each student to draw the arrangement of dots on his paper and then write the corresponding addition sentence. Next have the student turn his domino around (so that the dots are on opposite sides of where they were), copy the new arrangement of dots, and write its addition sentence. After each student has written two addition sentences for his domino, have students exchange dominoes and repeat the activity. Have students continue in the same manner until they have worked with five dominoes.

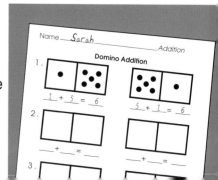

Math-Fact Fun

Help students memorize addition and subtraction facts with this partner game. Each student will need a deck of identical flash cards. To make a deck of flash cards, cut 3" x 5" index cards in half and program each card half with an addition or subtraction fact. Write each problem's answer on the back of its card. To play, each player shuffles and stacks his cards faceup (problems showing). In turn, the players read and answer their top problems, then flip their cards to check. If both players answered correctly, the player with the larger solution wins and places both cards on the bottom of his card stack. If one player answers incorrectly, his opponent wins and keeps both cards. If both players answer incorrectly, they exchange cards. The player with the most cards at the end of game time wins!

BEACH-BALL MATH

This adaptable math activity is sure to become a class favorite! Use a permanent marker to write a different numeral on each section of an inflated beach ball. Toss the ball to a child. When she catches the ball, have her hold the ball without moving her hands and determine which two numerals are nearest her hands. Have the student use those two numerals to create an addition or a subtraction sentence. After announcing the sentence and answering it, have the child toss the ball to a classmate. Continue in the same manner until each child has had at least one turn to catch and toss the ball. What a blast!

Table Tents

This partner activity is a great review for addition or subtraction facts. For each student pair, fold a piece of construction paper into thirds. Unfold the paper, turn it over, and then program each outer section with different math facts (as shown). Then turn the paper back over and assemble as shown. To begin the activity, pair students and distribute a table tent to each pair. Have each student sit across from his partner with the table tent in between them. Have students, in turn, announce the problems for their partners to answer. What a fun way for students to memorize their basic addition and subtraction facts!

$2 + 2 = 4$
$2 + 3 = 5$
$2 + 4 = 6$
$2 + 1 = 3$
$2 + 0 = 2$

$3 + 1 = 4$
$3 + 3 = 6$
$3 + 2 = 5$
$3 + 4 = 7$
$3 + 0 = 3$

Related Literature

These books add up to great reading!
— *Mouse Count* by Ellen Stoll Walsh (Harcourt Brace & Company, 1995)
— *The M & M's® Counting Book* by Barbara B. McGrath (Charlesbridge Publishing, Inc.; 1994)
— *How Many How Many How Many* by Rick Walton (Candlewick Press, 1996)
— *Ready, Set, Hop!* by Stuart J. Murphy (HarperCollins Children's Books, 1996)
— *Counting Our Way To Maine* by Maggie Smith (Orchard Books, 1995)

SHAPES, PATTERNS, and SYMMETRY

SYMMETRICAL PICTURES

Help students get a handle on symmetry with this artistic activity. Search through magazines for objects that are symmetrical, such as faces, chairs, or candy bars. Cut out each object, cut the object in half, and then glue one half of each object onto a piece of drawing paper. After a discussion of symmetry, have each student choose a picture and draw the missing side to make the picture symmetrical.

Shape Search

Looking for a unique way to review flat shapes? Try this easy-to-prepare activity. Provide each child with a magazine and a piece of drawing paper. Have each student search for shapes in the magazines. Each student then cuts out a picture, glues it to the paper, and traces the shape with a black marker. He then writes a sentence labeling his chosen shape. Compile the completed pages between two construction-paper covers, staple them together, and add the title "The First-Grade Shape Search."

Geometric Scavenger Hunt

Students are sure to give this scavenger-hunt activity a thumbs-up! Make a list of solid shapes; then duplicate a class supply and provide each child with a copy. Instruct each student to search in your classroom or on your school grounds to find an example of each shape. Have each student record where he found each shape beside its name. Set a time limit before the hunt begins. After the game, let students share the various objects they found for each shape.

Geometric Art

Combine art and geometry into one lesson with this simple tip. Cut a supply of art paper in each of several different geometric shapes, such as circles, triangles, and rectangles. Each week introduce and feature a new shape of art paper for students to draw upon. As students become more familiar with the basic geometric shapes, introduce more difficult shapes, such as octagons and parallelograms.

Tasty Patterns

Students are sure to love this delicious exercise in patterning! Provide each child with a plastic bag of snack mix (toasted oats cereal, peanuts, and chcolate chips) and a copy of a reproducible similar to the one shown. Have each student use his snack mix to create each pattern on the reproducible. After creating each pattern, have the student use crayons to draw the pattern onto the reproducible. Students can then munch on their tasty manipulatives.

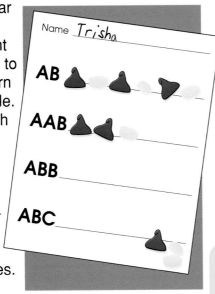

Name *Trisha*

AB

AAB

ABB

ABC

People-Pattern Person

Patterning will get creative when you use People-Pattern Persons. Each day choose a person to place several of her classmates according to a pattern of her choice. She may, for example, place her classmates in a boy, boy, girl pattern or in a pattern according to the color of clothing each child is wearing. When the students are in order, have children guess what pattern the People-Pattern Person has created.

Shapely Stories

Get your students' reading skills in shape with these great books:
— *The Greedy Triangle* by Marilyn Burns (Scholastic Inc.,1995)
— *Grandfather Tang's Story* by Ann Tompert (Crown Books For Young Readers, 1990)
— *The Shapes Game* by Paul Rogers (Henry Holt And Company, Inc.; 1990)
— *The Shape Of Me & Other Stuff* by Dr. Seuss (Random House Books For Young Readers, 1973)

Ready! Go!

This fast-moving game will get your students in shape with patterns. Gather students together and seat them in a circle. Give each student a six-inch red, green, or blue construction-paper square. Announce two colors and a pattern sequence, such as AB, ABB, or AAB. Have students holding those color squares meet in a designated spot in the classroom and work together to form themselves into the announced pattern. Enlist the help of the students still sitting to verify that the resulting pattern matches the one stated. Repeat the activity several times using different color combinations.

PATTERN SNACKS

Put your youngsters' patterning and cooking skills together in a tasty way! Ask parents to send in blocks of cheese and fruit such as grapes, bananas, strawberries, watermelons, and pineapples. Wash the fruit; then use a knife to cut the fruit into chunks. Have children make pattern snacks by putting fruit and cheese chunks onto shish-kebab skewers. Before students eat their snacks, encourage them to name their classmates' patterns and predict what comes next in the patterns.

MONEY

Coin Observations

Draw attention to the details on the front and back of coins with this money-recognition activity. Pair students; then provide each pair of students with a magnifying glass, and a real penny, nickel, and dime. Have students look at the coins as you use the list shown to ask questions about each coin. If desired, encourage students to create their own questions about the coins.

Who is the man on the coin?
What do the words on the coin say?
What is the building on the coin?
When was the coin made?
Does the coin have rough edges or smooth edges?

The Exchange Game

Invite your youngsters to try their hands at coin trading. Divide students into groups of five; then provide each student with a gameboard (page 229) and an envelope of paper coins (page 230) including 25 pennies, five nickels, two dimes, and a quarter. To play, each student in turn rolls a die and takes an equivalent number of pennies and places them atop the penny spaces on his gameboard. When a player has filled all of his penny spaces, he may trade five pennies for a nickel rather than rolling the die. Play continues in this manner with each player in turn rolling the die or trading for other coins. The person who trades up to a quarter first is the winner. For an added challenge, have students play the game without using the gameboard.

$4 + 3 = 7$

HEADS OR TAILS?

This center activity gives student pairs practice with counting coins of the same denomination. Place a handful of pennies and a carpet square at a center. To begin, have a child gently shake the handful of coins and then drop them on the carpet square. Both students sort the coins based on the side that lands faceup (head or tails). One student then counts the coins that landed with heads showing while the other child counts the coins that landed with tails showing. The students then add both amounts together. Have students continue in this same manner for a predetermined amount of time.

Money Lotto

This money game is sure to be a whole "lotto" fun! Distribute an unprogrammed lotto board (similar to the one shown) and a copy of the coins on page 230 to each student. Instruct each child to color and cut out the coins. Next announce an amount of money. Have each student count out the coins needed to make that amount and then glue them in any square on the board. While students are gluing their coins, write the announced amount on a small piece of paper. Continue announcing amounts in this same manner until all squares on students' boards are filled in. Place the pieces of paper labeled with the amounts in a container. Also distribute 16 markers to each child.

To play the game, draw an amount from the container and announce it to students. Have each student use a marker to cover the announced amount. The first student to cover four squares in a row on his board announces, "Money! Money!" To win the game, he must read aloud the value of the coins in each square on the row for verification. If desired award the winning student with a sticker or piece of sugar-free gum.

Magnetic Money

This whole-group activity gives hands-on practice in counting coins. Draw several large circles on the chalkboard and label each with a different amount of money. Then, beside the circles, attach sets of magnetic money to the chalkboard. For each circle, choose a student and instruct him to place coins in the circle to equal the amount shown. After checking the coins in each circle, have additional students use different coins to make the same amounts. Since there are numerous possibilities, continue in this same manner until each student has had a turn.

Coupon Math

Cash in with this soon-to-be-favorite activity! Pair students; then give each child a grocery-store coupon and a supply of coins. Instruct each student to use the coins to show the amount of money he saves with the coupon. Have each student check his partner's work. Then, on a given signal, have each student exchange coupons with a classmate. Students continue in this same manner for a predetermined amount of time.

Books That Make "Cents"!

Share some of these valuable stories with your youngsters:
— *A Chair For My Mother* by Vera B. Williams (Greenwillow Books, 1982)
— *General Store* by Rachel Field (Little, Brown And Company; 1988)
— *If You Made A Million* by David M. Schwartz (Morrow Junior Books, 1994)
— *Our Garage Sale* by Anne Rockwell (Greenwillow Books, 1984)
— *Alexander, Who Used To Be Rich Last Sunday* by Judith Viorst (Aladdin Paperbacks, 1987)

The Grouchy Ladybug

Eric Carle's timely account of a grouchy, ill-mannered ladybug is a great way to begin your unit on telling time. Each time the ladybug encounters a different foe, the time of their meeting is depicted on a clock. After sharing this story with your youngsters, use its illustrations to introduce telling time to the hour. Have students carefully examine each hourly clock illustration before having one of them point to the corresponding time written in the text.

As a follow-up activity, provide each child with a copy of the clock pattern on page 231 and a brad. Assist students in attaching the hands to their clocks. Then announce the hourly times used in the book, and have students use their clocks to show the time. Tick-tock, tick-tock!

DAILY TIMETABLE

With a daily timetable students can easily see how much time they spend on each daily school activity. Enlist students' help in making a list on the chalkboard of their daily school activities. Then record each activity and its time on a 9" x 12" piece of white construction paper. Divide students into as many groups as there are activities. Distribute an activity sheet to each group, and have the members work together to illustrate the activity. Compile the completed activity sheets in chronological order between two construction-paper covers. If desired have students make their own daily timetable booklet that includes their before- and after-school activities.

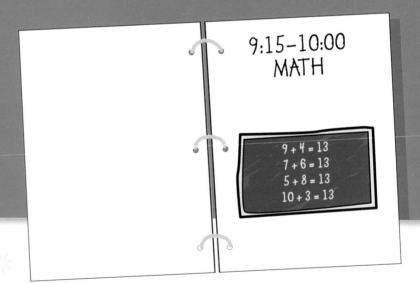

The Magic Of A Minute

A minute, is a minute, is a minute—but sometimes it sure doesn't seem like it! Help your students explore the consistency of time with this activity. Obtain a clock that you can set for one minute. First ask your students to do something that is relatively challenging or tiresome for one minute, such as standing on one foot. Time the chosen task for one minute. Then ask students to discuss whether that minute felt long or short. Next, time students doing something they enjoy for a minute, such as talking to a friend. Then discuss how that minute felt. Lead students to conclude that the time elapsed was exactly the same even though it might have felt very different.

Time Check

It's time—time for a time check, that is! Create a recording sheet similar to the one shown. Attach a slip to each student's desk every morning. Then, at five various hour and half-hour intervals throughout the day, declare, "Time Check!" Write the time on your own Daily Time Check sheet while students check the classroom clock and log the time. At the end of the day, check students' times during a group review.

Name _____

TIME CHECK!

1. _____ : _____

2. _____ : _____

3. _____ : _____

4. _____ : _____

5. _____ : _____

Through The Year

This poster will serve as a great visual reminder of the 12 months of the year. To make a poster, have each child fold a large sheet of construction paper in half horizontally, then in half again vertically. Next have him fold it in thirds vertically and crease along all the folds. Ask the child to unfold the paper, then draw a line along each fold line to make a 12-block grid. Instruct him to label, in sequence, each block with a month name, then draw a related picture in each block.

Only Time Will Tell!

This nifty activity reinforces the concept of time in relation to days, months, and years. Make a list of several activities, such as learning to ride a bike, building a treehouse, learning to swim, or reading a book. Then ask students to decide how long it would take to complete each activity—days, weeks, or months. Before long students will be experts with these concepts of time.

Timely Literature

Take some time to share these books with your youngsters.
— *Exploring Time* by Gillian Chapman and Pam Robson (The Millbrook Press, Inc.; 1995)
— *Pigs On A Blanket* by Amy Axelrod (Simon & Schuster Children's Books, 1996)

PLACE VALUE

PLACE-VALUE BASICS

A handy tens and ones chart is just what you need to introduce place value. Duplicate the chart on page 232 for each student. Then distribute a supply of base ten rods and cubes to each student (or duplicate page 233 for each student). To begin, have students place one cube at a time on the ones side of the chart until they can exchange ten cubes for one rod (to place on the tens side of the chart). Continue in this same manner until students have a good understanding of exchanging ten cubes for one rod. For an added challenge, use the tens and ones chart to review place value. Announce a number and have each student display the matching number on his place-value chart.

tens 10s

ones 1s

Tasty Place Value

Students are sure to enjoy this delicious place-value activity! Provide each student with a sandwich bag of toasted-oat cereal, raisins, or popcorn, and a napkin. Instruct the students to organize their snacks into groups of tens and ones. Then have each student announce the number of tens and ones she made and the total number of snack pieces she has. Conclude the activity by inviting students to munch on their snacks! Mmmm!

2 tens + 4 ones = 24

I Spy The Number!

Use this variation of the game I Spy to reinforce your students' understanding of place value. Post a hundreds chart (large enough for all students to view). Select one student to secretly choose a posted number. This student begins the game by announcing, "I spy a one- (or two-) digit number." The rest of the students try to identify the number by asking yes-or-no questions like, "Does the number have a three in the ones place?" or, "Does the number have a five in the tens place?" Stipulate that five or more place-value-related questions must be asked before the actual identity of the number may be guessed. The student who correctly names the secret number chooses the secret number for the next round of play.

Place-Value Lotto

This place-value game is sure to be a class favorite! Write any 25 numbers from 0 to 99 on the chalkboard. Provide each child with a blank lotto board. Instruct her to randomly program each of the 16 squares with a different number from the chalkboard. As students are programming their cards, write the 25 posted numbers on small pieces of paper and place the papers in a small container. Also distribute 16 markers, such as counters or dried beans, to each child. To play the game, draw a number from the container and announce each digit's value. For example, 43 would be announced as four tens and three ones. If a student has the announced number on her board, she covers it. The first student to cover all the numbers on her board, announces "Lotto!" To win the game she must read aloud the numbers on her board for verification. If desired award the winning student with a small prize.

PLACE-VALUE LOTTO

27	43		2
61	87		71
49	52	64	
80	10	14	58

Race To One Hundred

Looking for a place-value game to use at a math center? Then try this two-player game! Place 20 cubes and 20 rods (or duplicate and cut out copies of the cubes and rods on page 233) and a pair of dice at the center. To play the game, the first player rolls the dice and collects a matching number of cubes. The second player then takes his turn. Play continues in this manner. When a player collects ten *ones,* he trades them for a *ten* (rod). The first player to collect ten *tens* wins!

Related Literature

— *From One To One Hundred* by Teri Sloat (Puffin Books, 1995)
— *Dinner At The Panda Palace* by Stephanie Calmenson (HarperCollins Children's Books, 1995)

Playing The Numbers

This two-player game of chance is a quick review of place value. Make and laminate two gameboards similar to the one shown. Remove all face cards and tens from a deck of playing cards. To play, each player draws two cards and strategically places each number in a column on her gameboard in hopes of making the largest possible number. Numbers may not be moved once they have been placed on the gameboard. The player with the largest number wins the round.

tens	ones
6	3

MEASUREMENT

Handy Measurement

Improve students' nonstandard measurement skills with this handy activity. In advance create a recording form (similar to the one shown) that lists objects in the room for students to measure. To begin, have each student trace his hands onto construction paper and cut them out. Then refer to the illustration to show students how to measure using the handprints. Distribute a copy of the recording form to each student and have him use his hand cutouts to measure each object on the form. When students have finished measuring, have student volunteers share measurements for one object. Then ask students why the answers are different. Lead students to the conclusion that the measurements are different because everyone's hands are different sizes.

YARN MEASUREMENT

trash can

16 in.

Roll out a ball of yarn for this measurement activity. Provide each child with a length of yarn. Have each student choose a different object in the room. Instruct the student to measure it with the yarn and then cut the yarn the same length as the object. Next have the student use an inch ruler (see page 234) to measure the length of yarn. Provide each student with a piece of drawing paper. Have the student draw a picture of the object he measured, write the measurement, and then tape the yarn to the bottom of the picture. Display the completed pictures on a classroom wall for students to observe.

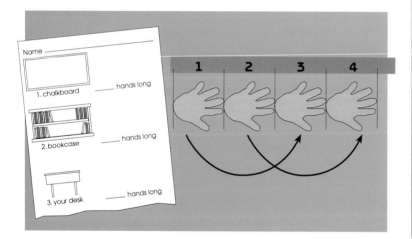

Name

1. chalkboard _____ hands long

2. bookcase _____ hands long

3. your desk _____ hands long

Estimating Length

Provide estimating and measurement practice with this easy-to-prepare activity. Create a reproducible with lines of various lengths—all in exact inches. Distribute a copy of the reproducible and an inch ruler (pattern on page 234) to each student. To begin, have each student record an estimate of the first line's length. Then have the student use the ruler to measure the line. Have the student record the actual measurement beside the estimate. Instruct students to continue estimating and measuring the other lines in this same manner. For an added challenge, create a similar reproducible for practice measuring in centimeters.

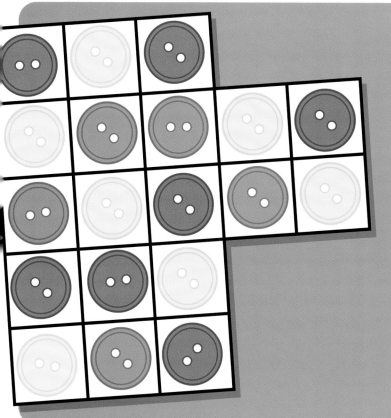

Getting The Area

To introduce area, cut a class supply of graph paper (page 234) into different sizes and shapes; then give each student a piece. Have each student use manipulatives—such as buttons, beans, or dry cereal—to measure the area of his shape. Then, on a predetermined signal, have students exchange shapes and repeat the activity. Continue in this same manner until each student has measured the area of ten shapes. Practicing area is fun!

Weigh In

This cooperative learning project carries its own weight! Give each group of four students a balance scale and a collection of objects to be weighed. To begin, have each student list his group's objects on his paper. Then have him write an estimate of each object's weight using a predetermined nonstandard unit of measurement, such as Unifix® cubes or clothespins. Next have each group member, in turn, place an item on the scale and balance the scale by putting the nonstandard units on the other side. Have the student count how many nonstandard units it took to balance the object. Then have each group member record the number on his paper. Continue in this same manner until all of the objects have been weighed.

Fill 'Er Up

This center activity gives students practice with measuring capacity. Place a large container of rice, a measuring cup, and containers of various capacities and shapes (cup, pint, quart, liter) at a center. Have the student use rice and the measuring cup to fill the containers, counting the cups as they work. Also have students observe the equal capacities by pouring the contents from one container into another container of the same capacity but of a different shape. What a great way for students to explore capacity!

Related Literature

Share these math-related books with your youngsters for some reading that's sure to measure up!
— *Twelve Snails To One Lizard* by Susan Hightower (Simon & Schuster Books For Young Readers, 1998)
— *How Big Is A Foot?* by Rolf Myller (Dell Publishing Company, Inc.; 1991)
— *Inch By Inch* by Leo Lionni (William Morrow And Company, Inc.; 1995)

ESTIMATION

Estimation Questions

Display a chart in the classroom that features the following questions. Refer to the chart when discussing whole-group estimating activities with your students.

- **?** What is the smallest estimate?

- **?** What is the greatest estimate?

- **?** What is the difference between your estimate and the actual result?

- **?** Did you make a reasonable estimate?

- **?** Which estimates are closest to the actual result?

- **?** Are most of the estimates too high, too low, or just right?

Tasty Estimation

This yummy estimation activity is sure to please your students and their taste buds! Give each child a plastic bag of popped popcorn and a napkin. Before opening their bags, have each child estimate how many pieces of popcorn are in his bag. Instruct each child to write his estimate on a piece of paper. Then have each student open his bag and eat one kernel at a time while tallying each one on the paper. Once students have finished eating and tallying their popcorn, have each student determine his total number of popcorn pieces. Then have students compare their estimates to their actual numbers.

Estimating More Or Less

Strengthen your youngsters' estimating skills by having them answer the questions below.

- Are there fewer than 40 people in this room?

- Are there more than 50 books in this room?

- Are there fewer than 20 pieces of paper in this room?

- Would it take more than 20 steps to get to the cafeteria?

- Can you hold more than 25 pennies in your hand?

- Are there fewer than ten chairs in this room?

- Are there more than eight cars in the school parking lot?

- Are there more than 15 boys in this room?

A Quick Peek

This whole-group activity will give students plenty of practice with estimation. Place a handful of manipulatives, such as beans or counters, on the overhead projector. Turn the projector on for students to look at the manipulatives for about five seconds. Then turn the projector off and have each student write on a piece of paper an estimate of the number of manipulatives shown. Turn the projector on again, and enlist students' help in counting the manipulatives to verify the estimates. Continue the activity in this same manner several more times.

The Feely Bag

This small-group activity will get your students feeling good about their estimation skills! In advance place a predetermined number of objects, such as counters or marbles, in a small paper or cloth bag. Gather a small group of students in a circle. Pass the bag to a student. Have the student quickly place her hand in the bag and feel the number of objects. Then have her record her estimate on a piece of paper (without anyone seeing it) and pass the bag to the student on her right. Have students continue in this manner until each child in the group has made an estimate. Then empty the objects from the bag and enlist students' help in counting them. Then have each child compare her estimate with the actual number of objects.

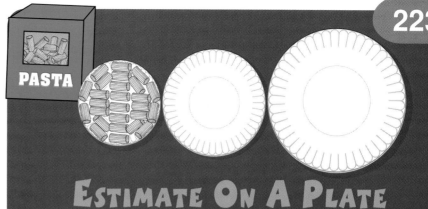

ESTIMATE ON A PLATE

Use paper plates for a variety of estimating experiences at your math center. Place several different-sized paper plates and a container of a food item, such as dried pasta noodles, at the center. Once at the center, have the student choose a plate and estimate how many of the food item is needed to cover it. After recording his estimate on a piece of paper, have the child count how many of the food item is needed to cover the plate. Instruct the child to write down the actual number needed beside his estimate. Have the student continue in this same manner with the other plates at the center.

Estimation Station

Challenge students to work on their estimating skills with this ongoing activity. At the beginning of the week, fill a clear, plastic jar with items for students to count. Items such as macaroni, peanuts, dried beans, buttons, and jelly beans work best. Secure the lid on the top of the jar; then display the jar for all students to see. At the end of the week, provide each student with an opportunity to estimate how many things are in the jar. If desired, write all of the guesses on the chalkboard and circle the highest and the lowest guesses. Then, as a class, count the items in the jar and discuss the results. Change the items in the jar each week, and continue in the same manner.

How many jelly beans are in the jar?

Guess Or Estimate?

Help students understand the difference between a *guess* and an *estimate* with this learning experience. Put a small, unopened bag of M&M's® in a lunch bag. Show the lunch bag to your students and tell them that it contains M&M's®. Then ask the class to *guess* how many M&M's® are in the bag, without offering any additional information. Then take out the bag, open it, and ask a student to count just the M&M's® he sees at the opening of the bag. Then instruct students to *estimate* how many M&M's® are in the bag. Ask students which they think are more accurate: their guesses or their estimates? Why? Children should determine that *guesses* result from having little information, while *estimates* are based on clues and what they already know.

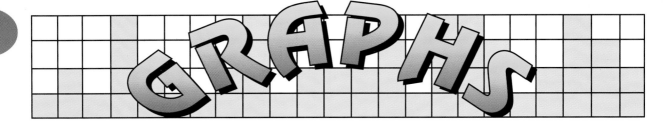

ALL ABOUT GRAPHS

There are three different kinds of graphs. *Real Graphs* use real objects on a table or the floor. *Representational Graphs* use pictures of real objects on a wall or chalkboard. *Abstract Graphs* use squares or circles of different colors to represent real objects and they are usually placed on a wall or chalkboard.

REAL

red	blue	green	yellow
red	blue	green	yellow
red	blue	green	yellow
red	blue		yellow
red	blue		
red			

REPRESENTATIONAL

red	blue	green	yellow
red	blue	green	yellow
red	blue		
red			

ABSTRACT

red	blue	green	yellow
Tia	Scott	Lee	Mandy
Alex	Debbie		Josh
Carly	Kevin		

Graphing Topics

- What month is your birthday?
- What is your favorite dessert?
- Are you left-handed or right-handed?
- What is your favorite color?
- How many letters are in your first name?
- How will you leave school today?
- Did you bring your lunch today?
- Are you a boy or a girl?
- What is your favorite sport?
- How many pockets do you have?
- Would you rather have a hot dog or a burger?
- How many teeth have you lost?
- Have you ever slept in a tent?
- Are you wearing sneakers?
- How many pets do you have?
- What is your favorite flavor of ice cream?

Suggested Graphing Questions

1. Which column has the fewest?
2. Which column has the most?
3. Are any columns the same?
4. How many _____ are there?
5. Are there more _____ or more _____?
6. Are there fewer_____ or fewer _____?
7. How many _____are there altogether?

Reusable Tally Graph

For a tally graph that can be used over and over again, program a grid on a sheet of poster board; then laminate the graph for durability. During a graphing activity, record student responses on the graph using a dry-erase marker. Afterward simply wipe the markings off with a wet paper towel and the graph is ready to be used again!

How many pockets are in our class?		
Monday	~~卌~~ ~~卌~~ ~~卌~~ ~~卌~~ ~~卌~~ ~~卌~~ l	31
Tuesday	~~卌~~ ~~卌~~ ~~卌~~ ~~卌~~ ~~卌~~ ~~卌~~ lll	33
Wednesday	~~卌~~ ~~卌~~ ~~卌~~ ~~卌~~ ~~卌~~ ll	
Thursday	~~卌~~ ~~卌~~ ~~卌~~ ~~卌~~ llll	
Friday	~~卌~~ ~~卌~~ ~~卌~~ ~~卌~~	

Tasty Graphing

Reinforce graphing skills with a tasty flair! Give each child a sheet of graph paper (page 234) and a snack-size bag of M&M's®, jelly beans, Skittles®, or candy hearts. Have each child sort and graph his candies by color on his graph paper. Then, using a corresponding crayon color, have him color one square for each candy of that color. Encourage each child to write the total number of each color on his graph. Then challenge each child to add the total number of candies.

CUTIE PIE

Picture-Perfect Graphs

Begin each day with a graphing activity that uses your students' smiling faces. Laminate a photograph of each child; then attach a magnet to the back of each laminated snapshot. On a magnetic board, prepare a bar-graph outline. Each morning select a subject for the graph and label the columns accordingly. After a student has unpacked, he attaches his magnet in the appropriate column. Take time each morning to discuss the results of the graph. It won't be long before your students' graphing skills are picture-perfect!

Graphing Board

Transform a science display board (or any large freestanding piece of cardboard) into a versatile graphing board. Cover the board with a solid color of adhesive covering. Use colored tape to make the grid. Post a question; then label the rows and/or columns using programmed cards. To graph results, have each child tape a personalized cutout in the appropriate place. Change the labels and questions frequently to keep student interest high!

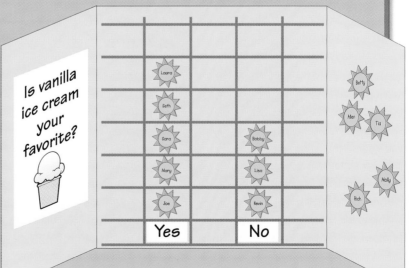

PROBLEM SOLVING

A LIBRARY OF WORD PROBLEMS

This small-group activity will provide students practice in learning what information should be included when writing a story problem. Divide your class into small groups and assign each group a number less than ten. Have the group members work together to write story problems that have an answer that equals the group's assigned number. (If desired, have students write each story problem on a separate page so there will be room for an illustration.) Encourage the students to work through the problems with manipulatives to make sure the necessary information is included. Compile each group's story problems to make a book; then place it in the classroom library for everyone to enjoy.

Story Problems That Equal 8

2 fish were in the pond. 1 more fish came along. How many fish were in the pond?

Problem-Solving Pros

Daily practice can make your students problem-solving pros. Each morning write a brainteaser or a word problem on the chalkboard. Challenge students to independently solve the displayed problem before a designated time later in the day. At that time, invite a student to share and discuss his solution to the problem. Periodically pair students and challenge each pair to create their own word problem or brainteaser for their classmates to solve.

Family Problem Solving

Spark interest in word-problem practice with this family approach. Each week choose a student to create a word problem with his family's help. Have the student record the word problem along with an illustration on an 8 1/2" x 11" piece of drawing paper. Then have the student return the word problem to school and share it with his classmates. Allow the student to call on volunteers to answer the problem. After his classmates respond, have the student explain the steps used in solving the problem. Punch holes in each student's paper and store it in a three-ring binder labeled "Family Word Problems."

Probable Outcomes

These two easy-to-implement activities will get your students thinking! For each activity, have students compile their own information to use in making future predictions.

• Have each student roll one die until he rolls a predetermined number, such as five. Have him record the number of turns it took to roll that number. Then have him repeat the activity several times using a different predetermined number each time. Have the student compare the number of rolls needed to reach each number.

• Have each student toss a coin in the air ten times and record which side the coin lands on for each toss.

The Skittles® Challenge

Sharpen students' logic skills with this tasty activity. Supply each child with three different-color Skittles®. Challenge each child to find and record the six different color combinations of his candies. After checking each child's answers, provide students with additional candies to eat.

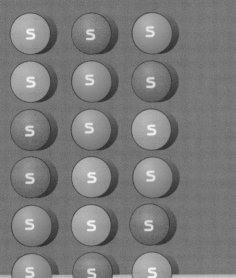

Calculator Math

Use the following activities to provide your students with practical calculator practice!

✚ Have each student write his seven-digit telephone number on a sheet of paper. Instruct students to find the sums of their phone numbers by adding together all seven numerals. Identify the student with the largest sum; then have the class recheck his calculations in unison.

✚ Provide each student with a page of the newspaper. Instruct each student to circle all the numbers on her newspaper and then find the sum of all the numbers. Identify the students with the largest sums and determine which sections of the newspaper have a large amount of numbers.

✚ Collect menus from a variety of restaurants. Have students choose a designated number of items to order from the menus, and then calculate the costs of the meals they ordered.

Names	Numbers	Objects
Katelyn	2	
Jake	4	
Jamie	10	
Chanda	6	
Riley	1	
Sean		

Riley had 2 cars. Jake had 1 car. How many cars were there in all?

A Multitude Of Word Problems

Provide students with problem-solving practice using this word-problem activity. Divide a bulletin board into three sections and label as follows: "Names," "Numbers," and "Objects." Mount paper strips labeled with students' names on the "Names" section and paper strips labeled with numerals on the "Numbers" section. Mount magazine pictures of a variety of objects (such as a car, a dog, or food) on the "Objects" section. To use the board, have a student choose two names, two numerals, and one object. Have the student record the information on a piece of paper and then choose either an addition or a subtraction function to solve the problem. Students can use this information to create and solve a variety of word problems.

Domino Addition

1.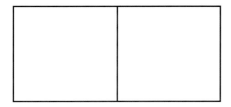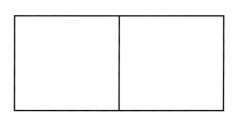

   _____ + _____ = _____   _____ + _____ = _____

2.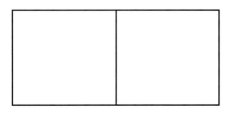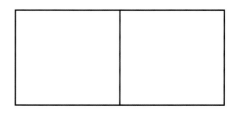

   _____ + _____ = _____   _____ + _____ = _____

3.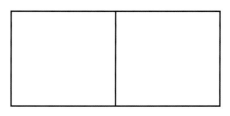

   _____ + _____ = _____   _____ + _____ = _____

4.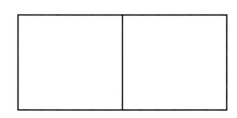

   _____ + _____ = _____   _____ + _____ = _____

5.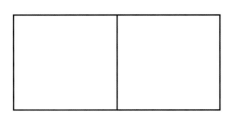

   _____ + _____ = _____   _____ + _____ = _____

Note To Teacher: Use with "Domino Addition" on page 210.

Name _____

The Exchange Game

Trade 2 dimes and a nickel for a quarter.

Trade 2 nickels for a dime.

Trade 2 nickels for a dime.

Trade 5 pennies for a nickel.

Trade 5 pennies for a nickel.

Trade 5 pennies for a nickel.

Trade 5 pennies for a nickel.

Trade 5 pennies for a nickel.

Note To Teacher: Use with "The Exchange Game" on page 214.

Patterns

Use with "The Exchange Game" on page 214 and "Money Lotto" on page 215.

©1998 The Education Center, Inc. • *The Mailbox® Superbook* • *Grade 1* • TEC450

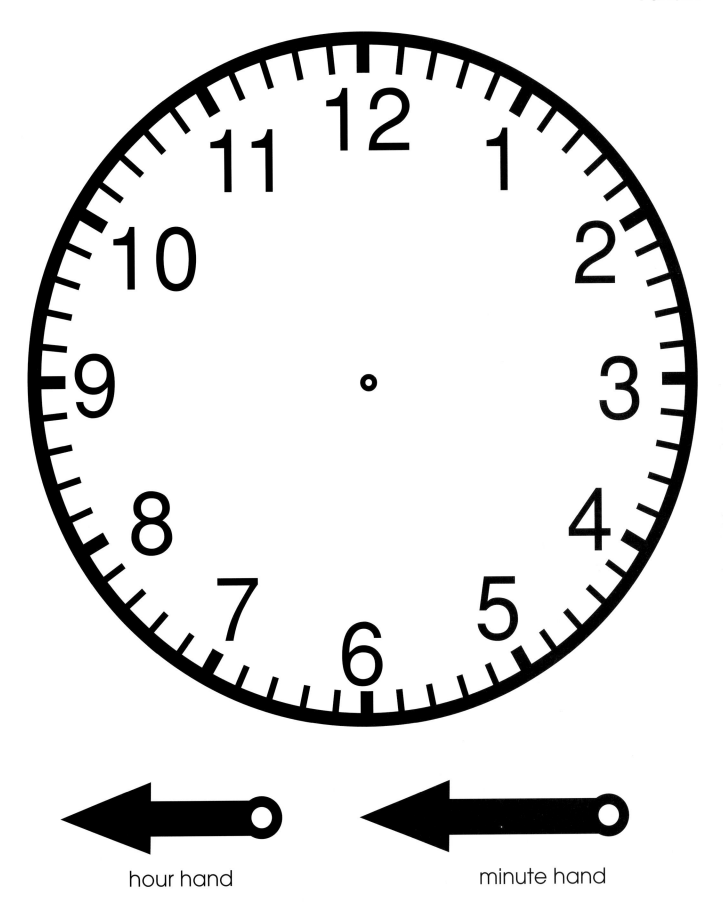

hour hand   minute hand

Chart

Use with "Place-Value Basics" on page 218.

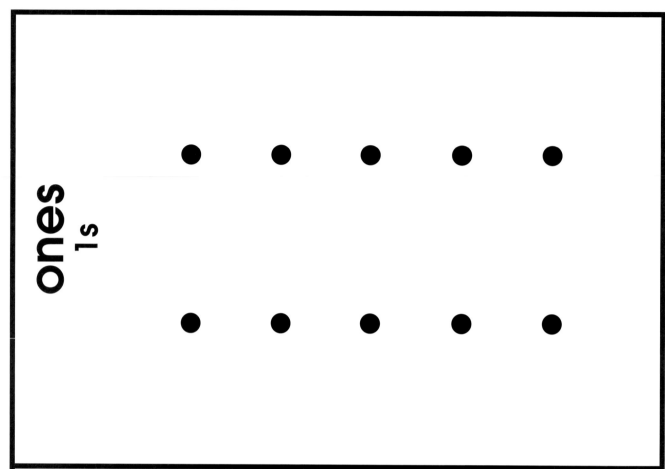

ones
1s

tens
10s

Use with "Place-Value Basics" on page 218 and "Race To One Hundred" on page 219.

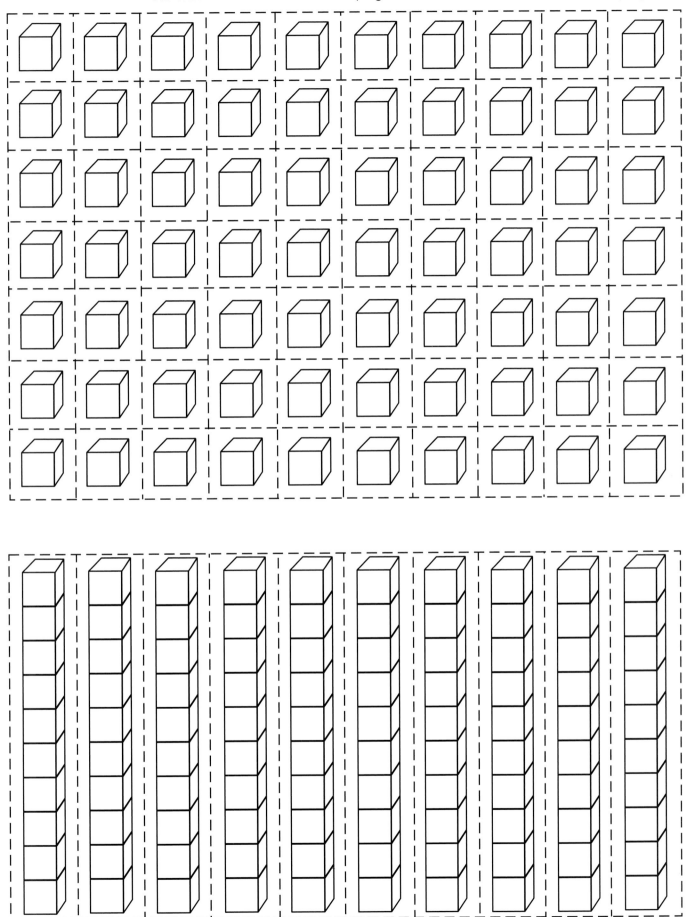

Ruler

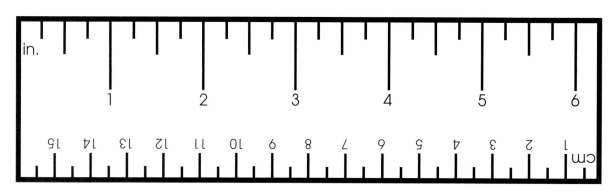

Graph Paper

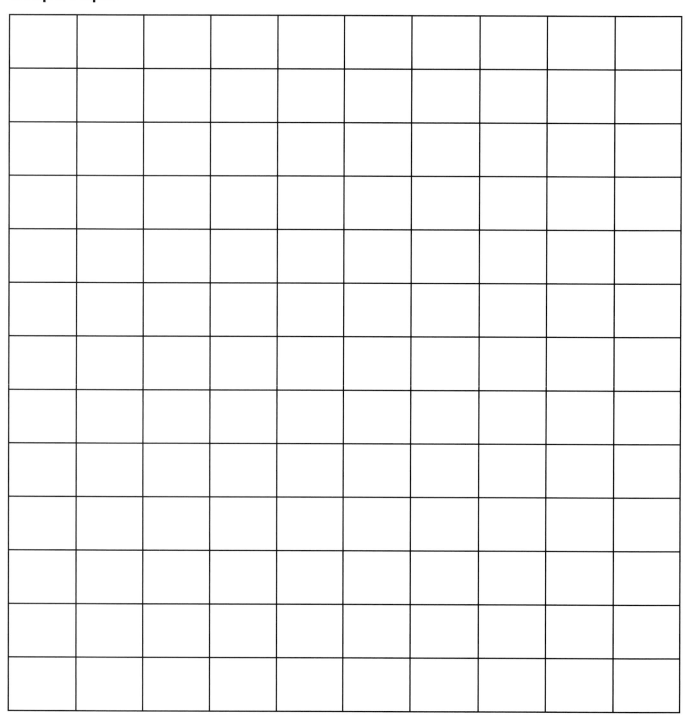

Note To Teacher: Use the ruler as needed with the measurement activities on page 220. Use the graph paper with "Getting The Area" on page 221 and "Tasty Graphing" on page 225.

SOCIAL STUDIES

My SUPER Self

Use this collection of ideas to focus on students' individuality and to help them learn about and appreciate their special traits and abilities.

What's Your Favorite?

Help students discover more about one another with this informative activity. Duplicate a class supply of the reproducible on page 255. Ask each child to complete the "My Favorite" column independently; then compare the results classwide for an overall view of your students' interests. Have students record the class similarities on their papers. If something is found to be a favorite of many, celebrate by featuring it in your classroom. For example, if popcorn is a favorite snack of most of your students, plan a popcorn party to celebrate!

ME TREE

These special creations will help students grow to know one another better. Have each child trace his hand and forearm on a sheet of brown construction paper; then have him cut out the shape and glue it onto a sheet of light-colored construction paper to resemble a tree. Next have students cut pictures from discarded magazines that depict their likes and interests. These cuttings become the leaves for each child's tree as they are glued in place. Display these special sprouts on a classroom wall and encourage students to compare their favorite things.

If you're looking for a quick self-esteem boost, look no farther. Have each student use a black marker to write his name in capital letters vertically on a 9" x 12" piece of poster board. Then have him write (in pencil) an acrostic poem that describes his positive qualities. Once his writing has been edited, the student traces over his writing with a fine-tipped marker and adds a colorful border using star stickers. If desired post the completed poems on a bulletin board before students take them home. For added fun, challenge students to write positive acrostics about their classmates, too!

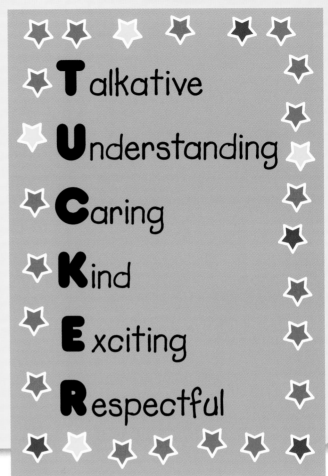

Talkative
Understanding
Caring
Kind
Exciting
Respectful

Me Or You

Students will appreciate themselves and others after playing this motivating game. Write the word "YOU" on five small index cards. Write the word "ME" on five index cards, also. Place the cards in a container. To play, arrange students in a circle. Pass the container to the first student and ask him to draw a card. If he draws a "ME" card, have him say something nice about himself. If he draws a "YOU" card, have him say a nice comment about the person to his left. Have the student place his card back in the container; then continue playing until each child has had a turn.

Self-Concept Stories

ABC I Like Me!
by Nancy Carlson
(Viking, 1997)

All About You
by Catherine And Laurence Anholt
(Viking Children's Books, 1992)

How Emily Blair Got Her Fabulous Hair
by Susan Garrison
(BridgeWater Books, 1995)

I Am Me!
by Alexa Brandenberg
(Harcourt Brace & Company, 1996)

Family FRAMEWORK

Emphasize the special qualities of each student's family makeup with the following activities.

FRAME A FAMILY

Make each child feel special with this sharing activity. Send home a parent note with each child asking her to bring in a family photograph. When the photos are brought to school, have each child share her photo with the class and tell something about each family member. After each child has shared, mount each family portrait in a construction-paper frame on a bulletin board titled "Our Family Album." Students will be eager to continue sharing family tales as long as the photos are displayed.

ONE BIG, HAPPY FAMILY

Encourage your students to capture their family images using this fun sponge-painting activity. Purchase or make a supply of people-shaped sponges (available at a craft store) in a variety of sizes. Give each student a 9" x 12" sheet of construction paper, and ask him to select the sponges that best represent the makeup of his family. Using tempera paint, have each child sponge-paint an image of his family. When the paint has dried, have students write their family members' names on the pictures; then display them in a hallway with the title "One Big, Happy Family!"

Families Hangin' Around

Your students will proudly share their family structures after creating these personal mobiles. To make a mobile, a child draws a likeness of each family member on poster board. Then he cuts out each drawing. On the opposite side of each cutout, he draws each family member as he or she appears from behind. Next he colors the front and back of all his cutouts. Then he hole-punches the top of each figure and attaches a length of yarn to each one. Next he ties each yarn length onto a wire coat hanger to form the mobile. Display the mobiles in your classroom and ask students to compare their families. Who has the most members? Who has the fewest?

FAMILY REFLECTIONS

This special project will help each child see how her family reflects on her. For each student, cover a sturdy paper plate with aluminum foil. Then give students a paper cupcake liner for each member in their families. Ask each child to write a different family member's name in each liner. Then have her write a sentence or phrase about how that person influences her life. After writing have each student glue the liners around the edge of the plate. When students look at their plates, they will see a shining reminder of how their family members are a reflection of themselves.

Mom teaches me to bake.

Dad helps me throw a ball.

Bobby asks me to play.

Julie helps with my homework.

Dad   Mom

Owen   Me

The Lassiter Family helps each other.

Family Flags

These family flags serve as symbols of your youngsters' families. For each student cut a flag shape from poster board. Have each student draw a picture of his family and then write a sentence explaining what makes his family great. Mount each flag on a large sheet of construction paper, and trim to within 3/4 inch of the white poster board. Then add a poster-board pole. Display the flags on a bulletin board titled "#1 Families" before sending them home with your students.

More Family Fellowship

Share these stories with your students for added enjoyment during your study of families.

➤ *Celebrating Families* by Rosmarie Hausherr (Scholastic Inc., 1997)

➤ *Fathers, Mothers, Sisters, Brothers* by Mary Ann Hoberman (Puffin Books, 1993)

➤ *I Love My Family* by Wade Hudson (Scholastic Inc., 1995)

➤ *Who's In A Family?* by Robert Skutch (Tricycle Press, 1995)

➤ *Who's Who In My Family?* by Loreen Leedy (Holiday House, Inc.; 1995)

Spoken As A Family Member

In advance, prepare a tape recorder to capture students' stories about family involvement. Ask each student to think about a time that his family spent together. Examples might be mealtimes, outings, vacations, or working together. One at a time, have students tell their family memories into the tape recorder. Place the tape in a listening center and encourage students to listen for similarities and differences in how each family spends its time together.

COMMUNITIES and NEIGHBORHOODS

Help students expand their knowledge of neighborhoods and communities by involving them in these neighborly activities.

Neighborhood Walk

Introduce the neighborhood concept by taking a walk through the neighborhood surrounding your school. Ask students to observe the places, people, and things that make up that neighborhood. Encourage students to comment about similarities and differences in their home neighborhoods. After returning to the classroom, set your class to work drawing and coloring a large neighborhood mural on bulletin-board paper. They'll enjoy capturing memories of their neighborhood walk on paper for all to see.

Everyone's Important

Emphasize to your class that the key to a *community,* a group of neighborhoods, is working together. To help students appreciate all the components of a community, have them imagine a community with something (or someone) missing. For example, ask students what it would be like if there wasn't a grocery store in their community. How would it change their daily routines? Repeat the question several times—taking away a different entity each time. What would it be like without any police officers? How would life change without a gas station? Students will soon see the importance of every part of a community through this valuable discussion.

MODEL COMMUNITY

Challenge your students to create a model community—that is, a miniature version of their own. To spark their imaginations about their own make-believe town, read aloud *Roxaboxen* by Alice McLerran (Lothrop, Lee & Shepard Books; 1991). Then begin by using a marker to draw streets and blocks on a large piece of bulletin-board paper. Have students decorate containers—such as milk cartons, gift boxes, and shoeboxes—using construction paper, paint, markers, and crayons to represent the buildings in your school's neighborhood. If desired park a few toy cars and trucks along the streets to make the community complete.

GOOD-NEIGHBOR AWARD

Put students in a neighborly mood with this good-behavior challenge. To begin, ask students about their neighbors at home. Are their neighbors friendly? What do they expect from their neighbors? What do their neighbors expect from them? Now ask your students to look at their classroom neighbors. Are the expectations the same? Have your class brainstorm a list of neighborly acts for the classroom. List their responses. When the list is complete, review the class standards of being a good neighbor. Then challenge each student to do his best to meet or exceed the good-neighbor qualities that the class listed. After a few days, award each deserving child with a "Good-Neighbor Badge" on page 256 for his neighborly behavior.

Giving Back

After studying all that a community environment provides, encourage your students to brainstorm ways they could help the community. Encourage students to consider community-service projects, such as picking up trash, recycling, or painting an unsightly fence or wall. Write students' responses on the chalkboard. Then have the class choose a project from the list that they would like to do after school or on a Saturday. Students can't help but feel proud as they give of themselves to help their community.

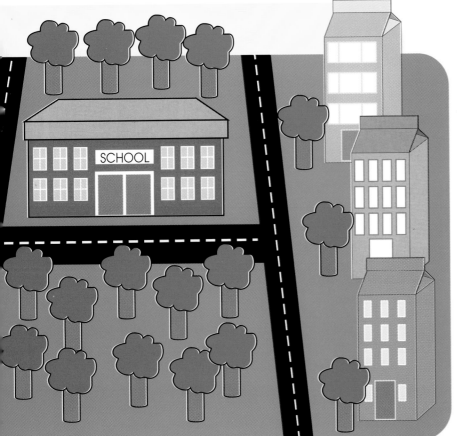

Community Reads

Get students caught up in the spirit of community by introducing them to these neighborly tales.

- *Arthur's Neighborhood*
  by Marc Brown
  (Random House, Inc.; 1996)

- *I Got Community*
  by Melrose Cooper
  (Henry Holt And Company, Inc.; 1995)

- *City Green*
  by DyAnne DiSalvo-Ryan
  (Morrow Junior Books, 1994)

- *Around Town*
  by Chris K. Soentpiet
  (Lothrop, Lee & Shepard Books; 1994)

Oh, Me!
WHAT CAN I BE?

Explore the world of work with your youngsters by investigating careers in your community. What will each of your students aspire to be after learning about many important jobs?

Read All About Them!

Acquaint your students with the roles of community helpers by sharing some of the career-centered literature listed below.

➤ *Jobs People Do*
by Christopher Maynard (Dorling Kindersley Publishing, Inc.; 1997)

➤ *Guess Who?*
by Margaret Miller
(Greenwillow Books, 1994)

➤ *Grandmother's Alphabet*
by Eve Shaw
(Pfeifer-Hamilton Publishers, 1997)

➤ *Who Are You, Sue Snue?*
by Tish Rabe
(Random House, Inc.; 1997)

➤ *Pig Pig Gets A Job*
by David McPhail
(Dutton Children's Books, 1990)

➤ Community Helpers series
(Bridgestone Books)

Career Charades!

Spotlight community helpers with this active game. In advance, write the job title of different community helpers on separate index cards. (See "Careers List" on page 254 for suggestions.) Create a class supply. Then, in turn, invite each student to choose a card and act out the profession. Challenge the remaining students to guess the career. The correct guesser becomes the next actor!

MYSTERY COMMUNITY MEMBER

This fun guessing game helps students learn who's who in their community. Have each child draw and color a community helper on a 9" x 12" sheet of construction paper. On writing paper, have the student write three clues about the worker he drew. Instruct each child to fold the construction paper in half. With the fold at the top, ask him to glue his clue sheet to the larger folded sheet as shown. In turn ask each student to share his clues while the remaining students try to determine the worker's identity. If desired, display each drawing on a wall outside your classroom so other students can have fun guessing, too.

Firefighter

This person uses water.

This person wears a special uniform.

This worker saves lives.

Classroom Careers

Bring the community to your classroom by trying this easy alteration on your helper chart. Rename your classroom jobs to incorporate jobs in your community. For example, change your messenger to a mail carrier, the snack helper to a waitperson, or the attendance keeper to the secretary. Not only will your students be eager to take on their new roles, they will also make the connection between their responsibilities in the classroom and the jobs performed by workers in the real world.

Picture That!

Students are eager to see themselves in career roles of the future. This activity will really help them picture themselves as anything they want to be! In advance photograph each student. After the photographs have been developed, ask each student to think of a job in the community that interests her. To make the picture, distribute a 9" x 12" sheet of white construction paper to each child. Instruct each student to cut only her head from the photograph and glue it near the top center of her paper. Then have each child draw and color the community helper whom she was thinking of, while incorporating her own photographed face into the picture. What a fun way for students to imagine their future roles in the community!

CAREER BOOKLET

Challenge students to summarize their favorite job interests by creating these career booklets. Have each child create a booklet by stapling five blank pages between construction-paper covers. On each page encourage each child to draw and write about a different community helper whom he particularly admires or desires to be. Challenge him to include sentences about why he feels each job is important. This is sure to be a successful career move!

I think stylists are important because they make people look nice.

Tara

AWAY WE GO!

Get your students on the move with these transportation activities.

AIR, LAND, OR WATER?

Transportation keeps our world on the move, whether it's in the air, on land, or on water. Explain to your students that a *vehicle* is a means of carrying or transporting something. Label the top of a piece of chart paper "Vehicles We Know." Then write a student-generated list of vehicles on the chart. Next inform students that there are three main types of transportation: air, land, and water. Then reread a vehicle on the chart. Beside each vehicle name, have a student volunteer draw a cloud if the vehicle travels through the air, grass if it travels on land, or water if it travels in the water. If desired have students count the vehicles for each group to determine which type of transportation includes the most vehicles.

Transportation Sort

Challenge your youngsters to create a collaborative mural of the three types of transportation. To prepare the mural, tape one piece each of blue, green, and white or light blue bulletin-board paper together and label as shown. Supply students with a large collection of discarded magazines. Encourage them to look for and cut out pictures of vehicles. Then have each student glue his pictures to the correct strip on the mural. Display the mural in the hallway for everyone to see.

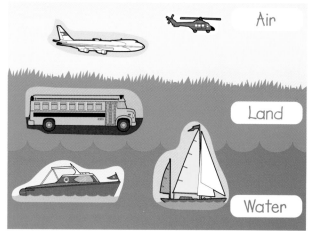

Transportation Book

Try incorporating this student-made book into your transportation unit. Cut construction paper into the shape of a vehicle to create the covers for a book. Cut a class supply of blank paper into the same shape as the covers. Distribute one sheet to each student and ask him to think about a place to which he would like to travel. Encourage each student to write about how he would travel to his desired location. When the pages are complete, compile and bind them between the book covers and add the title "Where We'd Like To Go And How To Get There." This class creation will be a joy to read while studying the many varieties of transportation.

Vehicles We Know

car

boat

train

airplane

motorcycle

Greg

I would like to go to Texas.

I would like to take a train.

Transportation Creations

Make the most of recyclable materials to teach your students about transportation. Prior to beginning this project, request that students bring in items such as empty soda bottles, plastic lids, and small boxes. Add to the collection glue, tape, construction paper, paper tubes, craft sticks, felt, buttons, yarn, and other small objects. As a class, brainstorm a list of transportation vehicles. Have each child select one transportation mode from the list and write three facts about it on a sheet of writing paper. Next have her create a model of her transportation vehicle using some of the collected supplies. Display each student's project with her facts on a table. If desired, invite parents to class to view these one-of-a-kind creations.

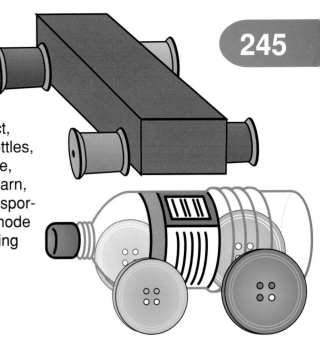

Riley

My Day As A Bus

If I were a school bus, I would sing to the students. I would also have softer seats. I would eat the

(over)

IF I WERE A CAR...

Ask each child to imagine that he is a form of transportation, such as a school bus, helicopter, or sailboat. Encourage the child to imagine his life as the vehicle. Have him think about what he would do all day, what he would eat, and whom he would meet. Next have each child write and illustrate a story titled "My Day As A [vehicle]." When every story is complete, provide class time for sharing the vehicles' adventures.

Tales Of Travel

Your little travelers will go far when you share these tales about travel.

⭐ *I Love Boats* by Flora McDonnell (Candlewick Press, 1995)

⭐ *I Fly* by Anne Rockwell (Crown Publishers, Inc.; 1997)

⭐ *I Spy A Freight Train* devised and selected by Lucy Micklethwait (Greenwillow Books, 1996)

⭐ *Peter's Trucks* by Sallie Wolf (Albert Whitman & Company, 1992)

⭐ *The Big Book Of Things That Go* (Dorling Kindersley Publishing, Inc.; 1994)

ALL-AMERICAN

Turn your little patriots into real Yankee-Doodle dandies with these terrific activities that help familiarize youngsters with symbols of the United States.

A NATIONAL SYMBOL

When the bald eagle was chosen as a symbol of America long ago, it did not make everyone happy. Other suggestions for our national symbol included the turkey and the rattlesnake. After sharing this information with your students, have each youngster draw her suggestion for a national symbol on a sheet of drawing paper. On the back of the paper, have her write a sentence explaining why she chose this symbol. Compile and bind the completed projects into a class book titled "Other Ideas For Our National Symbol." Then place the book in your reading center for everyone to enjoy.

SONG SALUTE

Put your students in a patriotic mood by involving them in this activity that appeals to the eyes and the ears. Teach your students several patriotic songs, such as "Yankee Doodle," "America The Beautiful," "This Land Is Your Land," and the national anthem, "The Star-Spangled Banner." Then read aloud the story *America The Beautiful* based on the poem by Katharine Lee Bates and illustrated by Neil Waldman (Atheneum, 1993). Next display photos, postcards, travel brochures, or posters from several of America's scenic landscapes. (Try to show landscapes from various regions of the country.) Then take a class vote to determine your students' favorite scene. If desired leave the visual displays on a bulletin board titled "America The Beautiful" throughout your All-American unit.

The Statue Of Liberty Comes To Life

With a few materials and a lot of imagination, you can bring the Statue of Liberty to life in your classroom. Don a green sheet (tied at the waist with some rope) and hold up a flashlight in your right hand and a large book in your left hand. Then share the following facts about the Statue of Liberty with your youngsters.

- In 1884 the statue was given to the people of the United States from the people of France as a gesture of friendship.

- The statue is of a woman wearing a robe. In her uplifted right hand, she holds a torch. In the other hand, she holds a tablet with the date of the Declaration of Independence. She also wears a crown with seven spikes that stand for the seven seas and the seven continents.

- The statue is on an island at the entrance of New York Harbor.

- It welcomed millions of immigrants who came to live in America.

- It is a symbol of the United States.

- It is an expression of freedom to people all over the world.

- Each year about two million people visit the Statue of Liberty.

Showing respect for the national flag demonstrates patriotism. Explain to students that the flag is sometimes called the *Stars and Stripes.* It is flown every day over government buildings, schools, and places where people want to show pride in America. Invite your youngsters to practice standing at attention with their right hands over their hearts and their eyes on the flag. Invite a member of the U.S. military or American Legion to give a demonstration on flag etiquette. Here are a few points they might share:

- The flag should be saluted when it passes you in a parade, when it is raised or lowered, when reciting the pledge, or when singing the national anthem in its presence.
- The flag should be displayed every day, weather permitting. It is customary to fly the flag from sunrise to sunset.
- The flag should never be allowed to touch the ground. It should be folded carefully and put away when not in use.
- The flag may be mended, dry-cleaned, or washed. A flag that is no longer fit for display should be destroyed, preferably by burning.

PATRIOTIC DISPLAY

This proud replica of our nation's flag will beat all others—hands down! Ask each child to trace his hand onto red, white, and blue construction paper. After your students cut out their handprints, have them sort them into piles by color. On a large sheet of white bulletin-board paper, draw a rectangle in the top left corner to represent the flag field. Assist students in gluing the blue hand shapes onto the rectangle. Then have students glue the red and white hand shapes in rows to create the flag's stripes. Complete the design by adding 50 star stickers or white star cutouts to the blue section. Display the resulting flag in the hallway or school lobby for all to see.

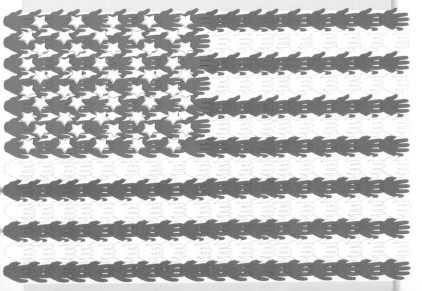

Let Freedom Ring

The Liberty Bell is a symbol of American patriotism. The bell rang on July 8, 1776, at the reading of the Declaration of Independence. It was also rung on special occasions, at celebrations, and at times of sorrow. Soon after its first ringing, it cracked. It was recast, only to crack again in 1835. The Liberty Bell has not been rung since. Today it can be found hanging in Liberty Bell Pavilion, in Philadelphia, Pennsylvania.

After sharing this information with your students, ask them what freedom means to them. Does it mean being able to do whatever they want? Encourage students to share different types of freedom, such as the freedom to be whatever they want when they get older, or the freedom to think what they want.

All-American Literature

- *America* by W. Nikola-Lisa (Lee & Low Books, Inc.; 1997)
- *The Flag We Love* by Pam Muñoz Ryan (Charlesbridge Publishing, Inc.; 1996)
- *The Statue Of Liberty* by Lucille Recht Penner (Random House, Inc.; 1995)
- *Yankee Doodle* by Gary Chalk (Dorling Kindersley Publishing, Inc.; 1993)

WHY WE BUY

Everyone is a *consumer,*
and every consumer has *needs* and *wants.*
Teach your students the meanings of these important words
by using these creative teaching tools.

NEEDS AND WANTS

Here's an activity that will really hit home with your students and will open a discussion about needs and wants. Give each child a sheet of paper and ask him to fold it in half. Instruct him to place the fold on the left side and draw two lines as shown. Then have him cut on the lines (through both layers) to form a house shape. After each child decorates the front of his house with crayons, ask him to unfold his paper and draw pictures of items that he actually has in his house. Encourage him to include items from several rooms in his house. After each child has drawn several items, discuss the difference between a want and a need. Ask students to circle their *needs* with a red crayon; then have them circle all their *wants* with a blue crayon. Have several volunteers share items from each of the categories to complete your discussion.

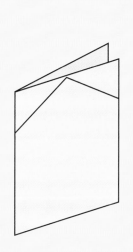

A Dynamic Display

The results of this activity will help students see the difference between wants and needs. In advance, divide a large sheet of bulletin-board paper into two halves. Label one half "wants" and the other half "needs." Then mount the chart on a classroom wall. To begin, have each child cut out five pictures that interest her from discarded magazines. Next ask student volunteers, one at a time, to glue each cutout onto the chart in its appropriate category. Leave the display in your classroom throughout your study of wants and needs for a quick visual reminder.

NEEDS ARE NEEDS, WHEREVER YOU GO

After students identify basic needs—such as food, shelter, and clothing—help them discover that these basic needs are found throughout the world. List basic needs on one side of your chalkboard. Share several non-fiction books from a variety of cultures past and present. List each culture studied along the top of the chalkboard and draw lines to form a graph. As each culture is studied, fill in the graph to identify how each of the basic needs are met, regardless of the location.

	Yucatan	India	France
food	meats, fruits, vegetables	rice	
clothing	shorts, dresses for hot weather	women: saris	
shelter	nas (clay in walls, thatched roofs)		

CONSUMER AWARENESS

Show your students how influential advertisements are with this fun awareness activity. To prepare, cut several advertisements from magazines or newspapers. Next cut out or cover the product name on each ad before gluing the ad to a sheet of construction paper. Write the corresponding product name on the back of each sheet of construction paper.

To begin, remind students that we are all *consumers*. Consumers are people who buy *goods* or *services* to satisfy their needs and wants. Then explain to students that we can also be *producers*. Producers are people who make products or provide services for sale to consumers. Producers advertise their products so consumers will buy them. Then, to reinforce this concept, display the advertisements one at a time and challenge students to guess each product's name. What kind of consumers do you have in your classroom?

SPECIAL T-shirt offer

The #1 cereal in America.

I Want, I Want, I Want!

Reinforce the concept that people have unlimited wants with this thought-provoking activity. To begin, ask each student to make a list or draw pictures of all the things he wants. After approximately five minutes, have students set aside their papers. Read aloud *The Berenstain Bears Get The Gimmies* by Stan and Jan Berenstain (Random House Books For Young Readers, 1988). After sharing the book, ask students if they sometimes get the gimmies. Then have each student revisit his list and choose the item that is most important to him. If desired have him circle the item and then share it with his classmates.

Todd

remote control car

new sneakers

football

basketball

book about soccer

TV

radio

basketball goal

MAP MATTERS

Help students bring the world into view through the magic of maps. After you teach them about the bird's-eye view, they will be anxious to map every place they go.

How Will I Get There?

This introductory activity will help students see the practical use of a map. Display a globe and several different maps including one each of the United States, your state, your city, and your school. Tell students that you need to find your way to the post office (or another location featured on your city map). Show students the globe, and ask them if that will help you with your travels. Discuss why or why not. Next feature your selection of maps and ask your students if they would be more helpful than the globe. Discuss each map and its features as students determine which map would show you the way. Finally post the city map on a wall and highlight your current location and your destination. Using a different color, highlight a route between the two places. If possible, walk or ride with your students along the mapped route to show how the map helps you reach a destination.

BIRD'S-EYE VIEW

To explain how a map is viewed, try this discovery activity. In advance arrange several objects from your desk on a serving tray. Give each student two sheets of white paper. Place the tray on a table where students can view it and ask each student to draw one of the items. Now place the tray on the floor next to the table. Ask students if they think their objects will look different from this view. Then display several maps to show that they are viewed as if you were a bird looking down. Next have students, in turn, stand next to the tray and look down onto it. While each student is viewing the tray from above, have him draw his object again on the other sheet of paper. When all the drawings are complete, post each child's pair of drawings on a bulletin board titled "Which Ones Are From A Bird's-Eye View?"

That's The Key!

Try this fun activity to teach your students how to make a map key. Explain that a *map key* is a list that explains the symbols on a map, and a *symbol* is a simple drawing that represents an actual object. With notebooks and pencils in hand, take your youngsters on a tour of your school and school grounds. Ask each student to create a symbol of particular objects you point out, such as a chair, a computer, a sidewalk, or a slide. When you return to your classroom, create a map key on a sheet of poster board using your students' suggestions. Have students use the key for future mapmaking activities.

Map Key

chair = ⌐

desk = ▭

slide = 🛝

tree = △

computer = 🖥

KEY CARDS

Reinforce the use of map symbols with this easy-to-make matching game. Take photographs of several things in your neighborhood, such as a road, bridge, tree, and fire station. Glue each photograph onto a colored 5" x 7" card. Show each photo to your class, and ask them to help you design a simple symbol for that landmark. Draw each symbol on a white 5" x 7" card. When each photographed place or object has a matching symbol card, place the cards at a center. Then have pairs of students play a game of Memory using the cards. With all the cards facedown, a child draws one colored card and one white card in search of a match. If the cards match, she keeps them. If the cards do not match, she turns them back over. The game continues until all the cards are matched. The player with the most matches wins. Later have your students use these symbols to draw a neighborhood map.

STUDENT ROOM ARRANGEMENTS

Students will jump at this chance to rearrange the classroom. In advance duplicate several copies of the classroom symbols on page 256. Then cut them apart, sort them, and place them in a central location. Next divide your class into four or five small groups, and give each group a sheet of paper. Tell each group that they are to work together to decide on a new arrangement for the classroom. (Remind students of the things that can't be moved from their current location.) Using the classroom symbol cards, have each group glue the cards onto the paper to achieve the desired room arrangement. If desired, allow each group to arrange the room according to its design for one day. Now, that's hands-on learning!

Cardinal Clues

Help students remember the order of the cardinal directions on a compass rose with this clever phrase. Beginning at north and moving clockwise, point to each direction as you say, "**N**ever **E**at **S**oggy **W**affles." To practice this memory aid, have students make several sets of intersecting lines on a sheet of paper, and then have them fill in the cardinal directions on each to create a compass rose. Have them repeat the sentence aloud as they fill in the directional symbols. Before long they'll have no trouble remembering where each direction belongs.

MAP MANEUVERING

Students will enjoy creating their own maps to use with this nifty activity. Provide each child with a sheet of graph paper that has two-inch squares. Ask him to create a map by adding symbols as desired. When the maps are complete, pair students for some map maneuvering. Have students in each pair exchange maps and ask each other questions about finding their way on the maps. For example, one child might ask how to get to the grocery store from the gas station. The person reading the map might respond, "Go three blocks north, then two blocks east." No doubt your youngsters will have fun maneuvering their way around these maps!

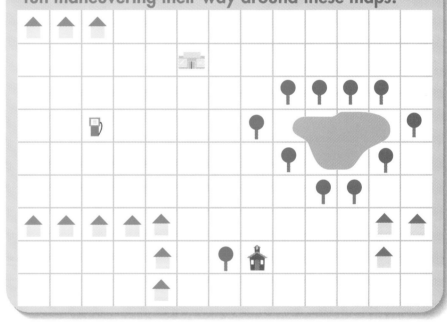

Cardinal Calls

Display the four cardinal directions in the appropriate places on your classroom walls. Refer to them frequently during the day for a variety of activities.

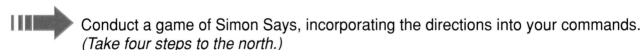

Conduct a game of Simon Says, incorporating the directions into your commands. *(Take four steps to the north.)*

Determine classroom helpers using cardinal locations. *(The student sitting the farthest north will be our line leader.)*

Collect assignments with the help of cardinal directions. *(Everyone pass their papers to the south.)*

Direct students to locations in the room using the directions. *(Please return your books to the reading table on the west side of the room.)*

DIRECTION DRAWINGS

Create a template using one-inch grid paper. Label the four cardinal directions, indicate a starting point, and then duplicate a class supply. Prior to this activity, prepare a few simple drawings to refer to when giving directions. With one picture in mind, give students verbal directions. Have students use a crayon to draw as they follow your commands. When your directions are finished, so are their pictures. Encourage your students to color and decorate them as desired.

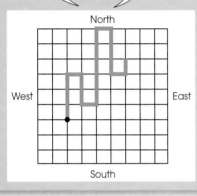

Start at the dot. Move three squares north. Now go one square east, two squares south, one square east...

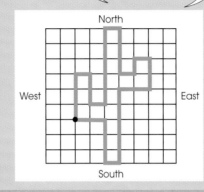

five squares north, one square east, three squares south, one square east, one square north...

one square east, two squares south, two squares west, five squares south...

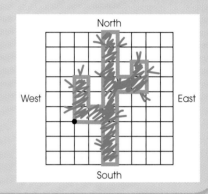

one square west, three squares north, then two squares west.

Treasure Hunt

This fun activity provides a challenging culmination to your study of maps. Hide a treasure (such as a shoebox filled with books) on your playground or in your school; then create a map to guide students to it. Challenge a small group of students to find the treasure by reading the map you created. Resupply your treasure before sending another group on the hunt, or change the map entirely for each small group. What an exciting way to practice map-reading skills!

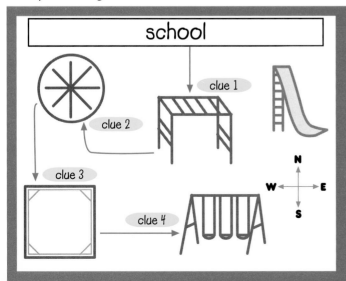

Find Your Way To These Great Books

A Bird's-Eye View by Harriet Wittels and Joan Greisman (Scholastic Inc., 1995)

As The Crow Flies by Gail Hartman (Aladdin Books, 1993)

Maps And Mapping by Barbara Taylor (Kingfisher, 1993)

Let's Investigate Marvelously Meaningful Maps by Madelyn Wood Carlisle (Barron's Educational Series, Inc.; 1992)

Me On The Map by Joan Sweeney (Crown Publishers, Inc.; 1996)

My Map Book by Sara Fanelli (HarperCollins Publishers, Inc.; 1995)

The Whole World In Your Hands by Melvin and Gilda Berger (Ideals Children's Books, 1993)

Careers List

accountant	farmer	news reporter
actor	firefighter	nurse
architect	flight attendant	
artist	florist	optometrist
astronaut		orthodontist
	garbage collector	
baker	gardener	painter
banker	geologist	pharmacist
barber	grocer	photographer
beautician		pilot
biologist	illustrator	plumber
bus driver	insurance agent	police officer
carpenter	janitor	race-car driver
cashier	jeweler	real estate agent
chef	judge	receptionist
chemist		
computer programmer	lawyer	salesperson
construction worker	librarian	scientist
	locksmith	seamstress
dentist	logger	secretary
designer		
doctor	mail carrier	teacher
	mechanic	travel agent
editor	meteorologist	truck driver
electrician	musician	
engineer		waitperson
		writer

What's Your Favorite?

Write your favorites.
Compare with your classmates.
Tally how many like the same.

	My Favorite	How Many Others Like It?
Animal		
Athlete		
Book		
Color		
Holiday		
Number		
Restaurant		
Snack Food		
Song		
Sport		
Subject		
TV Show		

©1998 The Education Center, Inc. • *The Mailbox® Superbook • Grade 1 • TEC450*

Note To Teacher: Use with "What's Your Favorite?" on page 236.

255

Good-Neighbor Badges

Use with "Good-Neighbor Award"
on page 241.

Classroom Symbols

Use with "Student Room Arrangements" on page 251.

desk	desk	desk	desk	desk	desk	desk	desk	desk	desk
desk	desk	desk	desk	desk	desk	desk	desk	desk	desk

desk	desk	desk
desk	desk	desk

teacher's desk

table

table

door

door

bookshelf

window

window

chalkboard

ABC

SCIENCE

Recycling

Three Cheers For The Three *R*s!

Have your students make these unique banners to remind others of the three *R*s—*reduce, reuse,* and *recycle.* Share the words and their definitions as shown. Invite students to brainstorm ways people can demonstrate each action. List students' responses on a sheet of chart paper. Then have each student make a banner promoting the three *R*s. To make a banner, a student labels three five-inch construction-paper squares as shown. Then he draws a picture to represent each action. Next he glues his squares in the appropriate order onto a 1" x 18" construction-paper strip, at evenly spaced intervals. Display the completed projects around your school to remind others about the three *R*s. Hip, hip, hooray!

Reduce: Create less trash by making careful shopping decisions. Buy food with less packaging material, and recycled paper products.

Reuse: Find new uses for items that would otherwise be thrown away. Before you recycle plastic grocery bags, use them at least three more times. Also save worn towels to use as cleaning rags.

Recycle: Turn used materials into new products. Sort your trash on garbage day and take recyclable materials (such as glass, cans, and newspapers) to a recycling center.

Recycle That Trash!

Invite students to set up a recycling station in their classroom. Have students discuss the kinds of materials that can be recycled, including plastics, aluminum, and paper. Then divide students into three groups. Assign each group a different material. Then have each group decorate and label a large box to use as a recycling container for its assigned material. Throughout the year, provide many opportunities for youngsters to recycle different items. When the containers in the classroom are filled, empty them into your school's recycling bin. (Or enlist the help of parent volunteers to take the containers to your town's recycling center.) Now that's a hands-on way to learn how to recycle!

Sensational Swap Box

Remind your youngsters of the importance of reusing products with this yearlong center. In advance, place some discarded items—such as books, games, or stuffed animals—into a box labeled "Swap Box." Invite students to bring in similar items from home and swap them for things in the Swap Box. Encourage youngsters to continue with this earth-friendly practice throughout the year. Your students will soon learn how easy it is to reuse products instead of throwing them away.

Must-Read Books About Recycling

- *Follow That Trash! All About Recycling* by Francine Jacobs (The Putnam & Grosset Group, 1996)
- *The Great Trash Bash* by Loreen Leedy (Holiday House, Inc.; 1991)
- *Recycle! A Handbook For Kids* by Gail Gibbons (Little, Brown And Company; 1992)
- *Round And Round Again* by Nancy Van Laan (Hyperion Books For Children, 1994)
- *Where Does The Garbage Go?* by Paul Showers (HarperCollins Children's Books, 1994)

Is It Living Or Nonliving?

Introduce the topic of living and nonliving things to your students by sharing *What's Alive?* by Kathleen Weidner Zoehfeld (HarperCollins Children's Books, 1995). The story's simple text and illustrations present the information in an easy-to-understand manner. After reading the book, guide your youngsters in a discussion about the basic life processes of all living things—eating, growing, and moving. Then take your class on a walk outside to look for living and nonliving things. When you return from the walk, have each student record his observations. First a student folds a sheet of drawing paper in half. Then he unfolds that paper and labels the halves "Living Things" and "Nonliving Things." Next he draws and labels pictures of the things he saw on his walk under the appropriate headings. As a culminating activity, have the students share their drawings with their classmates.

Sorting Living And Nonliving Things

Challenge youngsters to sort pictures of living and nonliving things. To begin remind students that living things need food, water, and air to grow and change. Then have students cut pictures of living and nonliving things from magazines. Ask each student to sort her pictures into two groups—*living* and *nonliving* things. Next challenge each student further by asking her to sort her pictures of living things into three more groups—*people, animals,* and *plants.* Then, as a class, mount the sorted pictures onto a piece of poster board divided and labeled as shown. Staple the chart to a bulletin board and add the title "Our Living And Nonliving Things." If desired have each student choose an item from the chart and write about it. Mount the students' work around the poster board to complete the display.

Look How We've Changed!

What better way to learn how living things grow and change than with baby photos? To prepare ask each student to bring from home a photo of herself when she was a baby. Then photograph each child with an instant camera. When the pictures from home have been collected, mount the photos on drawing paper. To do this, fold a sheet of drawing paper in half. Mount a student's baby photo to the front flap; then attach her current photo on the inside. Prepare the remaining photos in the same manner. Post the completed projects on a bulletin board with the title "Look How We've Changed!" Challenge students to guess the identity of each baby picture before lifting the flap to reveal the answer. As a follow-up, have youngsters discuss the changes they observed. What a fun way to see how living things grow and change!

Animals

Animal-Group Antics

Introduce your students to various animal groups with this one-of-a-kind game. To prepare, label a separate area of your classroom for each of the six animal groups listed below. Then involve students in a discussion about the different animal groups by sharing some of these interesting facts:

- **Fish** are animals that live in water. They are cold-blooded creatures that breathe by means of gills.
- **Insects** are small, six-legged animals. Most use tiny hairs on their bodies to hear and antennae to smell.
- **Amphibians** are cold-blooded animals with smooth, scaleless skin.
- **Birds** are animals with feathers and wings. They also hatch from eggs and can travel very fast.
- **Reptiles** are cold-blooded animals with dry, scaly skin. They lay eggs.
- **Mammals** are warm-blooded animals. They nurse their young and have hair that covers their bodies.

Have students name animals for each group. Record their responses on chart paper. Then have each student select a different animal from the chart and draw a picture of it on an index card. Collect the cards and redistribute one to each child. Have the student take his card to the corresponding area of the classroom. When all students have chosen a group, challenge members to decide if everyone belongs. Collect the cards and play additional rounds in the same manner.

Animals, Animals, Animals!

Have students use these encyclopedia booklets for recording facts about the animal groups. To make one booklet, stack four 8 1/2" x 11" sheets of paper and hold the pages vertically in front of you. Slide the top sheet upward approximately one inch; then repeat the process for the second sheet. Next fold the paper thickness forward to create eight graduated layers or pages (see the illustration). Staple close to the fold. Have each student write the title "[Child's Name]'s Animal Encyclopedia" on the front cover; then label the booklet pages as shown. Next have each student write interesting facts and draw pictures for each animal group. Youngsters will be flipping over animal facts!

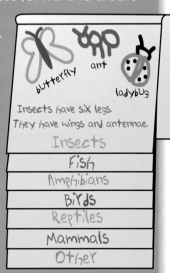

butterfly ant ladybug

Insects have six legs.
They have wings and antennae.

Insects
Fish
Amphibians
Birds
Reptiles
Mammals
Other

Creative Habitats

Introduce youngsters to animal habitats when you read Jim Arnosky's book *Crinkleroot's Guide To Knowing Animal Habitats* (Simon & Schuster Books For Young Readers, 1997). After sharing the story, remind students that animals need food, water, and cover to survive. Then make a student-generated list of different animals and their habitats on the chalkboard. Supply students with an assortment of construction paper, Styrofoam® trays, glue, and crayons. Instruct each student to use the materials to create an animal habitat by drawing and gluing animal pictures atop a construction-paper habitat background. Collect the completed projects and display them on a wall or bulletin board with the title "Creative Habitats."

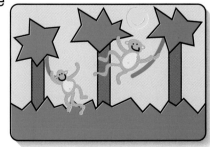

A Sorting Hoopla!

Challenge youngsters to sort animals by their characteristics. For each student cut an animal picture from a magazine and glue it to a 3" x 5" card. Begin by asking students to brainstorm animal characteristics. Write students' responses on 3" x 5" cards. (Some good characteristics to include: size, what they eat, where they live, number of legs, color, and body coverings.) Next gather students in a circle. Arrange two Hula-Hoops® on the floor to resemble a Venn diagram; then place a characteristic card at the top of each hoop. Next distribute one animal card to each child. Have students take turns placing their cards in the correct section on the diagram. Continue the hoopla by changing the characteristics and redistributing the animal cards with each new round.

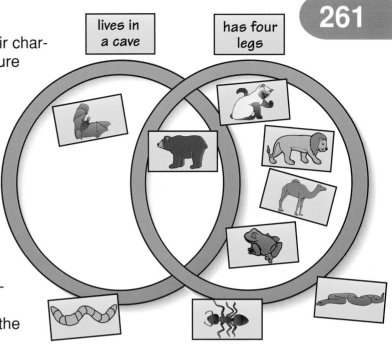

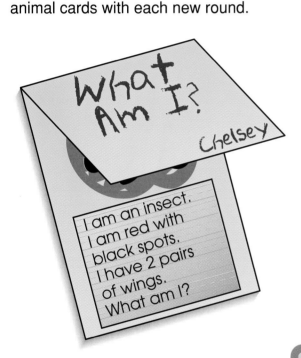

Guess What I Am

Have students demonstrate their knowledge about animals with this unique activity. Each child will need a large sheet of construction paper folded lengthwise into thirds, and a piece of writing paper one-third the size of the construction paper. Have each student choose a different animal, then write three clues about the animal on her writing paper. Each youngster then glues the clues to the bottom third of her construction paper, and illustrates a picture of the animal in the middle. Next she folds down the top third of her paper and adds the title "What Am I?" Provide time for students to share the clues with their classmates, revealing the picture when it is guessed correctly.

Animal Investigations

For additional reinforcement of animals and their characteristics, have each student research a desired animal and complete the reproducible on page 278. When your students have completed the activity, provide time for them to share their information with their classmates.

More About Animals

Share these stories with your students for added enjoyment during your study of animals.

- *Amazing Animal Babies* by Christopher Maynard (Alfred A. Knopf Books For Young Readers, 1993)
- *Atlas Of Animals* by Gallimard Jeunesse, Claude Delafosse, and René Mettler (Scholastic Inc., 1996)
- *No One Told The Aardvark* by Deborah Eaton and Susan Halter (Charlesbridge Publishing, Inc.; 1996)
- *Wonderful Nature, Wonderful You* by Karin Ireland (DAWN Publications, 1996)
- *Words About Animals* by David West (The Millbrook Press, Inc.; 1995)

Plant Needs

Students will sprout a new knowledge for the needs of plants with this banner project. For each student accordion-fold a 6" x 18" piece of construction paper into five equal sections. Instruct each student to vertically unfold his banner and write "Plants need…" and his name on the top section. The student then writes and illustrates a different plant need (air, soil, water, sunlight) in each of the remaining four sections. After completing these sections, the student turns his banner over and draws a picture of a growing plant. Clip these delightful projects to a clothesline suspended in the classroom.

Seeds Up Close

What better way for students to discover seed parts than by seeing them? To prepare, soak a bag of dried lima beans in water overnight. Also draw a picture of the seed diagram (shown) on the chalkboard.

Explain to your students that all seeds have three parts in common: the *embryo,* the *food-storage tissue,* and the *seed coat.* Point to the seed coat on the diagram and inform your students that it protects the inside of the seed from injury, loss of water, and insects. Have each student carefully remove the seed coat from her bean. Point to the embryo on the diagram and tell students that it is the baby plant. Have each student open her seed and find the embryo. Next point to the food-storage tissue on the diagram and explain that it contains all the food needed for the baby plant to begin to grow. Instruct each student to find the food-storage tissue in her bean. Now that's a hands-on way to dig into seeds!

What A View!

Uncovering the different parts of plants is easy with this activity. To begin explain to students that all plants have *roots, stems,* and *leaves,* although these parts may look different on different plants. Also share with students that many plants also have *flowers* and *fruit.* Then, to reinforce the different plant parts, have each student make a three-dimensional plant. To begin, a student staples the left edge of a 6" x 12" piece of brown construction paper to the bottom of a 12" x 18" sheet of drawing paper to resemble soil (as shown). Next she tightly rolls a 5" x 7" piece of green construction paper around her pencil and tapes it to prevent it from unrolling. She then carefully removes her pencil and glues the paper roll above the brown paper to create a stem. Next she folds back the brown paper and glues pieces of brown yarn to the bottom of the stem to create roots. Then she glues construction-paper leaves to the stem and uses tissue paper to create a flower as desired. To complete the project, she labels each part of the flower. This art activity is sure to make your youngsters more "part-smart" about plants!

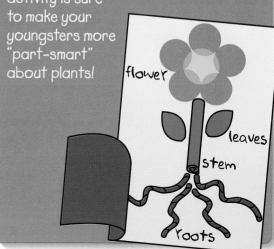

A Feast Of Plant Parts

Up to this point, students probably haven't considered that they eat parts of plants. Use the following demonstrations and tasting activities to tempt your youngsters' taste buds and learn about the important parts of plants.

Where Are Those Roots?

Set the stage for learning about roots by reading aloud *The Turnip* by Harriet Ziefert (Puffin Books, 1996). After sharing the book, explain to students that roots anchor the plant into the ground. They also absorb (and some store) water and minerals from the soil for the rest of the plant to use. If possible present a turnip with the leaves still intact. Pass the turnip around, cut it into pieces, and have students comment on its appearance, texture, and taste. Then challenge students to name other plants we eat that are roots. Be sure to have roots on hand—such as carrots, radishes, onions, potatoes, and beets—for students to examine and sample.

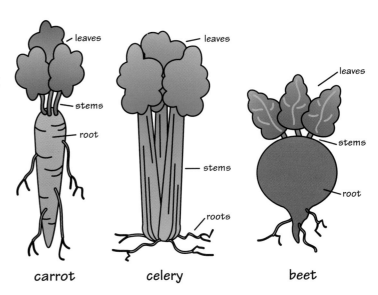

carrot   celery   beet

Going Up

Stems support the leaves and flowers of plants. They also carry water and minerals up from the roots to the leaves. To demonstrate this concept, cut one-half inch off the bottom of a leafy celery stalk. Then slice the stalk in half lengthwise from the bottom to about halfway up toward the top. Tie or tape the stem at the halfway point to prevent further splitting. Then place one end of the stalk into a clear plastic cup containing water tinted with red food coloring. Place the other celery end in a similar cup containing regular water. Ask students to predict what will happen to each celery half. Then leave the celery stalks in the water overnight. The next day check the celery, and have your students discuss the changes they observe. (Half of the stalk will be colored red.) Then remove the stalks from the cups, and slice them into several short lengths. Have students use magnifying glasses to view the tiny transport tubes. Explain to students that these tubes carry minerals from the soil to the plant cells. This process provides the flowers and leaves with necessary nutrients. Conclude the activity by serving each student a piece of fresh celery.

"Be-Leaf" It Or Not!

Students will be amazed to learn that they eat leaves. Bring to school some edible leaves, such as lettuce, spinach, and cabbage. Cut through the middles of the heads of lettuce and cabbage to show students the short stems. Tell students that the leaves of a plant are where the plant's food is produced. Then provide students with samples of the leaves to taste.

Books To Grow On

I'm A Seed by Jean Marzollo (Scholastic Inc., 1996)

From Seed To Plant by Gail Gibbons (Holiday House, Inc., 1993)

Little Green Fingers: A Kid's Guide To Growing Things by Clare Chandler (Whitecap Books Ltd., 1996)

All About Seeds: A Hands-On Science Book by Melvin Berger (Scholastic Inc., 1992)

Counting Wildflowers by Bruce McMillan (Mulberry Books, 1995)

Seasons

A Seasonal Sort

Introduce seasons to your youngsters by sharing *The Berenstain Bears' Four Seasons* by Stan and Jan Berenstain (Random House Books For Young Readers, 1996). After sharing the story, have students brainstorm items that relate to each season. Write the students' responses on chart paper. Then assign each child a different item from the list. The student illustrates a picture of his seasonal item on an index card. Then, with your students' help, sort the index cards by season before attaching them to a bulletin board. No doubt your youngsters will learn about the seasons in no time!

What's The Season?

Review the four seasons by involving youngsters in this hands-on game. Demonstrate each hand signal shown; then have students practice making each one. To play the game, announce a seasonal item mentioned in "A Seasonal Sort." Have each student make the corresponding hand signal for the item. To further challenge students, increase the rate at which you announce items. When necessary, involve students in a discussion of why more than one hand signal may be used with some of the items. For another variation, have a student volunteer announce items for his classmates.

Season	Hand Signal
Spring	palm up, fingers cupped (like a flower)
Summer	fingers spread (like a sun)
Fall	hand flat, fingers together (like a leaf)
Winter	make a fist (like a snowball)

Stories About The Seasons

Share these additional stories about the four seasons.
- *Ox-Cart Man* by Donald Hall (Viking, 1979)
- *Can't Sit Still* by Karen E. Lotz (Dutton Children's Books, 1993)
- *My Mama Had A Dancing Heart* by Libba Moore Gray (Orchard Books, 1995)
- *The Reasons For Seasons* by Gail Gibbons (Holiday House, Inc.; 1995)
- *A Circle Of Seasons* by Myra Cohn Livingston (Holiday House, Inc.; 1982)
- *Caps, Hats, Socks, And Mittens* by Louise Borden (Scholastic Inc., 1989)

A Booklet Of All Seasons

These creative booklets are a fun review of the four seasons. To prepare, gather one wallet-sized photograph of every child. Then duplicate four copies of each student's picture. To make a booklet, a student trims each of his duplicated photos and glues them to separate sheets of paper. On each sheet he draws a picture to represent a season, incorporating himself into the picture. Next he writes about each season. He staples the completed pages between two construction-paper covers and adds a title, such as "[Student's name] Through The Seasons," and illustrations. If desired display the seasonal booklets at a reading center for all to enjoy. What a great way to wrap up your unit about the four seasons!

I like to throw snowballs in winter.
It is cold.
My mom makes me hot chocolate.

What Is Weather?

Weather is the condition of air that blankets the Earth. The air, the Sun, the Earth, and water work together to make the weather.

Blowing In The Wind

Help students understand the amazing force of wind with these nifty activities. To begin, have each student hold a sheet of paper in front of himself. Then instruct students to gently blow on their papers. Ask students to describe what happened. Explain to students that they created *wind,* or moving air. Tell students that they cannot see the wind, but they can watch the wind move things, such as their papers or clouds. (If desired explain to students that wind is caused by the uneven heating of the Earth by the Sun.)

Next have each student take a deep breath and blow on his paper again. Ask students to compare what the paper looked like compared to when they blew gently. Lead students to understand that the wind blows at different speeds. Then share *The Beaufort Scale* (shown) with students and explain that it can be used to help decide how hard the wind is blowing.

The Beaufort Scale

Force	Strength	Effect
0	calm	Smoke goes up.
1	light air	Smoke drifts.
2	light breeze	Leaves rustle.
3	gentle breeze	A flag unfurls.
4	medium breeze	Paper blows away.
5	fresh breeze	Small trees sway.
6	strong breeze	An umbrella turns inside out.

To provide practice interpreting the scale, have students make wind murals. Divide students into seven groups, and provide each group with a sheet of drawing paper. Assign each group a different force from the scale. Instruct each group to draw a picture of an outdoor scene that illustrates the effect of its assigned force. Also have each group write its assigned force number on its paper. Glue the completed pictures in numerical order onto a large piece of bulletin-board paper. Then mount the display in a prominent location for students to refer to during their study of the weather.

Wind Direction

Students will see which direction the wind is blowing from by using windsocks. Explain to students that the wind is named by the direction from which it blows. For example, an east wind blows from east to west. To make a windsock, a student decorates a 6" x 18" strip of construction paper and then rolls it into a cylinder. Next he staples or glues the overlapping ends together. Then he glues 16-inch strips of colorful crepe paper inside the lower rim of the project. To prepare the project for hanging, punch two holes near the top of the cylinder so that the holes are on opposite sides of the project. Thread each end of a 16-inch length of yarn through a different hole and securely tie them. To use the windsock, the student takes it outside and observes which way the streamers are blowing. If desired post cardinal directions outside so students can determine from which direction the wind is blowing.

The Mighty Sun

These whole-group demonstrations will show students what effect sunlight has on water. Explain to students that water can *evaporate*, or turn into water vapor and rise into the air. Wet two paper towels. Place or suspend one paper towel in the sunlight and the other in the shade. Ask students to predict what will happen to both towels. Then have student volunteers check the towels every 15 minutes. Lead students to the conclusion that the paper towel in the sunlight dries faster because the heat from the Sun makes the water evaporate quicker.

To further extend the concept of evaporation, have students observe as you pour equal amounts of water into three containers, each with a different-sized opening. Next ask students to predict which container's water will evaporate first. Have students check the containers each day until the water from each container has evaporated. Students will make the discovery that the water from the container with the widest opening evaporated first because the water in this bowl has a larger surface area.

Cloud Discovery

Students will see how clouds are formed with this teacher-conducted experiment. Remind students that when water evaporates into the air to become *water vapor,* it cannot be seen. However, sometimes warm air that has lots of water vapor rises from the Earth, and as it meets cooler air, small water droplets can form to create clouds. Demonstrate this process to small groups of students by filling a can with hot water and another can with ice. Hold the can with ice above the can with hot water and instruct students to look closely until a small cloud forms. Then explain to students that rain falls when water drops in the clouds get bigger and heavier.

Many Different Clouds

For an informative look at the different types of clouds, read aloud *The Cloud Book* by Tomie dePaola (Holiday House, Inc.; 1975). After sharing the book, discuss with students the three major groups of clouds: *cirrus, cumulus,* and *stratus.* Draw and label an example of each of these clouds on the chalkboard. When students are familiar with the three cloud types, have them create cloud posters. To make a poster, a student folds a 12" x 18" sheet of light blue construction paper to create three equal sections. She then vertically unfolds the paper and uses cotton balls to create a different type of cloud at the top of each section. Then, at the bottom of each section, she labels each cloud with a black crayon. If desired have students observe the clouds each morning and then refer to their completed projects to determine the cloud type.

Cirrus

Cumulus

Stratus

A View Of The Weather

Provide students with views of many different types of weather conditions with this window-watching art project. Have students brainstorm as many different weather conditions as possible, such as strong winds, snow, or hail. Write students' responses on the chalkboard. Then have each student select a weather condition and draw that type of weather on an eight-inch square of white construction paper. Next the student glues the drawing onto a nine-inch brown construction-paper square. To complete the project, he glues two 2" x 8" strips of brown construction paper to create four equally sized windowpanes as shown. Enlist students' help in sorting the completed projects by their weather types; then mount pictures with similar weather conditions together on a bulletin board. Add a label for each weather condition and add the title "Many Views Of The Weather."

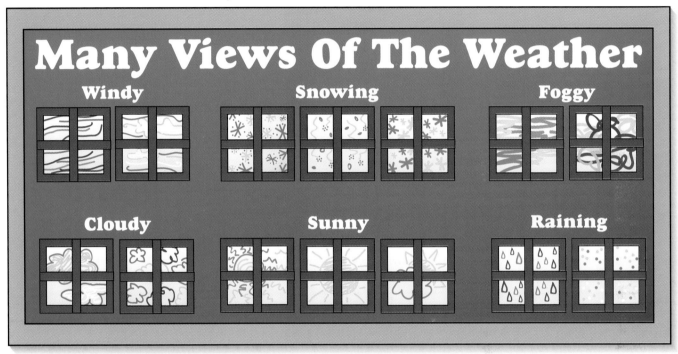

Weather Watchers

Reinforce your youngsters' weather observation skills with this daily weather-watching activity. For each student, duplicate five copies of the recording sheet on page 279; then stack the pages and staple them between two construction-paper covers. Distribute a booklet to each student, and have him personalize the front cover with weather words and pictures. Each morning have students observe, discuss, and record the weather on their recording sheets. For a fun follow-up, fill a box with articles of clothing for all possible types of weather conditions. Then have a student volunteer put on the appropriate clothing for the day's weather.

Weather-Related Reading

What Will The Weather Be Like Today? by Paul Rogers (Greenwillow Books, 1990)

Wild Weather Soup by Caroline Formby (Forest House Publishing Co., Inc.; 1996)

And Now...The Weather by Anita Ganeri (Simon & Schuster Children's, 1992)

Wind & Rain by Claire Llewellyn and Anthony Lewis (Barron's Educational Series, Inc.; 1995)

What Makes It Rain? by Susan Mayes (Usborne Publishing Limited, 1989)

Why Does Lightning Strike? Questions Children Ask About The Weather (Dorling Kindersley Publishing, Inc.; 1996)

Storms by Seymour Simon (Morrow Junior Books, 1989)

Matter

What Is Matter?

Help students better understand matter with this simple activity. Tell students that matter is anything that takes up space and has weight. Then have each student find three items in the classroom that are matter and illustrate them on a sheet of drawing paper. After students complete their drawings, invite each student to share his illustrations with the class. Lead students to the discovery that almost everything that can be seen and touched is matter.

Matter Takes Up Space

This small-group activity shows students that two things can't be in the same space at the same time. Divide students into small groups; then provide each group with a permanent marker, a rock, and a plastic cup half-filled with water. Ask a student from each group to draw a line on his group's cup to mark the water level. (Be sure to remind students to take the readings from eye level.) Then have each group carefully place a rock in the cup (without dispersing any water). Next have another student in each group mark the new water level. Have the students in each group compare their two water levels. Conclude the activity by explaining to students that the water level increased because the rock is matter.

The Many Properties Of Matter

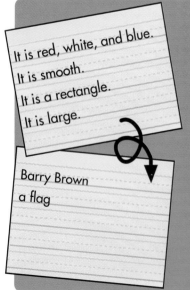

Provide students with the chance to explore properties of matter with this problem-solving activity. Explain to students that scientists describe matter using many different physical properties, such as color, texture, shape, size, and weight. Then have each student secretly choose an object from the classroom and list its physical characteristics on a sheet of writing paper. Encourage students to list properties that would help their classmates differentiate their objects from other objects. Also instruct each student to write his name and the object he chose on the back of his paper. Next collect the papers, and read each set of clues. Have students try to identify each object described. After sharing the clues, ask students to describe the properties the objects share. Also ask students why some objects are more difficult to identify than others.

Three States Of Matter

These nifty activities will help students better understand and identify the three physical states of matter—*solid, liquid,* and *gas.*

Solid: Send students on a scavenger hunt for solids. On a sheet of paper, write ten clues (similar to the ones shown) to describe solids; then duplicate a class supply. Distribute the list to each student and read the clues aloud. Challenge each student to find solids in the classroom with the given properties. Have her write the name of the solid or draw a picture of it in the space provided.

1. A solid that is heavy.
2. A solid that is red.
3. A solid that you can bend.
4. A solid that is soft.
5. A solid that smells good.
6. A solid that will not break if it is dropped.
7. A solid that is nonliving.
8. A solid that will float in water.
9. A solid that is very small.
10. A solid that can tear.

Liquid: Show students that a liquid has no shape of its own with this easy demonstration. Pour water into several different-sized containers. For each container, have a student volunteer draw on the chalkboard the shape of the water in the container. Guide students to understand that a liquid takes the shape of the container it is put in. Then, for a follow-up, write a student-generated list of different kinds of liquids on the chalkboard. Have students use the properties of matter to describe each liquid on the list.

Gas: These whole-group demonstrations will help students understand that gases are matter, they cannot be seen, and they spread out to fill containers. To begin, gather a small paper lunch bag near the top and hold it so that there is only a small opening. Then blow into the bag to fill it with air. Use your hand to hold the opening of the bag shut as you lead students to understand that there is air in the bag and that it takes up space.

Next tape a paper towel to the inside bottom of a glass. Then turn the glass upside down, and push it into a large container of water (keeping it straight). Lift the glass straight up from the container, and remove the paper towel for students to examine. Remind students that air takes up space. Then explain to students that air was trapped inside the glass and that it prevented the water from entering the glass and wetting the paper towel.

Matter Changes States

Prove to students that matter can change states with this simple demonstration. In advance create and display a chart similar to the one shown. To begin, place an ice cube in a clear, plastic cup. Remind students that the ice cube is a solid form of water. Then ask students to predict how long they think the ice will take to melt into a liquid. Have each student write her name under her prediction on the chart. Next ask students to predict how long it will take the water, or liquid matter, to evaporate into a gas. Again have students record their predictions on the chart. Then, periodically throughout the day, have student volunteers check the cup until the ice turns into a liquid. Circle the correct prediction on the chart. Then have students continue to check the cup until the water turns into a gas. Again circle the correct prediction on the chart. What a great way for students to see matter change right in front of their eyes!

The ice will melt into a liquid in...

less than an hour	a few hours	a few days	a few weeks
Janelle	Adam	Mario	Sharon
Max	Sonya	Phillip	Michelle
Beth	Juan	Alexa	Lawson
Timothy	Chelsea	Amy	
Leslie	Brenden		
Rodney	Natalie		
	Jonah		
	Trevor		
	Rachel		

The water will evaporate into a gas in...

less than an hour	a few hours	a few days	a few weeks
Chelsea	Leslie	Beth	Rachel
Amy	Max	Sonya	Jonah
Michelle	Timothy	Phillip	Trevor
Rodney	Alexa	Brenden	Adam
	Lawson	Juan	Janelle
		Sharon	
		Mario	
		Natalie	

Magnets

What Is A Magnet?

Introduce the force of magnetism by sharing these interesting facts with your students.

- *Magnets* attract iron, steel, nickel, and certain other materials.

- *Magnets* have a variety of uses—from holding a piece of paper to the refrigerator door, to changing electrical impulses in telephones and radios into sounds.

- *Magnetism* and electricity are closely related. Together they create a force called *electromagnetism*.

- The earth is a large magnet with poles at both ends—the north pole and the south pole.

- It's unclear how magnets were discovered. One story states that about 3,000 years ago in the country of Magnesia, a sheepherder named Magnes noticed that the iron nails in his shoes were attracted to certain rocks. Another story says that long ago in China, people discovered that certain rocks attracted pieces of iron.

An Attractive Learning Center!

Invite students to test objects for magnetism. Duplicate a class supply of the recording sheet on page 279. Also gather the magnetic and non-magnetic objects listed on the sheet. Place the objects, recording sheets, and different types of magnets at a center in your classroom. Encourage students to visit the center to determine each object's magnetism. As a student makes his predictions, he writes "yes" or "no" under the appropriate heading. Then he tests each object and makes a check in the correct column. When all of your students have visited the center, invite them to share ideas about why certain objects are attracted to magnets. No doubt this center will attract your youngsters!

Powerful Poles

Your students will discover that magnets are stronger at the poles during this cooperative-group activity. To begin, show students a bar magnet. Explain that magnets have two poles—*north* and *south*. Point out the poles on the magnet. Then divide your students into five groups. Give each group a bar magnet and a box of small paper clips. Tell the students that they will be using the materials to determine the strength of the poles. Have the members of the group hang as many paper-clip chains from the middle and ends of the bar magnet as possible. Instruct a member from each group to record the number of paper clips hanging from each part of the magnet. When the groups have finished the experiment, invite them to share their results with the class.

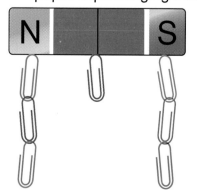

Magnetic Roadsters

Use this idea to teach students that sometimes magnets are strong enough to attract items through other objects. To prepare, cut one construction-paper car (similar to the one shown) for every student. Push one brad through each of the cars' wheels. Also cut one 12" x 16" piece of tagboard for each child. To begin, invite students to join you in a circle on the floor. Place a large paper clip on a paper plate. Hold a magnet under the plate and demonstrate moving the paper clip with the magnet. Encourage youngsters to talk about what happened. Then distribute one car, one piece of tagboard, and one magnet to every student. The student colors a road map on her tagboard and decorates her car with crayons. Then she places the magnet under the map and drives her car along the road!

Terrific Treasures

Your youngsters will really dig this learning center! To prepare, fill a medium-sized container with sand. Hide several magnetic objects under the sand (see the list shown). Place the container, a large magnet, and a supply of drawing paper at a center. Encourage students to visit the center and dig for buried treasure. To do this, a student moves the magnet under the sand until he finds an object. Then he draws a picture of the object on a sheet of paper. He continues in the same manner until he finds each treasure. No doubt your students will want to visit this center time and time again!

Magnetic Objects

paper clips
nuts and bolts
blunt scissors
screws
metal washers
metal spoons
metal key rings
thumbtacks
brads

Attract Or Repel?

Delight your students with this hands-on demonstration! Before the lesson, clearly label the poles of two bar magnets. To begin, gather your class in a circle on the floor. Pass around one of the magnets to prompt a discussion about the poles. Have students predict which ends of the poles will attract each other and which ends will repel (not attract). Next invite two students to stand at the front of the room. Give each volunteer a magnet. Have the students demonstrate placing the same and then opposite poles together. After the demonstration, have the youngsters talk about what happened. If time allows, repeat the demonstration with additional volunteers. Then place the magnets at a center for further investigations. Your youngsters will be amazed to find that opposites *do* attract!

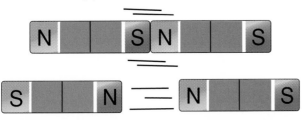

Rocks

A Rock Hunt

Introduce your first graders to the topic of rocks with a rock hunt. Provide each student with a plastic grocery bag (or shoebox) and a craft stick. Then, for homework, ask each student to use his materials to dig and collect seven to ten rocks. Set guidelines for the size of the rocks, such as smaller than the student's fist.

When the rocks have been brought to school, make sure each student's rock collection is labeled with his name. Next divide a sheet of poster board into four columns. Title the columns *shape, color, texture,* and *luster;* then explain each property as it relates to rocks. Have students examine their rock collections and brainstorm descriptive rock words. List students' responses under the correct headings. Then mount the word collection on a classroom wall for students to refer to throughout the rock unit.

shape	color
flat round oval	brown black white

texture	luster
smooth bumpy jagged	shiny dull sparkly

Comparing Rocks

Now that your rock hounds have rounded up some rock vocabulary, it's time to put it to use! In advance copy words from the poster created in "A Rock Hunt" onto sentence strips. Then use two Hula-Hoops® to form a Venn diagram in an open area of your classroom. To begin the activity, have each student choose a rock from her rock collection and place a personalized piece of masking tape on it. Then gather students in a circle around the Venn diagram. Place a labeled sentence strip in each of the outer sections of the diagram. Have each student examine her rock and, in turn, place her rock in the correct category. Rocks that fall into both categories should be placed in the overlapping section of the two circles. Rocks that do not fall into either category should be placed outside of the circles. After each student has had a turn, return students' rocks and repeat the activity using different categories.

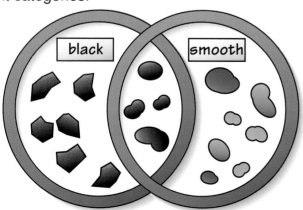

black   smooth

What A Great Pet!

To further encourage students to use their newfound rock vocabulary from "A Rock Hunt," have each student make and write about a pet rock. To make a pet rock, a student chooses a rock from his collection and uses craft glue to attach wiggle eyes. Next he uses paint pens to draw facial features and to write his initials on the bottom. He then adds yarn lengths for hair if desired. After creating his pet rock, the student writes a description of his rock on a sheet of writing paper. Next he glues the writing paper to a slightly larger sheet of construction paper and writes his name on the back.

For added fun, place five to ten rocks and their descriptions at a center. Challenge students to match the descriptions to the correct rocks. Keep interest high by routinely changing the rocks and descriptions. In no time at all, your youngsters' rock vocabulary will be polished!

A Gem Of A Book

Be sure to share *Let's Go Rock Collecting* by Roma Gans (HarperCollins Children's Books, 1997). In this informative book, your youngsters will join two adventurous, young rock hounds as they travel the world to collect many different types of rocks.

Investigating Rocks

Dig into the following rock tests to polish your youngsters' observation and scientific-thinking skills. Prepare the materials needed to set up each of the following experiments. Then distribute a copy of the recording sheet (page 280) to each student. A student chooses a rock from his collection (see "A Rock Hunt" on page 272) and places a small piece of personalized masking tape on it. On the recording sheet, he draws the rock and writes where it was found and a description of its texture. Then he performs each of the experiments and records the results on the remainder of the recording sheet. Dig in!

The Bubble Test

This test is another way to identify rocks. Have each student place a few drops of vinegar on her rock. Explain to students that if the vinegar on their rocks bubbles, their rocks contain *carbonate*. Rocks such as limestone and marble contain this mineral.

The Scratch Test

The scratch test demonstrates the hardness of rocks. Hardness is one way that minerals are identified and classified. To complete the test, a student uses his fingernail to try to scratch his rock. If he is unsuccessful, he uses a penny to try to scratch the rock. If he is still unsuccessful, he carefully uses a steel nail or file to try to scratch the rock. Lead students to understand that the harder the rock, the harder the object needed to scratch it. Then have students group their rocks based on their test results.

The Streak Test

This test reveals the true colors of rocks. Color is another way rocks are identified and classified. Explain to students that a rock's streak is the color of its powder, which is sometimes different than the color of the rock. A rock's appearance may be discolored by environmental factors, but rarely does its streak change. Have each child stroke her rock on the back of a piece of household ceramic tile, an unglazed white porcelain tile, or a concrete sidewalk. Then have students group the rocks together that leave the same colors of streaks. Explain to students that if a streak is not made, this indicates that the rock is harder than the tile or concrete.

Sink Or Float?

This simple test shows students whether their rocks sink or float when placed in water. Partially fill a large, widemouthed container with water and place it on a table with several towels. Have each student place his rock in the water to determine whether it floats or sinks. Provide towels for students to dry their rocks before they begin another experiment.

The Five Senses

Those "Sense-sational" Senses!

Invite youngsters to use their five senses as they describe different objects. Gather a variety of objects, such as sandpaper, a flower, an orange, a large shell, fresh or dried leaves, and a rock. Have students brainstorm everything they know about each of the five senses, and list their responses on a sheet of chart paper. Divide students into small groups, and provide each group with a different object. Challenge the groups to use as many senses as they can to describe their objects; then have them share their findings with the rest of the class. Display the list and the objects at a table or center for further investigations. "Sense-sational!"

Touchy-Feely Squares

Youngsters will explore their sense of touch when they make these unique creations. The day before the lesson, send home with each student a paper lunch sack. Ask each child to place in her bag a collection of an object that has a unique texture. Rice, cereal, macaroni, dried beans, buttons, and spaghetti noodles are good examples. When the bags have been brought in, have students think of words to describe any object's texture, such as *rough, smooth, bumpy, hard,* and *soft.* Then pair students. Have each student use her sense of touch to guess the contents of her partner's bag. When the contents of the bags are revealed, have each student glue her objects onto a posterboard square. Collect the squares and display them at a table or learning center. For added practice encourage youngsters to sort the squares by texture.

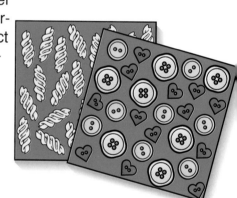

A Tasty Activity!

Tickle youngsters' taste buds with this appetizing activity! Begin the lesson with a tasting party. Provide an assortment of foods for youngsters to sample that represent each of the four kinds of tastes. Some good choices are chocolate chips (sweet), potato chips (salty), dill pickles (sour), and unsweetened chocolate (bitter). After sampling each food, have youngsters describe its taste using one of the following words: *sweet, salty, sour,* or *bitter.* Next challenge students to cut pictures from magazines for each of the four kinds of tastes. Collect the students' pictures. Then, as a class, sort the pictures on a large bulletin board decorated and labeled as shown. If desired provide time for students to name their favorite tastes. Mmmmmmmm!

How does it taste?

sweet

salty

sour

bitter

What Do You See?

Challenge youngsters to use their sense of sight when they create these one-of-a-kind pictures! Supply students with large sheets of construction paper, paint, and paintbrushes. Have each student fold her paper in half; then unfold it. The child then uses a paintbrush to drop some paint onto her paper. She then carefully refolds her paper, gently squashing the paint between the sides. Instruct her to open her paper up and set it aside to dry. When the paint has dried, encourage students to look at their pictures and imagine what they see in their ink blots; then have them copy and complete the sentence "I see_____" on their papers. Collect the students' projects, and bind the pages between two construction-paper covers. Then add the title "What Do You See?" before placing it at the reading center for all to enjoy.

I see a monster.

Nancy

Sounds Like...

Looking for a fun way to explore sound? Then this idea is for you! In advance, gather a classroom supply of paper-towel tubes and tape-record some different sounds, such as a telephone ringing, a knock at the door, and running water. To begin, share *Hey! What's That Sound?* by Veronika Charles (Stoddart Publishing Co. Limited, 1994). After reading the story, play the tape and challenge youngsters to guess each recorded sound. Then have students create sound sticks.

To make a sound stick, a student decorates one side of a 6" x 11" piece of construction paper with crayons or markers. Next he covers one end of a paper-towel tube with a scrap of construction paper and secures it to the tube with masking tape. He then fills his tube halfway with either rice or macaroni noodles, and seals the other end of the tube as he did before. Then he covers his tube with the decorated paper, and fastens it to the tube with clear tape. Youngsters will be delighted with the sounds their sticks make. Now, let's start shaking!

Name That Smell!

Entice youngsters as they sniff out different smells. Partially fill ten empty film canisters with different food items. Some good choices are vinegar, peppermint, cinnamon, coffee grounds, chopped onions, garlic, oranges, tuna fish, chocolate, and strawberries or peaches. Replace the tops on the canisters. Gather students in a circle on the floor. Pass a canister around the circle and have each youngster sniff its contents, keeping his guess to himself. After everyone has taken a turn, invite students to share their guesses about the canister's contents before revealing the source of the smell. Repeat the process with the remaining canisters. Next have students sort the canisters into favorite and least-favorite smells. Then have each youngster draw a picture and write about a favorite smell. Invite each youngster to share his picture with his classmates.

My favorite smell is cinnamon. I like it because I eat cinnamon toast every day!!

Jim

Books About The Five Senses

Share these additional titles about the five senses.

- *My Five Senses* by Aliki (HarperCollins Children's Books, 1989)
- *Sense Suspense* by Bruce McMillan (Scholastic Inc., 1994)
- *Touch* by Mandy Suhr (Carolrhoda Books, Inc.; 1994)
- *Hearing* by Mandy Suhr (Carolrhoda Books, Inc.; 1994)
- *Sight* by Mandy Suhr (Carolrhoda Books, Inc.; 1994)
- *Smell* by Mandy Suhr (Carolrhoda Books, Inc.; 1994)
- *Taste* by Mandy Suhr (Carolrhoda Books, Inc.; 1994)

Sun, Moon, Stars

Day Or Night?

Introduce the Sun when you share *Sun Up, Sun Down* by Gail Gibbons (Scholastic Inc., 1983). After discussing the story, display a globe for your students. Tape a small photo atop your state (or country) on the globe; then tape another photo on the opposite side. Ask a student to shine a flashlight on the first photo. Tell students that it is *daylight* in the areas where the light is shining and *nighttime* in the areas where the light is not. Then slowly spin the globe. Challenge youngsters to guess what will happen next. Lead students to the conclusion that the Sun shines all the time. The Sun is not always visible, because the Earth spins. The Sun shines on different parts of the Earth. As a follow-up activity, have students draw pictures illustrating daytime and nighttime.

Pictures In The Sky

Your youngsters will love learning about the constellations when they hear *Star Shapes* by Peter Malone (Chronicle Books, 1997). After listening to the story, invite students to share some of their favorite constellations from the book. Then have students create these star-studded pictures. To make a picture, a student attaches gummed stars to a sheet of black construction paper, creating a design of her favorite animal. To complete her drawing, she uses a white crayon to connect the stars and add details to her picture. If time allows, have students share their resulting constellations with their classmates. Then mount the constellations around the room for a starry display!

A Sunny Idea!

Youngsters will learn all about the Sun with this hands-on activity! To begin, share the following facts about the Sun:

- The Sun is a big star.
- The Sun is a very hot ball of gases.
- The Sun does not have any land on it.
- We get our light and heat from the Sun.
- The Earth travels around the Sun in an orbit.

Then have students create these sunny booklets. To make a booklet, a student paints a small paper plate yellow. When the paint has dried, he glues orange and yellow construction-paper triangles around the edge of the plate. Next the student copies each fact about the Sun onto a separate precut sheet of circular drawing paper (the same size as the plate); then he illustrates each fact. Next he staples the pages behind the Sun, and adds the title "The Sun" and his name to the cover. "Sun-sational!"

The Sun by Jack

The Marvelous Moon!

Mystify students with these marvelous Moon activities! To begin, have students brainstorm everything they know about the Moon. Then share some of these interesting Moon facts:

⭐ There is no water or air on the Moon.
⭐ It is very quiet on the Moon because there is no air to carry sounds.
⭐ The Moon is very dusty and dry because there is no water.
⭐ Craters are large spaces left from rocks that have crashed into the Moon.
⭐ There is less gravity on the Moon than on Earth. Gravity gives you weight and keeps you from floating away.
⭐ Astronauts' footprints are still on the Moon today. There is no wind or water to make them go away.

After sharing the facts, demonstrate the size of the Moon in proportion to the Earth. First ask students to estimate the size of the Moon. Then have a student hold up a baseball next to a globe. Explain that the baseball represents the size of the Moon as compared to the Earth. Lead students to determine that the Moon is much smaller than the Earth.

After the demonstration, have students discover how craters are formed. Fill a large container with sand and gather a variety of round objects, including tennis balls, golf balls, Ping-Pong® balls, and marbles. Ask a student to drop an object on the sand. Remove the object and have students talk about what they see. Then invite additional students to repeat the activity using the remaining objects. Challenge students to share ideas about the differences in the size of the craters with each drop.

Reinforce the crater concept by having your students create these magnificent Moons. To make a Moon, a student gently crumples a 10" x 12" piece of aluminum foil to create a crater-like appearance. He unfolds the foil and wraps it around a seven-inch tagboard circle, securing it to the back with tape. He then staples his Moon to the top of a 12" x 18" sheet of black construction paper. Next he writes a story about the Moon on a sheet of writing paper, then staples the story to the bottom of the black construction paper. Mount the Moon projects around the room for all to enjoy!

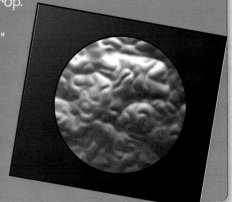

Journey Around The Sun

Take youngsters on a journey around the Sun as they re-create the orbits of the Earth and the Moon. To prepare, cut one large circle from each of the following colors of poster board: yellow, white, and blue. Label the yellow circle "Sun," the white circle "Moon," and the blue circle "Earth." Gather your students in a large, open area, such as a gym or playground. Have one student stand in the middle of the area holding the "Sun" sign. Ask another student to hold the "Earth" sign and stand about two yards from the sun. Instruct the Earth to walk *slowly* around the Sun. Explain that the Earth revolves (or moves) around the Sun. Next ask another child to hold the "Moon" sign. Have him stand next to the Earth. Tell students the Moon has its own orbit around the Earth. Then have the Moon revolve *slowly* around the Earth as the Earth revolves around the Sun. When the Earth has completed one revolution, enlist the help of additional students in re-creating the movements again. Now, let's start orbiting!

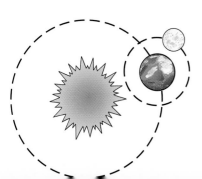

More About The Sun, The Moon, And The Stars

- *Floating Home* by David Getz (Henry Holt And Company, Inc.; 1997)
- *Here In Space* by David Milgrim (BridgeWater Books, 1997)
- *Look At The Moon* by May Garelick (Mondo Publishing, 1996)
- *The Sun And Moon* by Patrick Moore (Copper Beech Books, 1995)
- *Where Are The Stars During The Day?* by Melvin And Gilda Berger (Ideals Children's Books, 1993)

Animal Investigations

Draw and color a picture of your animal in its habitat.
Write the name of the animal on the line.

_____

Complete these sentences about your animal:

1. My animal lives in _____.

2. My animal eats _____.

3. My animal moves with _____.

4. My animal's body is covered with _____.

5. Interesting facts about my animal: _____

_____

_____

_____

Note To Teacher: Use with "Animal Investigations" on page 261.

MAGNETISM

Name Of Object	PREDICT: Is It Magnetic?	TEST: Magnetic	TEST: Non-magnetic						
paper clip									
rubber band									
eraser									
thumbtack									
metal spoon									
plastic spoon									
aluminum foil									
coin									
brad									
screw									

Name _____   Day _____

Time _____

What's today's weather?

1. **The ☀ is** ○ shining
   ○ not shining

2. **I see ☁ in the sky.**   ○ yes   ○ no

3. **The 🌡 reads** _____°.

4. **The temperature is**
   ○ cool   ○ warm
   ○ cold   ○ hot

5. **Today I will see 💧.**   ○ yes   ○ no

6. **Today I will see ❄.**   ○ yes   ○ no

Note To Teacher: Use the magnet recording sheet with "An Attractive Learning Center!" on page 270. Use the weather data sheet with "Weather Watchers" on page 267.

Rock Research

Draw your rock.

Write.

> **I found my rock** _____
>
> _____.
>
> **My rock feels** _____
>
> _____
>
> **when I touch it.**

Circle the correct
sentence.
Color a rock.

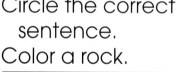

My rock floats.

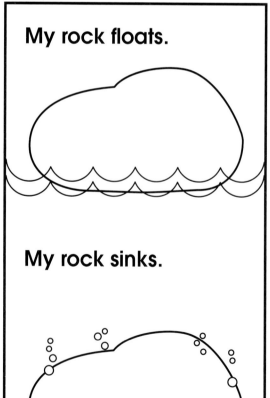

My rock sinks.

Color the correct circle.

> **I scratched my rock**
>
> ⃝ with my fingernail
>
> ⃝ with a penny
>
> ⃝ with a steel nail
>
> **I couldn't scratch it.** ⃝

Color the correct circle. Color.

> **My rock left a streak.**
>
> ⃝ yes   ⃝ no
>
> **This is the color of the streak.**
>
>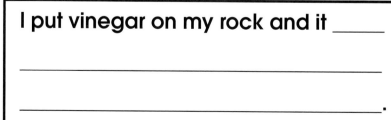

Write.

> **I put vinegar on my rock and it** _____
>
> _____
>
> _____.

HEALTH & SAFETY

TERRIFIC TEETH

Help your youngsters see the importance of sprucing up their pearly whites with these dynamic dental-health activities!

Smile Maintenance

Start your dental-health unit with a smile. Have each child wash her hands thoroughly; then provide each child or group of children with a mirror. Direct students to smile into the mirrors. Ask students to describe what they see. Next have each student open wide and take a peek at her teeth. Guide students to discover things about their teeth by asking questions such as, "How many teeth do you have?" or "Are any of your teeth missing?"

After the discussion, impress upon your students the importance of toothbrushing and flossing by sharing the following advice:

→ Brush your teeth after every meal with a soft toothbrush.

→ Use dental floss after brushing.

→ Replace a toothbrush when the bristles become worn—about every two to three months.

→ See a dentist for a checkup at least once a year.

→ Eat healthful foods such as vegetables, fruits, cheese, and yogurt.

→ Stay away from sugary foods such as candy, desserts, and sweetened cereal.

Front Teeth Graph

Students may enter first grade with their front teeth, but they often leave without them! Between the ages of six and eight, the 20 primary teeth begin to fall out, to be replaced by 32 permanent teeth. To illustrate the fact that students' smiles are ever changing, make a "Front Tooth Graph." In advance create and display a graph (as shown) for three different kinds of smiles—both front teeth, one front tooth, and neither front tooth. To begin the activity, have each student personalize a copy of the tooth pattern on page 288. Then have each younster attach his tooth-shaped cutout to the grid to indicate what type of smile he has. Conclude the activity by discussing the results of the graph.

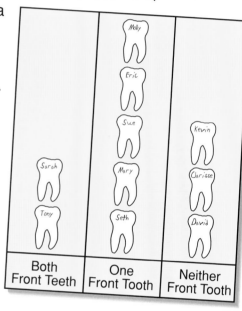

| Both Front Teeth | One Front Tooth | Neither Front Tooth |

Inside A Tooth

This activity will give students an inside look at a tooth. To make the tooth-shaped project, each child will need to fold in half a 9" x 12" sheet of white construction paper. He then positions a tooth-shaped template atop the folded paper so that one side of the pattern is flush with the fold. The student traces around three sides of the shape and cuts on the resulting outline. Next he uses templates to trace and cut the *dentin* from orange paper and the *pulp* from pink paper. He opens the tooth shape and glues the pulp and dentin in place. He uses blue and red crayons to draw nerves and blood vessels in the pulp section of the tooth, then labels the enamel, the dentin, and the pulp sections.

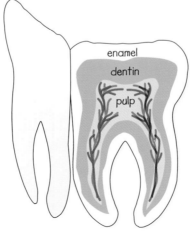

Attack That Plaque!

Sugar is an invisible enemy to teeth. Each time sugar is eaten, bacteria in the mouth produce tooth-decaying acids for about 20 minutes. Guide students to understand the importance of brushing to help keep sugar from making cavities with this nifty demonstration. In advance hard-boil two eggs. To begin the demonstration, place one egg in a jar of water, and one egg in a jar of cola. Set the eggs aside. The next day, remove the eggs and compare them. Students will observe the egg from the jar of cola is stained, but the other egg has retained its appearance. To extend the activity, use a toothbrush and toothpaste to remove the stain from the tainted egg. Conclude the activity by reminding students that proper toothbrushing helps to keep stains from forming on teeth.

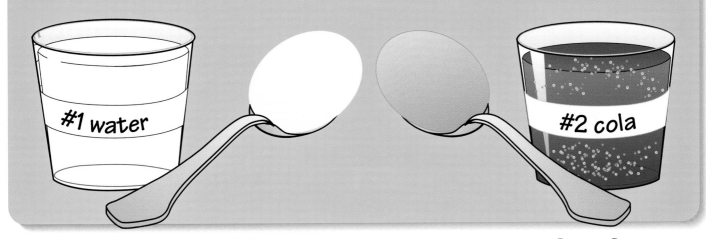

Dental-Health Booklets

This booklet-making project provides students with the opportunity to write about good dental-health practices. Enlist students' help in brainstorming a list of things involved in maintaining good dental health. Write students' ideas on the chalkboard. Then give each student six copies of the tooth pattern on page 288. To make the booklet, each student chooses five ideas from the list, then writes and illustrates one on each page of her booklet. Then she stacks her completed pages, places the blank tooth cutout on top, and staples the pages along the top edge. To complete the booklet, she personalizes the cover as desired. Encourage students to take their booklets home to share with their parents.

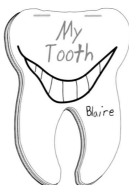

Tip-Top Tooth Tales

Students will be all smiles after they sink their teeth into these "tooth-erific" tales!

- *Arthur's Tooth* by Marc Brown (Little, Brown And Company; 1985)
- *Tooth Fairy* by Audrey Wood (Child's Play [International] Ltd., 1989)
- *The Bear's Toothache* by David McPhail (Little, Brown And Company; 1988)
- *Little Rabbit's Loose Tooth* by Lucy Bate (Crown Books For Young Readers, 1988)
- *Dr. De Soto* by William Steig (Farrar, Straus & Giroux, Inc.; 1990)
- *The Berenstain Bears Visit The Dentist* by Stan & Jan Berenstain (Random House, Inc.; 1981)
- *My Tooth Is About To Fall Out* by Grace Maccarone (Scholastic Inc., 1995)
- *How Many Teeth?* by Paul Showers (HarperCollins Children's Books, 1991)

Good NUTRITION For You

Serve your students a hearty helping of these activities that promote healthful eating habits!

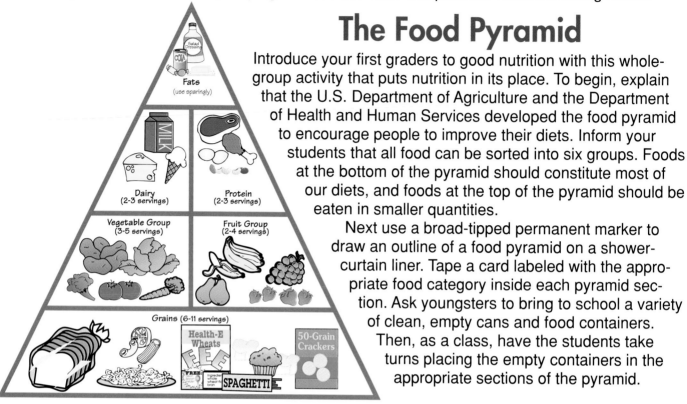

The Food Pyramid

Introduce your first graders to good nutrition with this whole-group activity that puts nutrition in its place. To begin, explain that the U.S. Department of Agriculture and the Department of Health and Human Services developed the food pyramid to encourage people to improve their diets. Inform your students that all food can be sorted into six groups. Foods at the bottom of the pyramid should constitute most of our diets, and foods at the top of the pyramid should be eaten in smaller quantities.

Next use a broad-tipped permanent marker to draw an outline of a food pyramid on a shower-curtain liner. Tape a card labeled with the appropriate food category inside each pyramid section. Ask youngsters to bring to school a variety of clean, empty cans and food containers. Then, as a class, have the students take turns placing the empty containers in the appropriate sections of the pyramid.

Food-Group Tag

Reinforce the concept of the Food Guide Pyramid with this outside activity. In advance create a large nametag for each of the six food groups. Designate a playing area and assign six players to be *It*—one to represent each food group. Have each of the six students wear a nametag to match his assigned food group. To begin the game, the remaining players run around in the designated area and try to avoid being tagged by one of the Its. If an It is close by, the student may quickly squat and name a food from the group represented by his pursuer. If the student is incorrect or isn't fast enough and gets tagged, he stays down. To be freed, he must be tagged by another player. What a fun way for students to actively learn about the food pyramid!

Magnificent Meals

Let your future restaurateurs plan their own nutritionally sound meals! In advance create a chart showing the recommended servings for each food group. To begin, divide students into groups of three. Provide each group with three paper plates and a supply of discarded magazines. Challenge each group of students to cut out pictures of food from the magazines and glue them to the paper plates to create three well-balanced meals—breakfast, lunch, and dinner. Remind each group to refer to the chart in planning their meals. After student groups have created their meals, invite one group at a time to share its delectables. If desired have students vote on their favorite set of meals.

Snack Sorting

Reinforce your youngsters' classification skills and knowledge of healthful snacks with this sorting activity. Remind students of the importance of choosing snacks that are low in sugar and fat, such as fruits and vegetables. Explain to students that the body needs some fat. However, if a person consumes too much fat, he increases his chance of having certain health problems. Place a large grocery bag labeled "Healthful Snacks" and another labeled "No-Nutrition Snacks" in a prominent location. Ask students to bring to school empty snack packages or pictures of snack-food items. Each morning have students place their packages or pictures in the appropriate grocery bag. Then, as students watch, empty each bag in turn and check its contents.

Pyramid Treats

This edible pyramid snack is perfect for reinforcing the basic food groups! Prepare and arrange the needed ingredients and utensils. Discuss the directions with your students and tell them that there is one food from each *layer* of the pyramid. Then invite students to make their treats and dig in!

Ingredients And Materials For One:
6 tablespoons crushed graham crackers
1 M&M's® candy
3 tablespoons drained fruit cocktail
3 tablespoons vanilla pudding
1 clear 8-ounce plastic cup
1 spoon

Directions For Each Student:
1. Put the crushed graham crackers in the bottom of the cup.
2. Spoon the fruit cocktail atop the graham crackers.
3. Spoon the pudding atop the fruit.
4. Place the M&M's® candy on the top.

Nutritious Reading

Motivate students to read by placing these appetizing books in a toy grocery cart.
Cloudy With A Chance Of Meatballs by Judi Barrett (Atheneum Books For Young Readers, 1978)
Gregory, The Terrible Eater by Mitchell Sharmat (Scholastic Inc., 1980)
The Berenstain Bears And Too Much Junk Food by Stan and Jan Berenstain (Random House Books For Young Readers, 1985)
D.W., The Picky Eater by Marc Brown (Little, Brown And Company; 1995)
Bread And Jam For Frances by Russell Hoban (HarperCollins Children's Books, 1986)
What Food Is This? by Rosemarie Hausherr (Scholastic Inc., 1994)
The Edible Pyramid: Good Eating Every Day by Loreen Leedy (Holiday House, Inc.; 1996)

PLAYING IT SAFE

Help students learn how to be safe at home, at school, and on the bus with these nifty ideas.

A Song About School-Bus Safety

Reinforce school-bus safety rules with this terrific tune!

School-Bus Safety
(sung to the tune of "The Farmer In The Dell")

Sit quietly on the bus, sit quietly on the bus;
Sit still and be real quiet while riding on the bus.

Obey your bus driver, obey your bus driver;
Listen to your driver while riding on the bus.

Keep your arms in the bus, keep your arms in the bus;
To keep from being injured, keep your arms in the bus.

No eating on the bus, no eating on the bus;
To help the bus stay neat and clean, no eating on the bus.

Don't throw things on the bus, don't throw things on the bus;
To keep from hurting other kids, don't throw things on the bus.

As the driver stops the bus, as the driver stops the bus,
Stay sitting in your seat until the driver stops the bus.

Stay-Safe Plan

Help students and their parents be prepared in case of a house fire. Invite parents to join students in the classroom for a fire-planning session. Begin the parent-student session by reviewing fire-safety rules. Then distribute a sheet of paper to each parent-student team. Ask them to work together to create a map of their home showing a safe escape, an alternate route, and a meeting place. If a child's parents can't attend, send the partially completed map home with the student for her and her family to complete. This is a great way to involve families in something very important—staying safe.

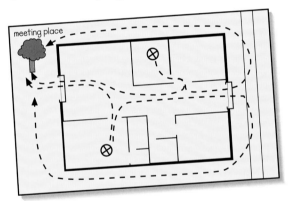

Cooperative Safety

Challenge students to work together to list fire-safety rules. Group students by fours or fives. Ask each group to brainstorm as many fire-safety rules as possible in a ten-minute period. Have each group elect one child to record their ideas on paper. Then gather the class and compare lists. Applaud each rule as it's read aloud by a group member. When all the lists have been read, create a master list for the classroom stating all the rules that were mentioned. Encourage students to refer to the rules often and to tell others about them, too.

Mr. Yuk Booklet

This safety booklet cautions youngsters about the dangers of poison. Have each youngster cut out pictures of several poisonous household items, such as cleaners, detergents, cosmetics, and medicine. Have each student glue each of his pictures to a separate piece of paper, then draw a frowny face beside each picture. Then have students staple their completed pages between construction-paper covers and decorate their front covers as desired.

What If...

Help your students become safety smart with this brainstorming activity. Create a list of possible scenarios, like the ones shown, that your youngsters might encounter. As a class, discuss solutions and determine the safety-smart course of action for each situation.

What will you do if...

➡ your smoke detector goes off?

➡ you're walking home and you think you're being followed?

➡ a stranger offers you a ride home?

➡ a friend invites you over to play, but you know it's time you're supposed to be home?

➡ a classmate is picking on you or someone you know?

Strangers Can Mean Danger

So who is a stranger? Ask students to name people who might be strangers to them. Then tell students that a stranger is anyone they or their parents don't know well. Remind students that all strangers should be treated with caution. Next display a copy of the stranger-safety rules (shown) with your students; then enlist their help in creating a bulletin board about stranger safety. Divide students into eight groups and assign each group a different stranger-safety rule. Have each student group draw a picture illustrating a child not following its rule on a large circle cutout. When the picture is finished, have each group draw a diagonal line across the circle to show their classmates that this could mean danger. Post the completed drawings on a bulletin board along with the title "Strangers Can Mean Danger." If desired have each student group write the rule on an index card and mount it under its drawing.

Stranger-Safety Rules:

1. Even a stranger can look friendly.
2. Never go anywhere with an unknown adult, even one who says she or he has been sent by your parents.
3. A stranger who knows your name is still a stranger.
4. Never open your door for a stranger.
5. Never tell a stranger your name, address, or telephone number.
6. Never accept anything from a stranger.
7. Never go near a stranger's car.
8. Never go for a walk with a stranger who says he or she needs to show you something.

Never go near a stranger's car.

YUCK! GERMS

Germy Jimmy

Promote healthful habits among your students with the help of Germy Jimmy. Use an old, discolored sock to create this puppet, sewing on buttons for eyes and tangled yarn for hair. Have him pay your students a visit and tell them about his unhealthy daily routine. Suggested items may include eating candy for breakfast, forgetting to brush his hair and teeth, not washing his hands, and wearing dirty clothes. Encourage your students to advise Jimmy on good hygiene. Then the next day, create a new Jimmy out of a new sock to give him a much more pleasant appearance. Invite Jimmy to share his new healthful habits with the class.

Related Literature

For a fun follow-up, have Germy Jimmy "read" aloud these informational books.
Achoo! All About Colds by Patricia Brennan Demuth (Grosset & Dunlap, 1997)
Germs! Germs! Germs! by Bobbi Katz (Scholastic Inc., 1996)

Pattern
Use with "Front Teeth Graph" on page 282 and "Dental-Health Booklets" on page 283.

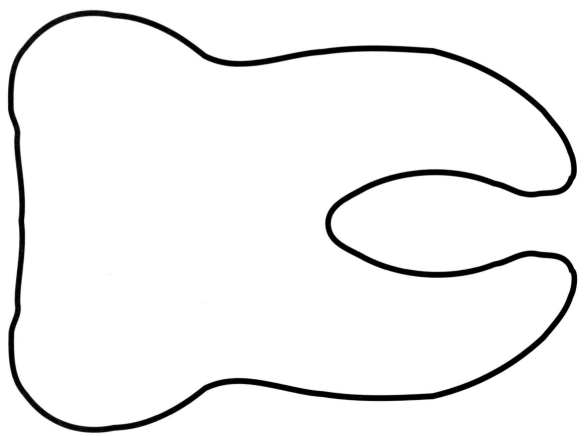

HOLIDAY & SEASONAL

GRANDPARENTS' LUNCH

Have students invite their grandparents (or other older adults) to enjoy a "PB&J Buffet" in honor of National Grandparents Day. Prepare for the event by gathering the necessary lunch ingredients and supplies with the help of parents. Menu items could include peanut butter and jelly sandwiches, fruit, chips or pickles, cookies, and juice. After students wash their hands, have them help you make the sandwiches and set up the buffet table with all the menu items. After everyone has enjoyed the buffet lunch, have your students read stories or sing favorite songs that they practiced in advance. A fun time will be had by all!

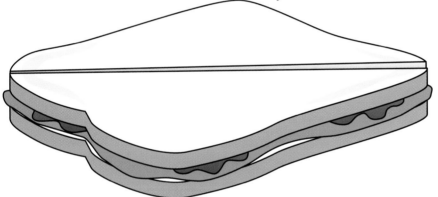

SHARE A STORY

This idea will help grandparents and grandchildren share their love of literature. Have each student invite a grandparent (or other older adult) to come to class and bring a favorite children's story to read. Meanwhile have each student select and practice reading a favorite story of his own. On the day of the visit, have each child-grandparent pair sit together and share their stories. After the book sharing, ask each child to introduce his grandparent and the title of his grandparent's book. Gather everyone for snacks when the event nears its end.

CANDY GRAPH

The weeks surrounding Halloween bring lots of miniature candy wrappers. Use a collection of these wrappers to graph your students' favorite candy choices. Create a grid on poster board; then tape a selection of wrappers to the grid. Give each child two dot stickers; then ask her to select her two favorite candy choices and mark them on the graph. Use the resulting graph to review graphing concepts with your students. The next day provide a sample of the students' favorite candy.

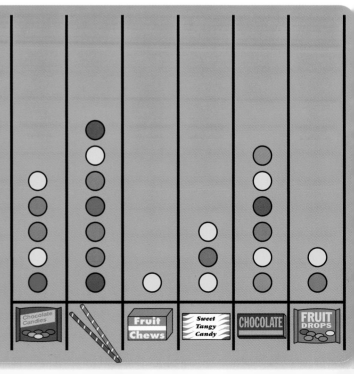

WHO'S THAT GHOST?

Turn this creative idea into a mystery bulletin board. Give each student a 6" x 9" piece of white construction paper and ask him to draw a picture of himself from head to toe. (Encourage each child to use the full length of the paper.) Have each student cut out his self-portrait and glue it to a 9" x 12" piece of colored construction paper. Next give each student another 6" x 9" piece of white construction paper and a ghost-shaped pattern. Have each child cut out a white ghost shape, then attach it at the top of the cutout with a dot of glue. At the bottom of the paper, have each student write three clues about himself (see the example). Mount the papers on a bulletin board with the title "Who's That Ghost?" Have students guess whom each ghost represents by reading the clues. By lifting the ghost shape, the answer will be revealed.

This ghost likes pizza, plays football, and has brown hair.

Pumpkin Suggestions

Take advantage of the abundance of pumpkins this fall to use them in a variety of creative learning experiences. Have students:
- estimate then measure the weight of a pumpkin.
- estimate then measure the circumference of a pumpkin.
- carve or design a funny face on a pumpkin.
- estimate then count the number of seeds in a pumpkin.
- salt and roast pumpkin seeds in an oven (with supervision), then eat them.
- cut shaped pieces of pumpkin shell; then use them with paint to make pumpkin prints.

FAMILY THOUGHTS ON THANKS

Include students' families in this thoughtful Thanksgiving project. Create a booklet with blank pages for each student. Have each student write the name of a family member on each page of his booklet. (Be sure each booklet has enough pages.) Ask your students to take the booklets home and invite each family member to draw or write a message telling what he is thankful for. When the messages have been entered, have the students decorate the covers and bring the booklets to school to share with their classmates. Allow students to take their booklets home again in time for the holiday.

THANKSGIVING-FEAST FAVORITES

Right after the Thanksgiving holiday, have students brainstorm a list of foods that were featured at their holiday dinners. Illustrate and label several of the food items along the bottom of a grid; then have each child graph one or two of his favorite foods on the list. Students will like finding out what foods were enjoyed most at the Thanksgiving feasts.

turkey	gravy	stuffing	corn	sweet potatoes	dinner rolls	cranberry sauce	pumpkin pie
		William					Cathy
		Jenny		Linda			Cordelia
Ralph		Alexander		Willow		Giles	Andy
Giles		Angel		Ralph	Jenny	William	Alexander
Cathy	Willow	Gina	Gina	Cordelia	Angel	Andy	Linda

WINTER

SHAPELY STARS

The six-pointed star—commonly associated with the Jewish holiday, Hanukkah—can be used to review some geometry skills with your students. From yellow construction paper, cut a class supply of hexagons; then cut six equilateral triangles per student (making the sides the same length as the hexagons' sides.) Distribute a hexagon and six triangles to each student along with a blue sheet of construction paper. If desired discuss the shapes that are being used, or have students measure the pieces. Next have each student glue the hexagon in the center of the blue paper, then attach each triangle to one side of the hexagon. Use the resulting star shape to introduce the Hanukkah holiday, and display the stars on a wall in your classroom.

Christmas Cookie Exchange

Bring the tradition of making and eating Christmas cookies into your classroom with this fun and tasty project. Ask five or six parent volunteers to each donate a class supply of homemade holiday cookies. (Plan in advance to have one batch be undecorated holiday-shaped sugar cookies.) On the day of the exchange, you will need a class supply of small paper plates and resealable plastic bags, and a selection of decorating icing (prepackaged in tubes). Have each child select a plain cookie and place it on a paper plate. Then invite each student to decorate his cookie using the icing tubes. While your students are enjoying their decorated treats, assemble the rest of the cookies into take-home treats. Place one each of the remaining cookies into a plastic bag for each student. Add a holiday sticker to each bag, and send your students out the door with smiles as you distribute the treat bags!

Hanukkah Gifts

Giving coins is a traditional part of the Hanukkah holiday. Make some coin coupons to give to your students in honor of this special Jewish celebration. Cut several yellow construction-paper circles per student and write a variety of redeemable items on the coins. Gather a class supply of resealable plastic bags; then place a few coins inside each one. Distribute a bag to each student and allow her to redeem the coin coupons as desired.

Good For 15 Minutes Free-Reading Time

Good For Your Choice Of Lunch Partner

Good For One Sticker!

Twelve Days—Revised

Turn your students into songwriters by having them rewrite lyrics for "The Twelve Days Of Christmas." Divide students into 12 groups and assign each group a verse from the song. Instruct each group to create a new verse for the song. Then use chart paper to record your students' new verses for each of the 12 days mentioned in the song. Practice the revised song after it's complete. If desired type and print a copy of the lyrics for each child to take home. Expand on the idea by relating art projects or curriculum to the 12 items students chose. This song also provides a fun way to review ordinal numbers.

Kwanzaa
Helping
Hands

Helping Hands For Kwanzaa

Kwanzaa is a holiday not only of giving handmade gifts, but also of celebrating many virtues. Students can explore both aspects of this African-American holiday by making helping-hand coupon book-lets to give to their families. Help each child make a booklet by placing four hand-shaped sheets of white paper between hand-shaped construction-paper covers as shown. Have the child decorate the cover in traditional Kwanzaa colors of red, green, and black. On each page of a student's book, have her write a chore that can be done to help the family or a family member. Have students present the books to their families on the third day of Kwanzaa, *ujima,* when collective work and responsibility is observed.

Kwanzaa Salad

Kwanzaa comes from a Swahili phrase meaning *first fruits.* Celebrate the holiday with a fresh fruit salad. Ask each student to bring a fresh fruit to school. Help each child clean and cut his fruit (using plastic cutlery) to make the salad. Combine all the fruit pieces in one bowl and mix. Serve individual portions of the salad for students to enjoy. This fresh treat is sure to brighten a bleak winter day.

Start The Year On The Right Foot!

I'm starting the year on the right foot...

Your students will enjoy making these New Year's cards to share with their families. To make a card, have each child trace his right foot onto colorful construction paper and cut it out. Next have each child fold a 9" x 12" piece of white construction paper in half to create a card; then have him glue the foot shape to the card's front. Instruct each student to write "I'm starting the year on the right foot…" on the front of the card. Encourage each student to complete the inside of his card by writing something that he plans to do in the new year. Have him complete the card by illustrating the inside. Encourage each child to present his card to his family for the New Year.

by keeping my room neat!

Involve your class in creating a timeline of Martin Luther King's life. Read aloud a story about Dr. King's life, such as *A Picture Book Of Martin Luther King, Jr.* by David Adler (Holiday House, Inc.) or *Martin Luther King, Jr.: A Biography For Young Children* by Carol Hilgartner Schlank and Barbara Metzger (Gryphon House, Inc.). After sharing the text, have students list important dates and events of Dr. King's life as you record each item on the chalkboard. On a long length of paper, have each child design a timeline of Martin Luther King's life using the information that was compiled. Soon students will get a clear picture of significant events in Dr. King's life.

PEACE TRAIN

Enlist students' help in completing this thoughtful bulletin board while remembering Dr. Martin Luther King, Jr. Place a cutout of a train engine on a bulletin board along with the title "Get On The Peace Train." Provide each student with a colorful index card and have her write a peaceful thought. Next have each child cut two black circles for wheels and glue them to the bottom of her card. Post each train car behind the engine to complete the display. All aboard!

CHINESE NEW YEAR MONEY FUN

To celebrate the New Year, Chinese children look forward to receiving gifts of money in red envelopes. Invest in this tradition by creating a money-practice game to enhance your classroom celebration of the Chinese New Year. Number a class supply of red envelopes; then place a combination of plastic coins in each envelope. Establish an answer key listing the number of each envelope and the coin value enclosed in each one. Distribute an envelope to each child and have him determine the coins' value, then check the answer key before trading with another student; or place the envelopes and answer key in a center for students to explore.

BRAGGIN' DRAGON

After introducing your students to a few customs of the Chinese New Year, have them design and make a dragon for a good-work display. Have your students use colored paper, glitter, and paint to decorate a large paper grocery bag to represent the dragon's head. After the bag is decorated, stuff it with paper and seal it with staples. Next attach an 18" x 60" strip of bulletin-board paper to the dragon's head as shown. Cut four-inch squares from red and green tissue paper; then have students crumple pieces of tissue and glue them to the dragon's body. When the dragon is complete, mount him on a classroom wall with the title "This Dragon's Braggin' About Good Work!" Display students' assignments beside the dragon.

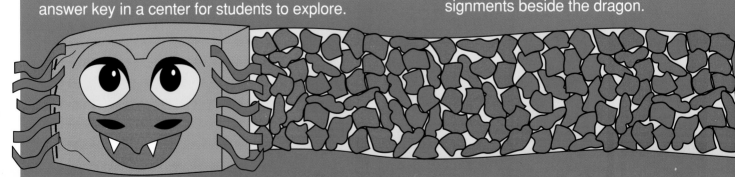

LOVE LINES

Your students will have fun making and displaying these love lines for Valentine's Day. Give each student a 6" x 18" piece of pink or red construction paper. Instruct students to accordion-fold their paper into four sections. With the paper folded, have each student draw a heart pattern similar to the one shown. (Be sure the connecting tabs reach the sides of the paper.) Have the child cut on the lines and unfold his paper to reveal a chain of four hearts. Next have him create a four-word phrase that includes the word *love;* then have him write the phrase on the hearts. Have students display their love lines on the fronts of their desks, on a wall, or on the classroom door. Valentine's Day will be filled with loving thoughts.

LOVE MAKES ME HAPPY!

Let me give you a kiss, Dad!

Mom, you're the sweetest!

VALENTINE KISSES

Encourage your students to give some love to a family member on Valentine's Day with this sweet project. Cut a six-inch candy-kiss shape from tagboard for each student. Then have each student write a message of love on a 1" x 12" strip of white paper using a blue marker. Then have the student glue the message strip to the top of the shape. To complete the project, have each student cover the tagboard shape with foil. Send each student home with his message of love, and encourage him to give it to a family member to show how much he cares.

LOVE IS...

Have your students compile a big book filled with their ideas of love. Give each student an 11-inch paper strip and have him write "Love is_____" (filling in his description). Then have him illustrate his sentence on a sheet of plain white paper. To create the book, have each child mount his sentence and picture on a 12" x 18" sheet of pink or red construction paper. Assemble the pages, add a cover and title, and then bind the pages with metal rings. Your students will enjoy reading the class collection of love definitions on *Valentine's Day.*

Love is ice cream.

SPRING

SEEING GREEN

Here's a fun activity to help your students see green on St. Patrick's Day. Have your class brainstorm a list of items that are green. List the responses on the chalkboard. Have each student choose one item from the list to depict. Provide students with a variety of green papers such as wallpaper, construction paper, tissue paper, or wrapping paper. Next have each student use the different papers to create his green item and then glue it to a 12" x 18" piece of white construction paper. Ask each child to write a caption about his picture. Display all the green pictures on a classroom wall and you'll find yourselves in a sea of green—or seeing green— just in time for St. Patrick's Day!

PEPPER PRINTS

Use this unique vegetable print to pep up your St. Patrick's Day celebration! Purchase a few fresh peppers and cut them in half around the middle. Prepare several shades of green tempera paint in aluminum pie plates. Allow each student to make a print design on a 12" x 18" piece of white construction paper. When the design is dry, have each child write a paragraph about her design or about St. Patrick's Day. Display the stories and pictures in the hallway for all to see.

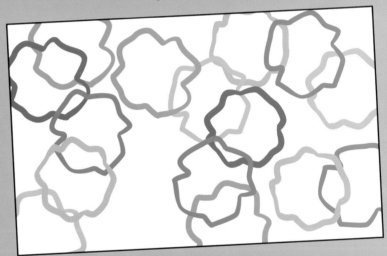

LEPRECHAUN WAND

I wish I had a horse!

Let your students try their leprechaun charm by waving this special wishing wand. Have students roll a 12" x 4" piece of black construction paper into a tight tube shape and secure it with tape. Next give each child two green shamrock-shaped cutouts. On one cutout have the child write a special wish; have him decorate the other shamrock with green glitter. Have the child glue his shamrocks back-to-back around one end of the wand. Now let your lucky leprechauns dance a jig around the classroom as they wave their wishing wands. Did any wishes come true?

Earth Day

Poster Pals

Use this Earth Day activity to send a message to your entire school or community while focusing on cooperation in your classroom. After discussing the significance of Earth Day, ask your students to brainstorm a list of vocabulary that relates to this event. Write the words on the chalkboard as they are presented. Pair students and ask each pair to create a poster in support of Earth Day. Encourage students to use words from the vocabulary list to create slogans for their posters. Display the finished posters in your school or in area businesses in time for Earth Day—April 22.

BUNNY TALES

Hop right into spring by having your students write rabbit stories. Cut booklet covers and writing paper into bunny shapes, and staple each booklet to secure the pages. Ask your students to compose rabbit-related stories on the booklet pages. Provide title suggestions such as "How The Bunny Got His Tail," or "The Bunny That Saved Easter!" After the stories have been written, have each student title her booklet "Bunny Tales"; then give each child a cotton ball to glue to the back cover of her booklet. Give each student an opportunity to read a story to her classmates before displaying the project.

Bunny Tales by Sally

GARBAGE GIANT

This garbage giant will make a big impression on your students while emphasizing the importance of reusing, reducing, and recycling trash. Cut a five-foot body shape from bulletin-board paper. Spend several days collecting trash from classroom activities and snacktime such as paper, food wrappers, and drink boxes. Each day have students glue the items to the cutout with craft glue (or assist them with a hot glue gun). When the giant is covered with trash, suspend it on your classroom door or in a hallway to stress the importance of making less waste. With the garbage giant's help, your students can make their world a beautiful place to live.

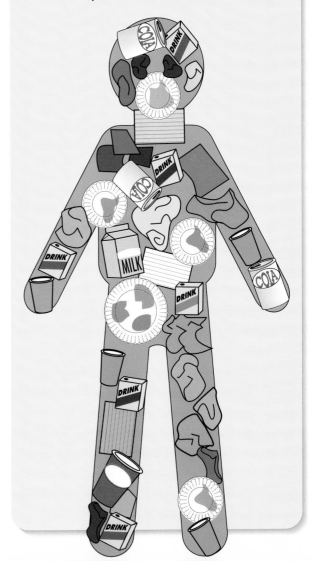

Jelly-Bean Count

Students will love sorting jelly-bean sweets for this simple graphing activity. Place a dish of assorted jelly beans in your math center. Then create a simple graph to correspond with the jelly-bean colors in your assortment, duplicate a class supply, and place the copies in the center with the candy. Have each student sort the jelly beans by color; then have her count and graph each amount. Conclude the activity with a treat your students can eat—a sampling of jelly beans, of course!

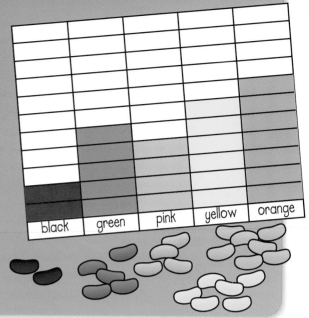

black	green	pink	yellow	orange

MEXICAN CAKEWALK

Many festivities are part of a traditional Cinco de Mayo celebration. Put students in a carnival mood with this fun cakewalk activity. Prepare by using chalk to draw a large circle on a paved area, such as a parking lot. Divide the circle into sections—one per student. Number the sections in order. Then create a corresponding card set by numbering index cards with the same numerals. To play, have each child stand in a section. Play some lively Mexican music, and have students walk around the circle. When the music stops, each child stays in a numbered section. Draw a card from the set and announce the number. Deliver a small prize to the child on the matching numbered section. (In a traditional cakewalk, the winning player selects a cake at this time.) Repeat the game several times; then provide a cupcake treat for all participants.

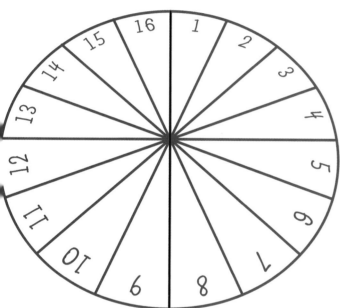

Personal Piñatas

After you arrange the necessary supplies in an art center, your students will be thrilled to know they can create their own personal piñatas. Supply a work area with small balloons, newsprint strips, and a pan of wheat paste. To make a piñata, help each child blow up and secure a small balloon. Then have him dip individual strips of newsprint into the paste and apply them to his balloon. The strips must overlap to completely cover the balloon's surface. After the balloons have dried, have students decorate them with tempera paint or colored tissue paper. Cut a small flap in the side of each piñata and add some individually wrapped candies. Secure a string from the top for hanging. Your students will love these festive treats!

MOM'S SPECIAL CARD

Creating a Mother's Day card will be a snap for your students with this creative method. Provide several *M* and *O* templates as well as a supply of colorful wallpaper samples. Have each child trace and cut out two *M*s and an *O* from different wallpaper designs. Provide each student with a 9" x 12" sheet of construction paper and have him fold it in half to form a card as shown. Then have each student glue his letters on the card's front to spell "MOM." Each child can then personalize the inside of his card with a special message.

NOW & THEN

I love you now...

Your students' moms will love this heartfelt Mother's Day gift. Before making the gift, ask each child to bring a baby picture from home. Also take current photographs of your students. To make the gift, have each child cut a large heart from construction paper. The heart should be slightly bigger than the photographs. Have each student glue her baby picture to one side of her heart; then have her glue a current snapshot to the other side. Encourage each child to write a statement on her crafted heart before presenting it to her mother.

like I loved you then!

Mother, may I wash the dishes?

MOTHER, MAY I?

Mothers will chuckle over your students' good intentions when they read these special booklets. Have each child staple several sheets of plain paper between construction-paper covers to create a booklet. Instruct each child to title his booklet "Mother, May I?" and add a byline to the cover. Ask students to fill their booklets with good deeds they intend to do in honor of Mother's Day. The statements should be written in this style: "Mother, may I water the flowers in your garden tonight?" or "Mother, may I do all the dishes after supper?" A final question might read, "Mother, may I love you even more on Mother's Day?" Each mother will cherish her child's genuine gestures of love.

Time Capsule

Use this creative idea to share your end-of-the-year treasures with your students. Use a plastic canister, a shoebox, or simply a large envelope to create a time capsule for each child. Personalize each container with a student's name, and add the date and your name. Now fill each student's capsule with papers and projects from the year, photographs from the school year, a special book, and a note or poem. Students will cherish these portable time capsules as mementos of their year in first grade.

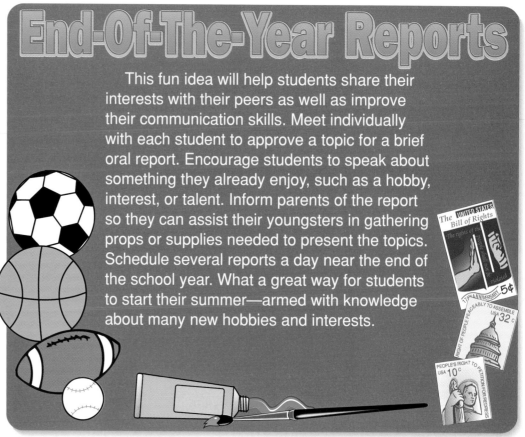

End-Of-The-Year Reports

This fun idea will help students share their interests with their peers as well as improve their communication skills. Meet individually with each student to approve a topic for a brief oral report. Encourage students to speak about something they already enjoy, such as a hobby, interest, or talent. Inform parents of the report so they can assist their youngsters in gathering props or supplies needed to present the topics. Schedule several reports a day near the end of the school year. What a great way for students to start their summer—armed with knowledge about many new hobbies and interests.

Baby Face

During the final month of school, have each student privately bring you a baby photo of himself. Post each photo on a bulletin board and number the photos for identification. Provide copies of a class list and allow students to guess who's whom by writing the corresponding picture's number by each child's name. Other teachers or classes may want to give their best guesses, too. What better way to show students how they've matured during the school year than by comparing them to their baby photos!

Jody Barnes-8
Amy Cabe-3
Lilly Jones-12
Cameron Olsen-
Amy James-
Riley Wilson-
Tom Jacobs-
Sheila Shadinsky-
Ron Klunk-
Greta Eisenhauer-
John Coble-
Robert Black-
Sarah Daniels-
Rhonda Taggart-

At year's end have your current students help you create a bulletin board to welcome new students the following year. Ask each child to decorate a face shape to resemble herself. Then distribute segments of sentence strips and ask each child to write describing words about her year in your class. Post the comments and personalized pictures on a display; then cover the entire board with newsprint or other material for protection during the summer. As you prepare your class for the start of school, unveil the board for an attractive first-day display.

SCHOOL SURVEY

During the final month of school, survey your students about their most memorable experiences in first grade. On a sheet of drawing paper, ask each child to write and illustrate a description of an event or activity that he thought was special. Encourage children to capture as many events as desired. Display the memories around the room. On the final day of school, send each child home with his favorite first-grade memory.

Picture-Perfect Grandparent

Complete each sentence.
Draw pictures and color the frame.

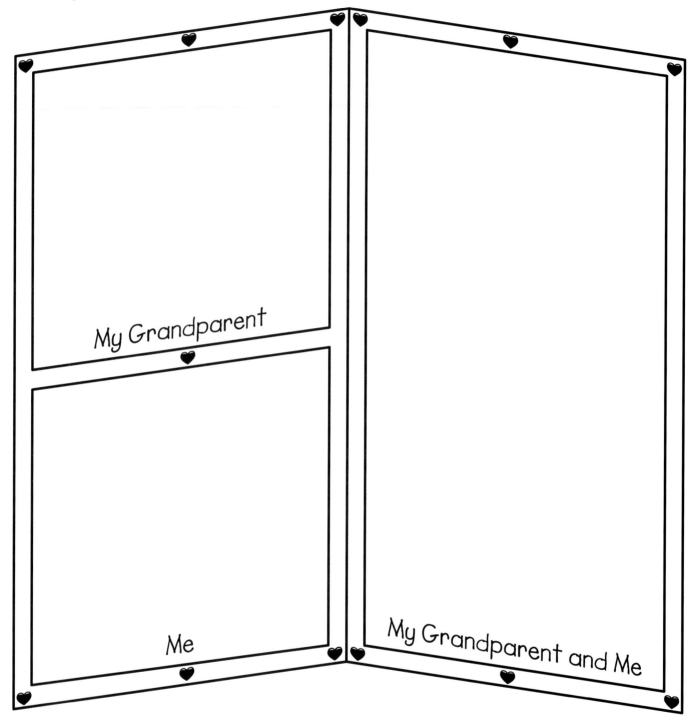

My Grandparent

Me

My Grandparent and Me

My grandparent has _____ eyes and _____

hair. We love to _____ and _____ together.

I call my grandparent _____.

Piles Of Pumpkins

Note To Teacher: Program pumpkins with math facts, vocabulary words, pumpkin activities, scrambled Halloween words, or other skills before duplicating. Add appropriate directions.

Trick Or Treat!

moon   costume
ghost   cat
candy   pumpkin
fun   treats

```
t  c  m  o  o  n  f
g  h  o  s  t  b  c
p  r  c  d  r  l  o
u  f  c  n  e  f  s
m  o  a  c  a  t  t
p  i  n  m  t  q  u
k  e  d  f  s  v  m
i  a  y  u  c  f  e
n  g  j  n  p  s  b
```

Who's Thankful?

What do you think makes each person or animal thankful?
Write.

teacher

Mom

Dad

dog

Draw what you are thankful for.

Observing Hanukkah

Match each activity to a picture.
Write.

play dreidel
make latkes
sing songs
light candles
give gifts

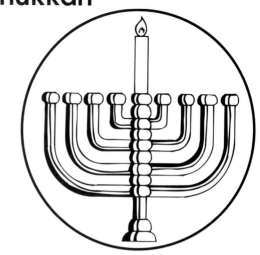

1. _____

2. _____   3. _____

4. _____   5. _____

Stocking Stuffers

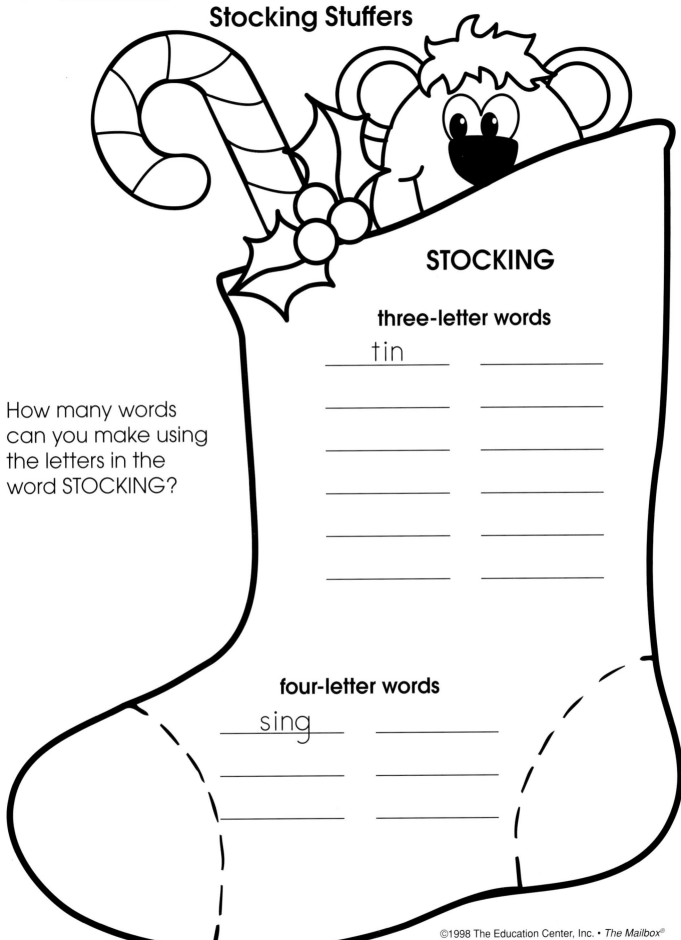

STOCKING

three-letter words

tin

How many words can you make using the letters in the word STOCKING?

four-letter words

sing

Time For A New Year!

Write each time.

____ : ____   ____ : ____   ____ : ____   ____ : ____

____ : ____   ____ : ____   ____ : ____   ____ : ____

____ : ____   ____ : ____

Happy New Year!

____ : ____   ____ : ____

Martin Luther King, Jr.

1. Cut out each strip on the heavy lines.
2. Glue each strip to a 5$\frac{1}{2}$" x 8$\frac{1}{2}$" sheet of paper.
3. Draw a picture to match each sentence.
4. Sequence the pages; then staple them to make a booklet.

Martin Luther King, Jr., studied hard in school. 1.

Martin Luther King, Jr.

Martin Luther King, Jr., studied hard in school.

1.

Martin became a preacher.

2.

Dr. King dreamed that all people would be treated the same.

3.

He gave speeches.

4.

We celebrate his birthday to remember how he helped people.

5.

Winter Wear

Note To Teacher: Program scarves and mittens with math facts, vocabulary words, winter activities, or other skills before duplicating. Add appropriate directions.

Celebrate Chinese New Year!

Find and circle the words below.
Color the fortune cookies as you go.

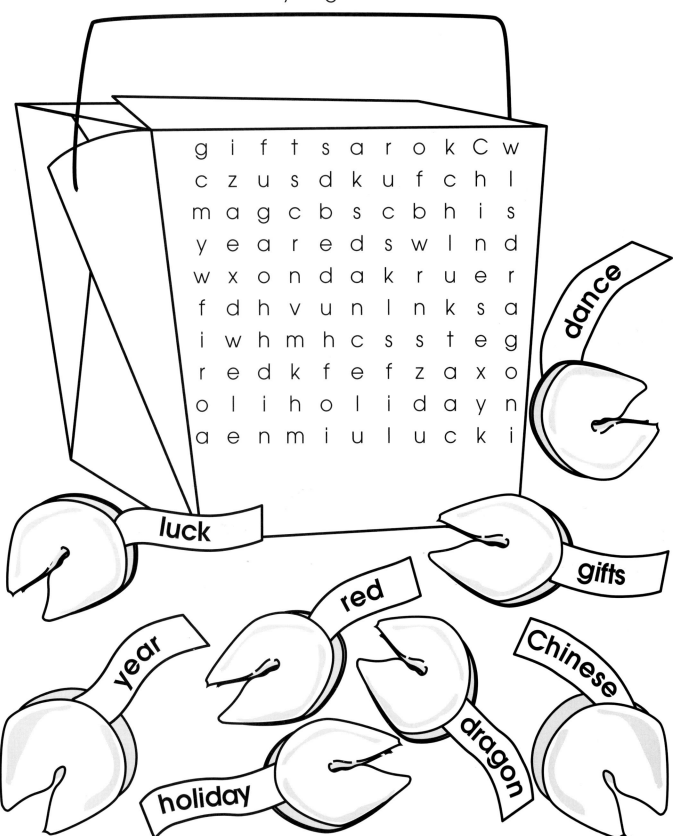

```
g  i  f  t  s  a  r  o  k  C  w
c  z  u  s  d  k  u  f  c  h  l
m  a  g  c  b  s  c  b  h  i  s
y  e  a  r  e  d  s  w  l  n  d
w  x  o  n  d  a  k  r  u  e  r
f  d  h  v  u  n  l  n  k  s  a
i  w  h  m  h  c  s  s  t  e  g
r  e  d  k  f  e  f  z  a  x  o
o  l  i  h  o  l  i  d  a  y  n
a  e  n  m  i  u  l  u  c  k  i
```

dance

luck

gifts

red

year

Chinese

dragon

holiday

Valentine's Deliveries

Note To Teacher: Program hearts and letters with math facts, vocabulary words, valentine activities,
312 scrambled valentine words, or other skills before duplicating. Add appropriate directions.

Name _____

Wearin' Of The Green

Read each word. If a word begins with the blend **gr,** color the area **green.**

green

play

grand

grin

snap

fly

spot

gray

grass

grape

grow

Bonus Box: Color the rest of the picture. Use any colors.

©1998 The Education Center, Inc. • *The Mailbox® Superbook* • Grade 1 • TEC450

Silly Signs Of Spring

Color each thing that is a sign of spring.

SCRAMBLED EGGS

Unscramble each Easter word.
Use the word box below.

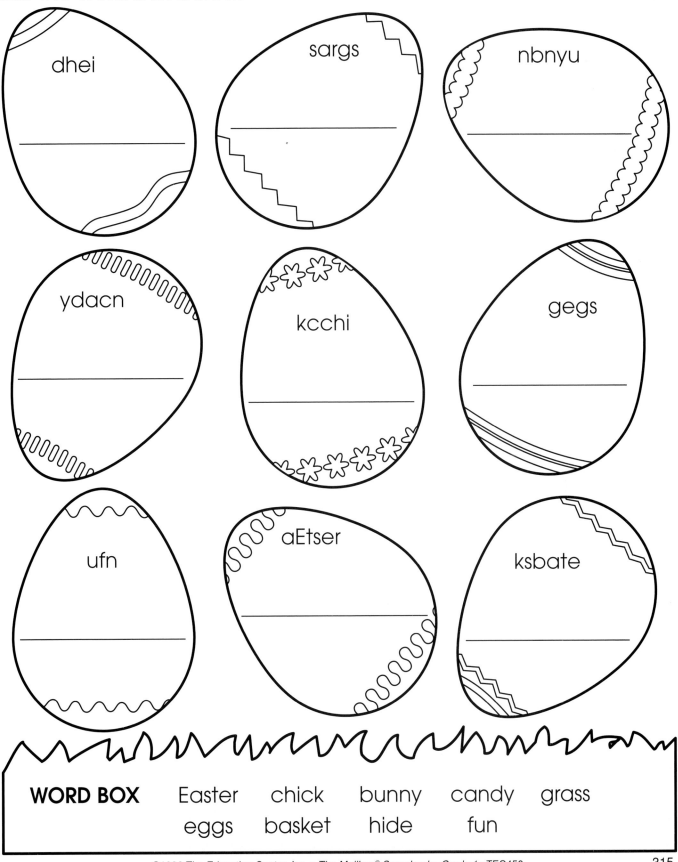

dhei

_____

sargs

_____

nbnyu

_____

ydacn

_____

kcchi

_____

gegs

_____

ufn

_____

aEtser

_____

ksbate

_____

WORD BOX   Easter   chick   bunny   candy   grass
eggs   basket   hide   fun

Earth's Friends

Cut and paste to show things that are good for the earth.

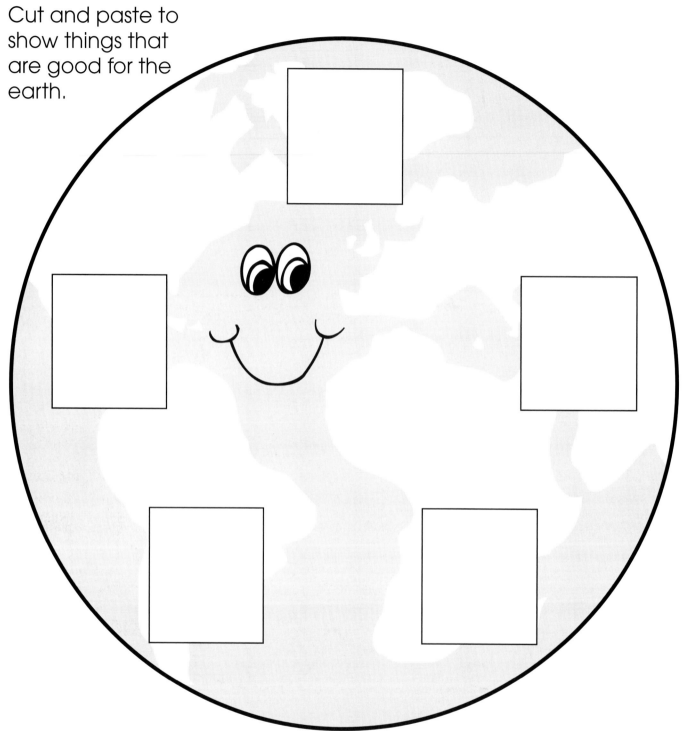

©1998 The Education Center, Inc. • *The Mailbox® Superbook* • Grade 1 • TEC450

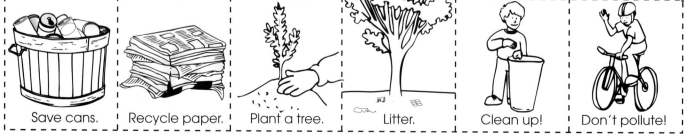

Save cans.   Recycle paper.   Plant a tree.   Litter.   Clean up!   Don't pollute!

First Grade Follow-Up

My Favorite Lunch

My Favorite Story

My Favorite Subject

My Teacher

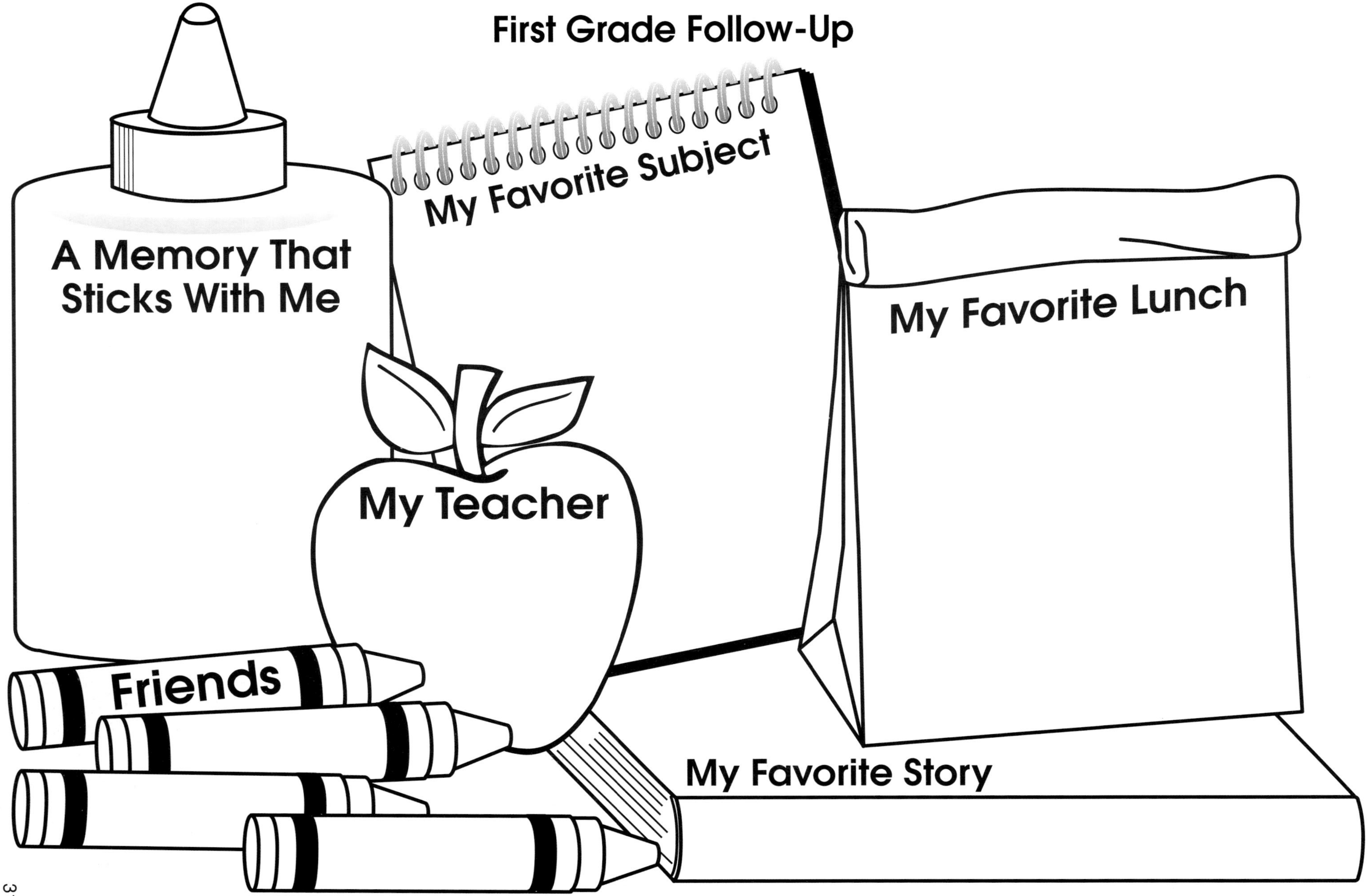

A Memory That Sticks With Me

Friends

I Learned A Lot This Year!

Things I Learned:

_____

_____

_____

_____

_____

_____

_____

_____

_____

_____

_____

What was the most important thing you learned this year? Put a ✓ beside it.

Seasonal Clip Art

Fun Clip Art